'THE TIME OF THE HARVEST HAS COME!'

Revolution, Reformation and the German Peasants' War

Martin Empson

b
Bookmarks
Publications

About the author

Martin Empson is a longstanding socialist and environmental activist. He is the author of several books including *'Kill All the Gentlemen': Class Struggle and Change in the English Countryside* and *Socialism or Extinction: The Meaning of Revolution in a Time of Ecological Crisis.*

Acknowledgements

Writing a book like this would have been impossible without the support and advice of many individuals. I would like to thank Justine Firnhaber-Baker, Donny Gluckstein and Graham Mustin for all their comments and suggestions on earlier drafts. Rosemarie Nünning offered detailed comments that helped me think about the role of women and how the German Peasants' War has been, and continues to be, understood centuries later. I would like to record particular thanks to Andrew Drummond, whose book on Thomas Müntzer has, as will become obvious, been a major source of inspiration. Andrew's willingness to offer advice, comments, translations and sources, often at short notice, was of incalculable help. All these individuals offered advice, comments and suggestions and made me think about events in new ways. Any remaining errors are mine alone.

Thanks are also due to Colm Bryce, who first agreed that a book on the German Peasants' War would be of interest to socialists and trade union activists five hundred years after the events. Mark L Thomas has been a supportive, insightful and enthusiastic editor. I owe him a great deal of thanks. I would also like to thank Oisin McGann for his map design, and Ben Windsor, Carol Williams and Camilla Royle for transforming my text into a finished book.

Finally, my thanks to Sarah Ensor, who once again has had to endure a prolonged period while I have been immersed in the history of agrarian and religious struggles. Without her support, this project would not have been possible.

The publisher would like to thank:

- Bloomsbury Publishing Plc for permission to use quotes from Peter Matheson, 1988, Collected Works of Thomas Müntzer, T&T Clark, an imprint of Bloomsbury Publishing Plc.
- Augsburg Fortress Publishers for permission to reproduce quotes from volumes 1 and 3 of The Selected Writings of Martin Luther by TG Tappert.

The Time of the Harvest Has Come:
Revolution, Reformation and the German Peasants' War
by Martin Empson

Published 2025 by Bookmarks Publications
c/o 1 Bloomsbury Street, London WC1B 3QE
© Bookmarks Publications

Cover design by Ben Windsor
Typeset by Ben Windsor
Printed by Halstan, Amersham HP6 6HJ

ISBN paperback 978-1-917020-213
Kindle 978-1-917020-29-9
ePub 978-1-917020-30-5
PDF 978-1-917020-31-2

Cover illustration: The siege of Frankenhausen culminates in the storming of the town and the retreat of the peasant army.
Source: Bamberger Burgenbuch StaBa Rb. H. bell. f1, B166.
Photo: Gerald Raab

What is the evil brew from which all usury, theft and robbery springs but the assumption of our lords and princes that all creatures are their property? The fish in the water, the birds in the air, the plants on the face of the earth – it all has to belong to them! To add insult to injury, they have God's commandment proclaimed to the poor: God has commanded that you should not steal. But it avails them nothing.

For while they do violence to everyone, flay and fleece the poor farm worker, tradesman and everything that breathes, yet should any of the latter commit the pettiest crime, he must hang... It is the lords themselves who make the poor man their enemy. If they refuse to do away with the causes of insurrection how can trouble be avoided in the long run? If saying that makes me an inciter to insurrection, so be it!

Thomas Müntzer
Vindication and Refutation, late 1524[1]

Contents

Introduction
1   The German Peasants' War?

Chapter 1
7   Germany on the Eve of Revolution

Chapter 2
26   Martin Luther and the German Reformation

Chapter 3
37   The Beginning of the Revolt

Chapter 4
47   The Twelve Articles

Chapter 5
53   Fear and Loathing at a Peasant Revolution

Chapter 6
61   The Spread of the Rebellion

Chapter 7
75   The Peasants' War in the Towns

Chapter 8
83   Thomas Müntzer and the Revolt in Thuringia

Chapter 9
117   Military Organisation

Chapter 10
123   The End of the Rising

Chapter 11
142   Michael Gaismair's Unchristian, Horrible Order against the Royal Domain of Tyrol

PART TWO: CAUSES AND CONSEQUENCES

Chapter 12
158 The Reformation, the German Peasants' War and the Bourgeois Revolution

Chapter 13
178 All Things in Common

Chapter 14
187 Anabaptism: The End of the Radical Reformation

210 Conclusion

Afterword
215 The strange afterlife of the German Peasants' War

Appendix
218 The Twelve Articles

224 Bibliography

227 Endnotes

242 Index

Introduction
The German Peasants' War?

In March 1525 about fifty representatives of one of the largest revolutionary movements in European history met in the small town of Memmingen, in the south-west of what is now known as Germany. Over a series of meetings, the elected delegates debated and condensed a set of demands into twelve articles summarising the anger and frustrations of the lower orders across a huge swathe of the southern parts of the Holy Roman Empire of the German Nation, including areas that are now part of France and Switzerland.[2] The mass movement of armed peasants, organised into armies, or bands, numbering tens of thousands, had spread rapidly, marching long distances to widen the rebellion and unite with other rebels. Towns and cities across the region fell in behind them, often raising their own demands and articles. The rebels were, at least in the short term, enormously successful at pushing back their enemies and capturing and destroying symbols of their oppression, at one point destroying two hundred castles alone in the bishopric of Bamberg in just ten days.[3]

The Twelve Articles, put together by their representatives, were widely disseminated, with an estimated twenty-five thousand copies distributed across the Empire. We know that thousands of people read and were inspired by them because elements were incorporated into hundreds of further local demands raised by other groups of rebels.

The enormous rebellion, which became known as the German Peasants' War, was very radical, and closely related to a wider ferment in European society. Europe was on the cusp of a period of great change. Less than three decades before the outbreak of the rebellion, Christopher Columbus had begun the process that led to the violent colonisation of the Americas, and the destruction through war, disease and famine of its Indigenous people. Ships from Spain and Portugal were travelling around Africa and into the Indian Ocean, opening up the areas for European commerce and colonisation. The slave trade had already begun. Even in its early years, hundreds of Africans were seized for forcible labour, the start of a violent, triangular exchange that would see millions forced across the Atlantic to work, and die, on European plantations in the Americas. The wealth from these nascent trades was beginning to make its way into the European countries, particularly England, France and Spain, who vied with each other for the greatest share of the riches.

At this time the Holy Roman Empire of the German Nation focused its ambitions closer to home, with particular attention on events in the Mediterranean. All Christian Europe was fearful of the spread of the then most powerful global force, the Ottoman Empire. Seventy-five years earlier, the Ottomans had captured one of Christendom's most important towns, Constantinople, and were pushing back Portuguese and Spanish trading posts, explorers and armies. Their weapons, technology and culture equalled and surpassed Europe in most regards.

As well as military conflict, Europe's rulers faced other crises. The rise of new economic forms was leading to tensions. For the previous few centuries, the old feudal order had been gradually changing and with it new economic motives were making themselves known. The emergence of a money economy and merchant trade, as well as agriculture and manufacture for profit, were the birth signs of a capitalist economy. Increasingly, the interests of those whose wealth relied on these new methods of production were in conflict with those of the old feudal order.

These economic changes were manifesting in numerous different ways – political, cultural and religious. In particular the power of the Christian Church, the head of which, the near all powerful Pope, was being challenged. As we shall see, the tensions within Christianity manifested themselves in the Reformation, which was unleashed by the theologian Martin Luther in 1517. Luther's early demands for religious reform quickly became a mass, radical movement of the "common people" which led to a schism within the Church itself. The Reformation's ideas are clearly visible in the Twelve Articles, and countless other Demands raised by German rebels in 1524 and 1525.

Those at the bottom of society had experienced a long period of economic stagnation and crisis. Conditions for the majority of

Europeans were poor, and hunger and poverty were common; as were the deprivations caused by regular wars as lords fought each other for land and power. The economic pressures on those at the bottom of society could be immense – especially through high levels of rents and taxes. In the town of Rothenburg people complained of paying "over half their income in rents and taxes".[4] As the historians Tom Scott and Bob Scribner summarise, "feudal dues or rents often accounted for as much as forty percent of production, along with ten percent in tithe".[5]

Pressured from outside and in, German society in the late 1510s and early 1520s was under enormous tension. In 1524 it exploded into an armed rebellion that would only be ended by the most violent repression as tens of thousands of ordinary people were murdered for daring to demand change. This book is the story of that rebellion.

The mass uprising that took place between 1524 and 1526 in central Europe has become known as the German Peasants' War. This title is inaccurate for three reasons. The first is that the rising took place far beyond the borders of what we now call Germany. There were connected events in Switzerland, parts of what is now France, the region we now know as Austria and even as far afield as Samland, then part of the Duchy of Prussia, a duchy of the Kingdom of Poland and now in the westernmost part of Russia.[6] The second is that the revolt involved far wider forces than peasants. Today we tend to understand the term peasants as referring solely to those who laboured on the land. But as Rodney Hilton famously argues in his classic study of the English Rising of 1381, "peasant communities" included people far beyond those who worked the land.[7] Individuals such as craftsmen, blacksmiths and millers had interests closely tied to those of the wider village community.

The same is true of sixteenth century rural Germany, and in the account that follows we will see plenty of examples of individuals who fought in the peasant armies yet do not fit the classic image of a peasant as someone who solely as a producer working on the land, either for themselves or for a lord. Nonetheless there are differences between the period that Hilton is discussing and sixteenth century Germany. For instance, there was much greater differentiation between the wealthy and poorer peasantry within locales, and the German Peasants' War also saw the involvement of wage labourers, particularly miners, who played a significant role in the uprising. So this was very much a rising of the people who formed peasant communities, and their opponents understood them as such.

Peter Blickle, an important historian of these events, developed an interesting thesis that the Peasants' War was a "revolution of the Common Man", and argues that the "bearer of the revolution was not the peasant – as a rule he dominated only the first phase of the rebellion, the formulation of grievances and demands. Rather, it was the 'common man': peasants, miners, the citizens of territorial towns, the politically disenfranchised citizens of imperial cities".[8] I discuss this thesis later, but it mistakes the nature of the revolution, confusing participants with the class that was central to the events itself.

The final inaccuracy is that it was not a war. There were military confrontations and the peasants certainly armed themselves, built armies, organised military operations, stormed castles and towns and fought pitched battles. However, to see the rising as simply a war is to miss the way that social, religious, economic and political issues came together and contributed to the wider revolution.

Leon Trotsky prefaced his monumental history of the 1917 Russian Revolution, a revolution in which he himself played a leading part, by saying that "The history of a revolution is for us first of all a history of the forcible entrance of the masses into the realm of rulership over their own destiny."[9] This was certainly true in Germany in 1524 and 1525. While there are major differences between sixteenth century "peasants" in central Europe and the workers and peasants who seized power in Russia in 1917, the rebels of 1524 were trying to establish control over their own lives, communities and futures. Tens of thousands of them laid down their tools, armed themselves and left their homes and villages to join armies to confront their lords and masters. They could not be successful in the way that their compatriots four centuries later were, and the reason for this is closely linked to the emerging development of capitalism.

The centuries that followed the turmoil of the 1520s in Germany would see the further progress of the Reformation. Old certainties were shattered. Numerous monarchs, princes, aristocrats and clergy were toppled in the wars, discontent, political crises and rebellions that followed. Accompanying this, and intimately connected to it, was the rise of capitalism. It would not be until the nineteenth century that bourgeois society would finally break through, victorious throughout Europe. But when it did so, it completed a process whose beginnings were just visible in the years preceding the sixteenth century. This was one reason why, in 1850, the German Marxist revolutionary Friedrich Engels would turn to the sixteenth century to shine a light on the events of the revolutionary year of 1848. It is also, I would like to suggest, another reason why the story of what took place in 1524 and 1525 remains of interest and importance to us today, for it helps understand our own society and can serve to inspire the rebels and revolutionaries of today.

In the account that follows, I have tried to draw, as much as possible, on contemporary accounts and to explore themes raised by the rebellion. The reader should be aware that these sixteenth century quotes occasionally have language that is antisemitic and sexist.

The title of this book comes from Thomas Müntzer's Prague Manifesto of 1521, "All the extremes of scoundrelly behaviour had to come to the light. O ho, how ripe the rotten apples are! O ho, how rotten the elect have become! The time of the harvest has come! That is why he himself has hired me for his harvest. I have sharpened my sickle, for my thoughts yearn for the truth and with my lips, skin, hands, hair, soul, body and life I call down curses on the unbelievers".[10]

Key areas of the German Peasants' War in 1524-25

Chapter 1
Germany on the Eve of Revolution

The sixteenth century was a period of rapid change and development across Europe. In 1492 Columbus arrived in the Americas, ushering in a period of colonial exploitation that saw the continent's people, natural resources and ecology become tied to a global market, with genocidal consequences for the Indigenous people. The influx of wealth in the form of precious metals, minerals, wood and animal furs and skins would have a marked impact on European society, encouraging economic developments that had already begun to challenge the existing feudal order.

Germany would not be immune to these changes. But in the sixteenth century agriculture dominated its economy. About 80 percent of the population worked the land, and society was shaped by the relationship between these peasants and the landowners, their princes. Across the Empire there was a great variety of agriculture, from cereals, animal husbandry and dairy, to the growing of flax to produce linen and winemaking. While much of this production was still for local use and sale, some parts of the economy were already producing for extensive markets. Some regions of the Empire were associated with particular forms of agriculture. Even today places like the Rhineland or Alsace are known for their wine and dairy production. But within this agricultural economy other industries were developing. Some towns and cities became known for their wool and linen production. Strasbourg, for instance, then part of the Holy Roman Empire, became "one of the largest cities in the Empire, with a population of around 25,000 at the turn of the fifteenth century" based on wool. Products like these, together with the cereals and animals produced in vast areas in the east of the Empire, were sold in Western Europe. This, as well as other emerging industries such as mining, weaving and iron production, pointed towards a new economic reality.[11]

*

Most people in Germany in the sixteenth century were peasants. But what exactly defines a sixteenth century peasant, and who the peasants were, is surprisingly complex to explain. Those who took part in the German Peasants' War were not simply people who worked on the land. They included others who lived in rural communities such as blacksmiths or innkeepers, people whose lives and labour were intrinsically linked to the agricultural economy. To confuse things further, these individuals may have also worked their own land or land belonging to others.

Germany was a highly structured, rigidly hierarchical society that had changed little over the previous centuries. Almost everyone was under the authority of their lord, though this lord might be very distant, and it was likely that most peasants never met them. On a day-to-day basis the immediate authority over the peasants was the seigneur, a local feudal lord. This lord might have been an individual noble, but it could also have been an institution such as a monastery or the church, in which case the peasants owed their allegiance to that bodies' head.

The peasants themselves had a bewildering array of names and labels, which reflected the different social positions they held and their place in the social hierarchy. In the classic feudal period, which ran from about the ninth to the fifteenth centuries in Europe, most peasants were serfs. Serfdom gave little rights or freedom to those at the bottom of society. Serfs were bound to their lord and their manorial lands and required to labour for them. This obligated labour took a number of forms. It might have meant a certain number of days work on the manorial lands every week or month, as well as extra labour at busy times of the agricultural year such as harvest time.

Serfs were also restricted in other ways – bound to the land, forbidden to marry without permission, and obliged to pay taxes to their lord for a plethora of different reasons. When a serf died, their family might have to compensate the lord, or pay a fee on taking over some land. A serf's lord had enormous power over them, including the right to use violent punishments. Such iniquities were the source of much of the discontent that fuelled peasant rebellions.

By the sixteenth century, German rural relations were beginning to change. Serfdom was gradually being eroded. It was an inefficient use of land, and growing numbers of lords were leasing land to peasants for rent or other forms of payment. There were other reasons to move away from serfdom. One important factor was the drop in population following the Black Death (1347-1350), which decimated Europe – Germany lost about a third of its population – making it possible for serfs to better their position in the context of a shortage of labour. This depopulation also led to areas of arable land not being cultivated, reducing lordly income and raising prices. It was an era of crisis for the feudal order, which only saw a recovery as the population in Germany began to grow, as it did in the sixteenth century: from between seven and ten million in 1470 the population reached fourteen million by 1560.[12]

Alongside this was further development of the money economy with the production of crops and livestock for market.[13] As the population expanded, more land was needed, and this was found by reclaiming uncultivated land through the draining of marshes or by clearing forests. Older field patterns had been lost as the land had become disused during the period of population crash. While the price of agricultural crops rose, wages for peasants failed to rise at the same rate, so profits went up. Consequently, landowners sought to intensify their production to meet growing demands for food and raise their profits further. The intensification of land use, alongside changes in farming practices such as crop rotations and the introduction of new crops improved yields. All these factors reflected a turn towards agriculture for profit, not for use. A minority of peasants benefited from these changes, though the main beneficiaries were large farmers. There was a consequent increase in the "social distance between a tiny upper stratum of the peasantry and the great number of small farmers".[14] In eastern Germany in particular, the growth of "estate farming" saw the consolidation of former and current peasant lands into manors. This contrasted with farming in the south and west of Germany, where "the sixteenth century witnessed no formation of extensive estate farming; rather, these areas were dominated by tenant farming for landlords, on the basis of rents in money or kind".[15]

One contradiction in these changes in rural relations was that some parts of Germany, and eastern Europe in general, saw a renewal of serfdom, sometimes called a "second serfdom". This saw rulers reasserting and increasing the rights of lords to manage serfs, and, in the words of historian Tom Scott, permitting a "distinctive entrepreneurial domain economy…to develop, in which the peasantry was subordinated by feudal ties…to a capitalist mode of production supplying overseas markets".[16]

German agriculture took multiple different legal and economic forms across the Empire, but everywhere this was based on an exploitative relationship between landowner and peasant. Serfdom was being slowly replaced, though the nobility were fighting to keep its legal structures, even while they understood it was an inefficient way of producing wealth. But if the number of serfs was changing, what was replacing them? Who were the other, non-serf, peasants of the sixteenth century?

The hierarchical, stratified nature of rural society at the time was most obvious in the differences between the wealthiest of people and the poorest – the lord and the peasants, for instance. But there were differences among the peasants themselves, who were separated by wealth and property ownership; each individual knew their place in village society. A peasant's legal position determined their income and hence the social position of the peasant's family. Exact income was mostly determined by the amount of land a peasant farmed. A wealthy peasant, with multiple holdings of land, was much higher up in the village hierarchy than one who only farmed one holding, or part of one. The poorest of the village community were the many landless peasants who worked other peoples' land as wage labourers.

So, the peasants cannot be understood as a single, homogenous block. Rather a group of people with common interests, but who were also differentiated by their wealth and social position. This complex mix of legal, economic and social factors meant that individuals could find themselves beholden to different masters from their neighbours, friends and other family members. As Christopher Friedrichs points out, because land might be inherited from a peasants' father, but status from the mother, it was possible that "a single person might hold his land from one seigneur but be in personal bondage to another".[17]

These differences are reflected in the different demands made by the peasants during the rebellion. While many Articles called for the abolition of serfdom, others demanded lower taxes and rents, reflecting the peasants' different interests. This meant that the nobles could divide the peasantry by offering concessions to some but not others.

These social and political developments were driven, across Europe, by new technology. New navigation and ship building techniques were opening up the world to European colonialism. Guns and cannon were transforming warfare, devices such as clocks were beginning to change how people lived and worked and new agricultural implements were changing farming. Producing the materials needed to make all these things was having an enormous impact on the world. One important example is the blast furnaces needed to make iron. The historian Jean Gimpel notes how the Middle Ages had seen vast forests cut down to produce fuel for the furnaces, which were built in their thousands.[18]

One of the reasons explorers and colonists were expanding outward from Europe in this period is that the natural resources of places such as the Americas were extremely attractive to merchants, manufacturers and rulers who needed them to continue expanding their wealth. But these resources also existed in Europe. In Germany, for instance, silver mines were enormously important to the economy, and the miners in these, and others who dug iron ore, gold, copper and so on, would become central to the class struggles that marked the German sixteenth century.

These economic and technological developments were gradually changing European society. They would also encourage wider developments. As Marxist historian Chris Harman notes, Columbus might have found the Americas without the Arab astrolabe and the Chinese compass, but he needed them to chart the route that made multiple voyages and the Spanish conquest possible.[19] Similarly, Luther's ideas gained rapid traction not simply because they addressed common concerns and complaints, but because the invention of the printing press allowed the mass production of pamphlets and posters, making Luther's ideas readily accessible to ordinary people. Indeed, as one author notes, Luther made a conscious attempt to develop "Brand Luther" through the mass production of material by bringing a printer to Wittenberg and developing a "brand" using similar designs and layouts.[20] This interaction between technological development and social change fed back on itself, encouraging further change.

The Middle Ages, the period prior to the sixteenth century, was an era in which societies were dominated by peasant production for their feudal lords. These lords owed their position to a distant historical era when they could promise to organise military forces to protect the populations of their lands who in turn owed allegiance to them. In return for this protection, the peasantry were obligated to give over a large percentage of their production to the lord for their personal use. Over time, this lordly rule became embodied in an extremely repressive and exploitative society, which, as we have seen, strictly controlled peasants' lives. This unequal and oppressive system drove class struggle. The lords tried to force more out of their peasants, and the peasants would resist using a myriad of forms of protest from limited legal avenues to open rebellion.

Vestiges of this feudal relationship continued to exist into the sixteenth and seventeenth centuries. But some things, such as the manorial system, had changed. Most lords "had long since divested themselves of their demesne", which was rented out, and made most of their "feudal revenues" from rents. It was, says historian Tom Scott, a "petrified" form of the feudal system. However, as he cautions, the system still provided "the framework for the sociolegal subjection of the peasantry" even if it was being transformed.[21]

Emperors, kings and queens still sat at the top of the hierarchy in countries across Europe, and while the nobility, princes and lords were below the monarchs, they controlled the lives of hundreds of thousands of peasants. But as the Middle Ages progressed, new forms of production began to change society. Under feudalism, peasant agricultural production dominated and was geared entirely towards satisfying the wants of the lords (non-agricultural production such as the production of clothing or tools was also bound up in peasant family units, such as blacksmiths). So, for feudal lords, wealth was determined by the amount of land they owned and the peasants who could work it. In Marxist terms, the feudal economy was organised for the production of use-values. A lord was mostly content to exploit their peasants enough to produce food and goods to keep the lord, their family and retinue in luxury and to ensure that their position was protected by hiring servants and guards to facilitate this. The amount of land owned by a specific lord determined just how much luxury they enjoyed because the only source of their wealth was peasant labour. But this was not production for the sake of production. There was a limit to the exploitation of the peasants as there was only so much one lord needed, and this had caused a stagnation in technological development during the Middle Ages.

As the Middle Ages progressed, things began to change. Production for exchange value – in order to sell products on the market – became more and more important. Increasingly the cash economy came to dominate, and merchants trading goods across the European continent grew in economic and political importance. Some urban areas grew wealthy from this developing market system. The German city of Freiburg, for instance, sat at the junction of various trade routes and rivers that merchants used, and the city's council attempted to control this trade to bring wealth to the city through taxes and controlling production within Freiburg itself.

We get a good sense of this change in Silesia and Upper Lusatia. There, as Scott explains, by the mid-sixteenth century:

> The feudal lords used their concerted seigneurial power to promote crafts and textile production. Rather than expropriating tenants, they released demesne and common land for new settlement by cottagers, and encouraged the transfer of linen manufacturing away from the towns to their own estates, where it was integrated into the system of feudal rents.

But in other areas, such as Lower Saxony, Thuringia, Saxony and Upper Austria, where much of the Peasants' War was centred, there was an

> interval type of landlordship, using both wage-labour from free peasants and the labour-services of serfs to manage sizable estates... In one such area, the district around Magdeburg, commercial leases on the larger peasant farms co-existed with a landless servile workforce within one estate. Such domains certainly developed in response to the

market, but that demand was as much local as international, and was geared towards the main crop, barley.[22]

These new agrarian economic relationships, developing in the period before and after the Peasants' War, illustrate the enormous upheaval in rural society, and the way that lords were trying to adapt to the rise of the market and new economic realities.

Money was increasingly important to the European economy. Some merchants became extremely wealthy and were able to move from trading to using their wealth to make more money from banking or manufacturing. The German Fugger family began as merchants trading textiles and cloth. They then became fabulously rich by lending money to monarchs and popes, as well as other merchants, and their "bank" became the single most powerful economic institution in Europe. The Fuggers' wealth allowed them to shape European society, funding wars, breaking or making princes, as well as, on the one hand, selling indulgences[23] on behalf of the Pope and, on the other, lobbying the Catholic Church to change its prohibitions on making interest from loans.

These economic developments were also changing the landscape. Increasingly, agriculture was becoming geared to growing cash crops that could be sold for money. This began to create new groups of rural labourers who worked some, or all, of the time as wage labourers. They were now producing commodities for trade, rather than products for immediate use. A new "putting out" system, while still based on household groupings, saw merchants providing raw materials to be manufactured into commodities for sale. Production was becoming tied to a market and broken from the immediate needs of landowners and rulers. At the same time, newer urban industries were developing "organised on capitalist lines". The development of rural and urban industry in this way saw the beginnings of wage labour in towns and the countryside.[24]

All these changes created great tensions. The old feudal lords resented their loss of power and prestige as new individuals rose to prominence having made their money through trade and finance. The continuous wars of the Middle Ages between various factions of the feudal order vying for control of land continued, often on an enormous scale. The German Peasants' War itself was shaped in no small part by conflicts between the Holy Roman Empire and other European powers. The mercenary armies that proved so decisive against the peasantry on battlefields such as Frankenhausen and Böblingen were often temporarily redeployed by the nobility from other arenas. A quarter of a century after the Peasants' War, Germany was engulfed in the "Princes' Revolt" as Protestant princes rebelled against the Catholic emperor.

These wars and conflicts of sixteenth century Germany were not separate from the conflicts between classes. The Middle Ages was a period of constant class struggle as those at the bottom of society tried to resist their exploitation at the hands of their lords. This book argues that the Peasants' War was both an extension of this process and a development as wider economic changes brought new social groupings into conflict. This is most clearly seen in urban areas with the interaction between peasant and rural communities and their urban compatriots. Cities and towns were no longer simply centred on markets. They became places of production, that were independent sources of wealth, and places to get rich. Many of those who tried to enter the towns from the countryside, often illegally leaving their lord's land, would retain their cultural and social links with the peasantry, creating the potential for powerful unity in the battles that were to come. The historian Roy Pascal, who was influenced by Marxist ideas, notes:

> It was the policy of many cities to refuse civic rights to the peasants who constantly flocked to the towns, and thus a real class of non-possessors was created. In the economic crisis of the sixteenth century these lower classes were…hit hardest, for while there was a great increase in the prices of industrial products, the price of agricultural produce and wages increased more slowly, often only at the cost of a struggle. With the exploitation of the journeymen there was joined a sort of colonial policy towards the peasants. Thus in the peasant wars of this century we find the proletariat involved on the side of the peasants.[25]

The Peasants' War was not just dominated by class war directed against landowners. The new rich, such as the Fuggers, drove class conflict through their exploitative practices and became the targets of that discontent. As we shall see, one leading radical, Michael Gaismair, raged against the likes of the Fugger family in his vision for a radically new, equal society in Tyrol.

These changes marked a new era for European society. Production was breaking away from the old feudal order, as capitalist relations developed. Millions of people across the continent were finding that the lives that they, and generations before them, had lived, were being transformed. Traditional practices were under assault as production developed for the market as opposed to immediate use. As Chris Harman explains, capitalism emerged "as a network of productive units in both handicrafts (in town and country) and agricultural production using free labour separated to varying degrees from real control over the means and materials of production, a network bound together by the activity of a section of merchant capital which itself was centred on the towns".[26]

Along with these changes came adjustments to how many peasants owned their land, taking different forms throughout the Empire. In eastern Germany, hereditary possession was gradually replaced by what Werner Rösener describes as "unfavourable rights of occupancy". This, he says, was done to "promote estate farming... by tying the peasants to the soil", reducing the total number of peasants and increasing the "servile obligations of the remaining peasants". The peasant now increasingly "counted as part of the estate's possessions and was obliged to perform heavy labour service". The estate farming that came to dominate in eastern Germany, which grew predominantly between 1480 and 1624, had far-reaching consequences. It meant a renewal of serfdom for the peasantry, but this time geared towards production for the market.[27]

But in south-west Germany, where the Peasants' War was centred, this was not the case as tenant farming was the norm and the peasants themselves were relatively free. These regional differences strongly influenced the nature of rural class struggle and the future development of the German economy.

All these changes would have profound consequences. As Chris Harman summarises:

There was frenzied money making among the rich of the country and town alike. The gold lust of Columbus, Cortes and Pizarro was one expression of this. Another was the church's trade in indulgences which led to Luther's first outburst. So too was the turn to renewed serfdom in eastern Europe and to the first forms of capitalist farming in parts of western Europe. Money was becoming the measure of everything. Yet the official values of society were still those embodied in the hierarchy of the old feudalism.[28]

This is not to say that Europe was now capitalist. It was a society in transition. Capitalist processes and interests were developing within the old feudal economy, forcing change and transforming relations. But the old order, as Harman emphasises, remained and this was no more true than in Germany, where society was marked by dozens of competing lordships – but now challenged by radical new ideas that were being taken up by the mass of the population.

There were other social changes taking place as well. Merry E. Wiesner argues that between 1300 and 1600 "work" in Germany was dominated by agriculture, which saw a gendered division of labour. She explains that women were "largely responsible for tasks within or close to the house". This included looking after animals, growing flax to make cloth, preparing beer, bread and dairy products. At busy times of the agricultural calendar such as harvest, women would work in the fields, "manuscript illuminations and woodcuts show women and men working side by side with sickles well into the eighteenth century". Both men and women would also go to market and work as day labourers. Wiesner notes that while in some parts of Germany men and women earned the same, in most places women earned less – both for the same work and for work traditionally done by women.[29] This, Wiesner argues, was the consequence of a process that saw the creation of gendered work and the exclusion of women from areas of production. In 1300 there was "no sharp split between the realms of production and reproduction for either sex", even while there were jobs specific to different genders and the work of men was usually "more highly valued". The point is that women's tasks were considered "work". By the end of the period, "women were excluded from some areas of production, but, more importantly, their productive tasks were increasingly defined as reproductive, as related to 'housekeeping'. Women worked, but what they did was no longer thought of as 'work'."

Wiesner argues that these changes were related to the development of capitalism and production for the market. But she also relates it to wider changes taking place through this period – firstly the growth of the idea that education was to "prepare one for a career", from which women who could not get an education were excluded. Secondly the rise of the Protestant idea that women's role was that of wife and mother, and finally "guild notions of honour, which increasingly defined production in a shop as what the apprentices, journeymen and masters did" while the women "assisted".[30] Across Germany, various laws were being introduced that encouraged such divisions, leading to situations where labourers themselves would police and manage the separation between gendered work. Wiesner gives an example:

> When the knitting-frame was introduced into Germany, men began to argue that using it was so complicated that only men could possibly learn; the frame actually made knitting easier and much faster, but women were prohibited from using it anyway with the excuse that they were unskilled. The amount they could earn from hand-knitting was thus much less than their male counterparts using a frame, but by the end of the sixteenth century male knitters were pressuring for laws which would exclude women altogether, with the argument that all knitting was so skilled that it should be the province of men alone."[31]

This, it should be emphasised, took place in the context of the "church and state" reinforcing "gender roles through sermons, published advice books, laws and ordinances". The Reformation, which emphasised "family life" with the husband at the head of the household and women in the role of wives and mothers, was the context for this assault on women's work by some men and institutions such as guilds.[32] These changes were then enshrined in laws "which divided skilled from unskilled labour, and productive from domestic tasks".[33]

The potential for radical revolt to overcome these ideas was real. After the Peasants' War, a contemporary writer, Andreas Musculus, linked its radicalism with the position of women in society. He wrote in 1556 that having a woman as head of a household was like the rebellion "when the subjects wanted to be lords".[34] The Peasants' War here embodies the establishment fear of a world turned upside down, where women were equal or even above men in society.

In the run up to the Peasants' War, the German ruling class was terrified of rebellion from below. They had good reason. During the Middle Ages, the exploitative nature of feudalism meant a continuity of struggle, with rebellions and discontent threatening the status quo. Peasant rebellion might not have been directed towards the overthrow of society, but it could easily lead to the burning of castles and manor houses, the killing of lords and their families, and the destruction of property.

But events in the early sixteenth century also raised fear among the ruling classes of Germany of wider turmoil. In his history of the period, the German Marxist Karl Kautsky argued that there was a sixteenth century "communist movement" in Germany which was the precursor to later revolutionary socialist movements. He wrote that "antagonism to the Papal power" was the most important feature of such radical groups because the Papacy was "in the front rank of the propertied classes of the Middle Ages".[35] Kautsky overemphasises both the existence of a proto-communist movement and its links to later working class movements. But he is right to note that movements such as the Taborites, a radical Christian sect that arose from the Hussite rebellion in Bohemia (now in the Czech Republic), argued for a communal society that rejected the established church.[36] The Taborites preceded Luther's Reformation by nearly a century, but they were an indication of the potential for radical ideas to seize the hearts and minds of the peasantry. Kautsky says that "emissaries" of the Taborites travelled in the south of Germany to spread their ideas among discontented sections of rural society.[37]

The Bundschuh Rebellions

But it was the last years of the fifteenth and early years of the sixteenth century that saw precursor rebellions that gave an inkling of what was to come and terrified Germany's rulers. In the 1490s south-west Germany was in a state of "perpetual uproar" as ordinary people expressed their discontent at their rulers.[38]

These are known as the Bundschuh rebellions, and they were marked by violence and anti-clericalism. The name comes from the laced shoes worn by the peasantry, which became a symbol of the rebellions, and was inscribed on peasant banners much as the clenched fist has become a symbol of radical movements today. There was a popular belief that the capture of Jerusalem during the First Crusade (1095–1099) had been completed by peasants under such a banner.[39] These rebellions were sporadic, but took place over several decades, and represented real discontent across the region. The Bundschuh rebellions had a number of different causes, including anger at taxes, crushing debt and so on. Inability to pay back loans to money-lenders, who included Jewish people, also led to some examples of antisemitism within these rebellions.[40]

Joss Fritz was the peasant leader of several Bundschuh rebellions around the Rhineland, and a sadly neglected figure in the history of peasant struggle. We will encounter him again in our account of the Peasants' War, but before that he was involved in several local risings which preceded it. Little is known of Fritz's background though we do know he was an "episcopal bondman", a serf tied to the church. Fritz's ideas are summarised by Tom Scott:

> Fritz contemplated more than simply a savage destruction of the ecclesiastical hierarchy. He aimed to purge and purify the Church in accordance with the tenets of divine justice. This religious inspiration was manifested in the ritual of the Speyer Bundschuh. Those who joined were required to recite five Paternosters and five Ave Marias on their knees; the Bundschuh password ran, 'God greet you, fellow. How fares the world?' with the reply, 'We cannot rid ourselves of the plague of priests'.[41]

Like the Peasants' War, these rebellions used religious ideas to argue for a different society. A slogan on a banner during Fritz's rebellion of 1502 read "Lord, stand by Thy divine justice" – emphasising the importance of "godly law" as opposed to those imposed by earthly rulers.[42]

The 1502 rebellion was discovered and suppressed before it could start, and many of those involved were tortured into revealing the demands of their "conspiracy". These included plans to attack and pillage religious institutions, to "annihilate all authority and government" and "never again to pay a tithe, either to the clergy or to secular lords and nobility." The appointment of clerics and priests was to be overseen by the peasantry, who would control all church institutions. As with the later rebellion, peasants were also concerned about how their livelihoods were destroyed by the rich and powerful. The 1502 Bundschuh demanded:

> That hunting, fishing, grazing, lumbering and every other thing that had become a princely prerogative be returned to the public so that a peasant might hunt and fish whenever and wherever he had a mind to, without being hindered or oppressed by anyone.[43]

These demands, or "articles", were collected by hostile torturers, and we must be wary of putting them directly into the mouths of the rebels who planned the conspiracy. But they do give an indication of what those at the top of society thought the rebels were demanding. Fritz himself disappeared, reappearing a decade later to prepare another rebellion across a large number of villages in Breisgau, around Freiburg. Interestingly this new rebellion seems to have been less anti-clerical, the new rebel password, in reply to the question "how fares the world?", was "in all the world the common man can find no comfort." In September 1513 the rebels were ready. They had completed a revolutionary flag, which had been in storage since 1502, "with a Bundschuh on one side, and on the other Christ crucified, the Virgin Mary and St John the Baptist with a peasant kneeling before them, along with the insignia of Pope and Emperor and the legend: Lord stand by Thy Divine Justice". An elaborate and complex plan to capture significant towns around Breisgau had been agreed, a march that, had it happened, would have had many similarities to the marches of the bands in the Peasants' War to come just over a decade later. But the march did not take place. The authorities had advance warning from spies in the rebel camp and Fritz barely escaped.[44]

Another rebellion was launched in 1514, this time caused by the actions of the duke of Württemberg, Ulrich, who we will meet again due to his later role in the Peasants' War when he portrayed himself as the voice of peasant discontent. In 1514, however, he was firmly on the side of the lords, and tried to increase his own wealth by adjusting the weights and measures that he taxed. The consequent rebellion against this became known as the Poor Conrad movement, from the German Armer Konrad. Konrad was a name associated with the rural poor, and Armer, in German, carries the same dual meaning of poor as in English. The phrase "Armer Konrad" began as a derogatory term for the situation of the rural population but was taken up by that population in rebellion.[45]

In 1517 Joss Fritz tried again, organising groups of rebels in dozens of towns and villages along the Rhine. Fritz was too well known, so he appointed organisers to travel between villages and towns – "beggars, vagabonds, strolling players, ballad-mongers, hawkers, questionnaires (sellers of holy relics), and quacks and the discharged mercenaries who thronged the highways of the Empire".[46] This time the rebels demanded the cancellation of debts and the abolition of feudal obligations, "intended to strike at the heart of all seigneurial authority in city and countryside".[47] But once again the Bundschuh was discovered – this time a peasant lost his nerve and confessed to a priest. The priest, conveniently ignoring the seal of the confessional which was supposed to keep confessions secret, promptly told the authorities. Attempts to arrest the leaders were limited until one conspirator, Michael von Dinkelsbühl, was caught and provided the names of hundreds of other rebels. Once again, Fritz escaped, alongside, in this case, most of the other rebels. Rather inspiringly though, we hear of Fritz again during the Peasants' War, "by then a grey-bearded veteran, still agitating among the peasantry".[48]

Adolf Laube says that the Poor Conrad movement was "less revolutionary and anti-feudal" than the Bundschuh rebellions. Nonetheless, it must have been a significant shock to Ulrich, as the rebellion spread rapidly across the whole Duchy, involving peasants and town dwellers. It was only through a combination of "compromise" and "armed force" that the duke regained control. The Bundschuh and Armer Konrad movements were part of a continuum of struggle in the period, and were, according to Laube, an "expression of a deep social crisis at the threshold of the transition from feudalism to capitalism in which all classes and social groups experienced a process of dislocation and differentiation of unprecedented extent, and which also caused grave difficulties for the ruling classes."[49]

While these precursors to the Peasants' War were easily defeated, they fuelled the general worries of the rulers about further rebellions and left a well of experience and knowledge for the great struggles of 1524-25.

By the start of the sixteenth century, the gradual changes within European economies had created a variety of new forces whose interests clashed, both with the existing social order and with each other. The tensions between those whose wealth was based on old feudal relations and those whose interests came from making profits through mercantilism was one source of discontent. But more important were those at the base of society – as hundreds of thousands of peasants and urban labourers struggled for a more equitable society. The principal ideological expression of this discontent would come from Martin Luther's challenge to the established church, and those who ruled in its name. This would, as we have seen, provide fertile ground for new, more radical, egalitarian politics to break through, which would deepen the antagonism between those at the bottom of society and its rulers.

As Roy Pascal summarises, "by 1500…the balance of power of the Middle Ages, such as it had been, had completely broken down, and had split up into a number of antagonistic interests, all of which were self-conscious enough to make a sharp clash of policy inevitable."[50]

The exploitative relationships between those at the top of society in the sixteenth century Holy Roman Empire and those at the bottom drove discontent and provoked repeated revolts. But to fully understand the scale and events of the German Peasants' War, we must look further at another factor that was transforming German society, closely related to other social and economic changes. This was the religious crisis within German society.

In sixteenth century Europe, Christianity was how almost everyone, whatever their class position, understood the world around them. For the lower classes this religious understanding was mediated through the church, clergy and religious institutions. Religion, however, was not universally accessible. The Bible was not available in vernacular languages. Church services were usually performed in Latin. Priests were selected by lords, and their sermons parroted the interests and ideas of the ruling class. Religion shaped the day-to-day life of the peasant in particular – from explaining natural disasters and being reflected in the agricultural rhythms by which rural populations planted and harvested crops. Religion was reality. People lived in a world where the devil was real and where demons existed to tempt people away from God. Luther, for instance, thought that he had regularly been tormented by and fought with the devil.

But religion did not simply play an ideological role for the mass of the population, contributing to the general oppression of the lower orders. Its contradiction was famously summed up by Marx's famous comment that

> Religious suffering is, at one and the same time, the expression of real suffering and a protest against real suffering. Religion is the sigh of the oppressed creature, the heart of a heartless world, and the soul of soulless conditions. It is the opium of the people.[51]

In other words, religion was the ideology of society that both explained the world and offered comfort from its day-to-day realities and hope for a future without the harshness of those realities. It was how people understood the world around them and how they hoped to escape it. Thus, when ordinary people rebelled against their exploitation, they usually did so in religious terms, seeking explanations for their oppression and arguments for an alternative from religious texts, scripture and the Bible. We will repeatedly see this as we look at the progress of the Peasants' War. In his account of events, Engels expands on this:

> Even the so-called religious wars of the sixteenth century mainly concerned very positive class interests; those wars were class wars, too, just as the later internal collisions in England and France. Although

the class struggles of those days were clothed in religious shibboleths, and though the interests, requirements and demands of the various classes were concealed behind a religious screen, this changed nothing at all and is easily explained by the conditions of the times.

He continues:

This supremacy of ideology in the entire realm of intellectual activity was at the same time an inevitable consequence of the fact that the church was the all-embracing synthesis and the most general sanction of the existing feudal order.[52]

But in Germany in the 1520s, Christianity was in crisis. In 1517 the theologian and academic Martin Luther had begun events that became known as the Reformation, challenging the established church in fundamental ways. This challenge was to help fuel the ideological, political and social discontent that formed the basis for the Peasants' War.

Chapter 2
Martin Luther and the German Reformation

In order to fully understand the events of the Peasants' War, it is necessary to place the rebellion in its wider context. We have already seen how the uprising arose out of growing discontent at the economic situation. Rebellions against poverty and the oppressive reality of feudal society were not uncommon in Europe in the fifteenth and sixteenth centuries. But one major difference between the rebellions of 1524-5 and preceding ones was the context of the German Reformation. The Reformation, which began in Wittenberg, Germany in 1517, is the movement that led to the split in the Christian Church between Catholicism and Protestantism. It was rooted in discontent at the established church and its practices (the Church was highly repressive and exploitative) as well economic developments within feudal society. A huge landowner, whose priests and functionaries were part of the economic exploitation of the peasantry, the Church was also the key instrument of rule providing an ideological framework which shaped and justified feudal society, placing the mass of the population subordinate to a tiny elite.

In October 1517, Martin Luther, an academic, monk and theologian, published Ninety-five Theses criticising the Church's practice of selling indulgences. Discontent among ordinary people at the Church was common, and within the Church itself there was great discord and disagreement. The five year long Fifth Lateran Council, which ended in March 1517, had been called in response to growing rifts within the Church. In some cases, these rifts represented the different interests of European rulers who had various disagreements with the Church over issues such as jurisdiction. The calls for reform stemmed from the contradictions caused by a Church that was enormously powerful, wealthy, a massive landowner and at the same time was supposed to be overseeing the spiritual wellbeing of millions of impoverished people. Luther's initial attack on indulgences rapidly exploded into a general critique of the Church, spreading discontent, confusion and debate throughout European society in general, and Germany in particular. Luther himself quickly moved on from a focus on indulgences, into a generalised critique of the Church, its institutions, practice and hierarchy.

Before publishing his Theses, Luther was an unknown academic living and working in a provincial German town, overlooked by almost everyone in the Empire. Despite this relative obscurity, Luther rapidly found himself the centre of a storm of change that swept Europe. His early life had given no real indication that he would become the radical thinker who would threaten the whole edifice of Catholic power. He was born in the small town of Eisleben in 1483, before his family moved to Mansfeld, where he spent his childhood. Mansfeld was a small mining town, and Luther's family worked in the metal mining industry. In later life, Luther claimed he was the son of a peasant family. But while his ancestors had been peasants, his parents were no longer so humble. Hans Luder, Luther's father, was a mine manager responsible for some 200 workers.[53] Mining had been the preserve of small, independent producers, but that was changing. Lyndal Roper gives a sense of the social relations:

> Hans Luder would have been caught between several competing forces: the counts, who leased the mines and constantly sought to extract more money by altering the legal terms; the other mine managers…the miners, whose labour actually produced the wealth from the ground, and who were beginning to organise collectively; and the capitalists in faraway Nuremberg and Leipzig, who drove hard bargains and to whom it was only too easy to become irrevocably indebted.[54]

Miners were to be a key force during the Peasants' War. But the importance of this background to Luther's life lies in the economic context that he came from. Initially Luther trained as a lawyer, not least because such a role would have been important to strengthening the family's business. His father had invested highly in this cause. But two factors changed things. The first was Luther's personal religious experience. A key moment, expressed in Luther's own account of his life, was being caught in the open during a major thunderstorm.

Luther prayed that he would be spared, notably invoking Saint Anna, the patron saint of miners, and vowed that he would become a monk if his life was spared. When he survived, he made true on his promise and entered the Order of Saint Augustine in 1505. This change of direction came as a shock to everyone who knew Luther, and led to a major break between him and his father.

The Fifth Lateran Council was intended by Pope Julius II to strengthen the position of the Pope and bring peace to the Church. But in his history of the Reformation, Diarmaid MacCulloch argues the Council "failed to achieve anything important". He goes on to say, "No one was prepared to offend vested interests by enacting concrete proposals which would significantly change anything".[55] While this may have made the Pope more comfortable, it did nothing to quieten the growing demands for reform. Figures like the humanist theologian Desiderius Erasmus were fuelling calls for reform by challenging the ideas and practices of the Church. Erasmus built a network of contacts around Europe, exchanging correspondence and debating ideas. His new translation of the New Testament challenged accepted Church dogma. His work became "crucial to the Protestant revolution" peaking, according to MacCulloch, in "a brief period after 1517".[56]

Despite Luther's relative isolation and obscurity, his attack on indulgences fell on fertile ground. What seemed like a very specific demand rapidly evolved into a great criticism of the whole Church, the Pope at its head and his representatives across Europe. It was rapidly disseminated through Europe using the latest communications technology – the printing press. It is worth exploring Luther's demands to understand how they spread so rapidly, generalising discontent through Germany, and then Europe.

Indulgences were a way that believers could purchase remission for their earthly sins. This was usually understood to mean a reduction in time spent in purgatory, the state of suffering after death for sinners to make amends before entering heaven. The sale of indulgences had been used to raise funds, for instance to pay for the costs of crusades in the Middle East. But by the time of Luther, income from indulgences was increasingly being used to pay for other Church projects. In particular, and to Luther's great anger, the Church was raising money to fund the cost of rebuilding the spectacular St. Peter's Basilica in Rome.

The sale of indulgences angered Luther. It was seen as a way of raising money from the most oppressed people, often through the use of high-pressure sales tactics that used guilt to encourage peasants to pay. The highly successful indulgence seller Johann Tetzel, who famously set up shop in Jüterbog, a small town near Luther's Wittenberg, was adept at raising money in this way. Tetzel was said, for instance, to use rhyme to encourage donation, one such being "Place your penny on the drum; the Pearly Gates open, and in strolls mum".[57] Tetzel was, according to Peter Stanford, someone who "personified the Catholic Church's habit of making a business out of religion" and was thus the trigger for Luther's initial criticism of the Church. This also indicates a second point of discontent for Luther. The sale of indulgences brought together the economic interests of the Church and the local lords and princes.

Indeed, indulgence sales in Brandenburg in 1517 emphasise the complex relations between local and regional rulers and the Church hierarchy. When, in 1515, Pope Leo X asked for the sale of indulgences in Brandenburg to pay for St Peter's, he tasked the local archbishop, Albrecht, to administer the process. Albrecht took this on because he was in debt to the Pope and the Fugger bank, debts incurred in becoming Archbishop. Fugger representatives accompanied the indulgence sellers, checking the money and then taking half of it.

Luther's anger at indulgence sales was not only economic; it was also spiritual. Indulgences sold in Brandenburg by people like Tetzel offered

> complete remission of the penance for all sins, the promise of divine grace, and deliverance from purgatory; the right to confess to any priest, so that the sinner could choose a lenient priest from whom absolution was certain, and was freed from the control of his parish priest; participation in the general merits of the Church; and, to souls in purgatory, remission of the sins they had committed during their life-time.[58]

This was a significant offer and people flocked to buy them. But Luther objected by saying that salvation could not be purchased; it had to be granted by God. He was concerned about the relationship between the individual and God, and here we begin to discern why Luther's objections were radical. Essentially his criticism of indulgences opened the door to criticism of the Church itself, which, for Luther, was not buildings, hierarchy and structure but was the "community of believers".[59] Luther was not the first person to criticise indulgences, and his opposition to them did not develop overnight with the arrival of Tetzel in the neighbouring town. Rather his concerns had grown over time[60] and were expressed in the Ninety-five Theses, which skilfully raised a series of objections that directly challenged the Church.

Reading the *Theses* today one is struck by the clarity of Luther's polemic. He builds up an argument that skewers the role of the Church, and specifically the Pope, in individual salvation. This underpins an explicit criticism of indulgences, but also the role of the Church itself. To illustrate, here are some of the *Theses*:

> Therefore the pope, when he uses the words "plenary remission of all penalties," does not actually mean "all penalties," but only those imposed by himself. [Thesis 20]

> ...most people are necessarily deceived by that indiscriminate and high-sounding promise of release from penalty. [24]

> They preach only human doctrines who say that as soon as the money clinks into the money chest, the soul flies out of purgatory. [27]

> Christians are to be taught that the pope does not intend that the buying of indulgences should in any way be compared with works of mercy. [42]

> Christians are to be taught that if the pope knew the exactions of the indulgence preachers, he would rather that the basilica of St Peter were burned to ashes than built up with the skin, flesh and bones of his sheep. [50]

> Christians are to be taught that the pope would and should wish to give of his own money, even though he had to sell the basilica of St Peter, to many of those from whom certain hawkers of indulgences cajole money. [51]

Luther contrasts the practice of the Church in the sale of indulgences with its use of religious ideas:

> ...the treasurers of the gospel are nets with which one formerly fished for men of wealth [65]

> The treasurers of indulgences are nets with which one now fishes for the wealth of men [66]

He asks direct questions about the role of the Pope that go to the heart of the contradiction exposed by the selling of indulgences:

> Why does not the pope empty purgatory for the sake of holy love and the dire need of the souls that are there if he redeems an infinite number of souls for the sake of miserable money with which to build a church? [82]

> Why does not the pope, whose wealth is today greater than the wealth of the richest Crassus, build this one basilica of St. Peter with his own money rather than with the money of poor believers? [86] [61]

Thus, the *Theses* both expose the illogical nature of indulgence selling and turn this into a criticism of a Church that was immensely wealthy but was happy to take coins from the poor to fund its projects. Perhaps the most powerful points are those that expose the hypocrisy of the approach pushed by the Church – that if the Pope can grant remission from purgatory, why does he not simply do so out of "holy love" rather than financial gain.

Today, many people believe that Luther nailed his Ninety-five Theses to the door of the Castle Church in Wittenberg, the town in whose university he lectured in theology. As popular as this belief is, whether Luther actually posted his theses on the door or simply sent it to close friends and the Archbishop, is immaterial. What matters is the explosive effect the *Theses* had throughout Europe, but particularly in Germany. Within weeks, the *Theses* had been widely reprinted and read across Germany. By March 1518 a copy had even been sent to Henry VIII's chancellor Thomas More in England.[62]

With the publication of the *Theses*, Martin Luther placed himself at the centre of a growing movement for reform of the Church, becoming an iconic figure of resistance to the Church hierarchy and to the Emperor. One of Luther's recent biographers, Peter Stanford, explains:

> By the language of the street that he used, the ecclesiastical corruption and incompetence that he highlighted, and even his own relatively humble beginnings, Luther had a strong appeal for the lower orders... As he took his stand against the two great powers of the age – the Pope and the emperor – he excited an anticipation of more to come as his reform programme easily...became conflated with the prospect of better circumstances in daily lives, where economic woes would be addressed and that widespread sense of being excluded finally tackled. In the minds of his hearers, the religious and the political were one.[63]

Luther's criticism of the Church did not stop with indulgences. Nor did it remain his property. Once he had opened up the debate, dozens of other theologians, clerics and thinkers took up their pens. Initially there was unanimity among critics of the established Church. Everyone agreed with Luther's basic tenets.

As the Reformation developed further, cracks in Luther's camp appeared, often between the more conservative-minded theologians (of which Luther was soon to be the most significant) and more radical thinkers. Massive debates took place, which saw heated discussions, long polemics and the publication of hundreds of pamphlets and broadsheets. These discussions were primarily theological and we cannot cover the depth of ideas here. But we should note the way Luther's theological differences with the existing Church began from opposition to the behaviour of the Church itself – the selling of indulgences and so on – but then moved in an entirely new direction. In particular, Luther argued that only God could grant salvation and what mattered was solely individual faith. This dramatically differed from the understanding prevalent at the time, that salvation could also come through the actions of humans - doing "good works" for instance, or buying indulgences. This challenged the Church's belief that its power to grant indulgences was because it could redistribute the "treasury of merits" that had come from Jesus' sacrifice on the cross.

By rejecting this, Luther was essentially arguing that the Church had no special role. Its hierarchy, from parish priest to the Pope, were, in Luther's assessment, essentially unimportant except in how they could help individual worshippers to reach a better understanding of the Gospel. This was the basis for the Church's attempt to prevent Luther from publishing through excommunication, expulsion from the Church, and the order to destroy his works.

Luther's ideas were attractive to many people, not least those who were sick of paying tithes to support priests or those who had to pay rent to a religious institution for the use of their land.

These Reformation ideas also began to open up wider criticisms of how society functioned. After all, if people were questioning the authority of the Church, it was easier to take the next step and question the wider hierarchies that depended on, and were so closely associated with, the Church itself.

So, while Luther, and most of the other key figures of the Reformation, were conservative and preached against rebellion and in favour of obedience to authority, the Reformation itself opened up a space for wider discontent. In Germany the Reformation became the property of countless numbers of people who looked initially to Luther, but who then carried the movement forward – protesting against priests who refused to change, destroying icons and statues of saints that they saw as blasphemous, and demanding change. Such actions brought them into conflict with the authorities, and indeed Luther himself, and helped to solidify a religious movement that won towns and cities across the Empire to Protestant ideas.[64]

Luther's antisemitism

One further aspect of Luther's thought should be discussed here – his attitude to Jews. This is relevant to our discussion of sixteenth century German society because antisemitic ideas were occasionally part of rebellions and protests. As we shall see, a small number of demands raised by urban rebels in 1524 and 1525 contained attacks on Jewish people. Some of these arose out of existing antisemitic ideas. But Luther's own arguments need to be discussed.

Luther's attitude towards Jews changed over time. Before the Reformation he "reflected standard anti-Jewish views".[65] In the initial period of the Reformation, he believed that his reforms and challenge to the Pope would lead to Jewish people returning to the Christian faith. Indeed, his writings of this period, such as the 1523 pamphlet *That Christ was Born a Jew*, reflect this position and display a sympathy to Jews and their persecution, which was unusual at the time. However, as Lyndal Roper notes, the end of this pamphlet "made it clear that toleration of the Jews was dependent ultimately on the dissolution of Jewry".[66]

While in the aftermath of the Peasants' War his attitude to Jews hardened considerably, antisemitism was often present in his writings. But by the 1540s Luther's antisemitism had reached new levels. In 1543, he wrote a long tract, *On the Jews and Their Lies*, which attacks Jewish belief and religious practice. Here Luther calls for destruction of Jewish places of worship and their homes, burning their religious books and banning them from loaning money. Roper describes it as a "programme of complete cultural eradication".[67] Roper concludes:

> Luther's views were not a medieval relic but a development of it. Even more disturbingly, it was not incidental to his theology, a lamentable prejudice taken over from contemporary attitudes. Rather, it was integral to his thought; his insistence that the true Christians – that is, the evangelicals – had become the chosen people and had displaced the Jews would become fundamental to Protestant identity. It was the central plank of his understanding of the Lutherans' providential role in history, and to secure it the Jews had to be pushed aside, discredited and, if necessary, eliminated.[68]

Luther and the German Peasants' War

The story of the Reformation as it began in Germany is inseparable from Luther. Indeed, for Karl Marx, the Reformation began "in the brain of the monk".[69] Luther's position within the Reformation, and the way that the Reformation was linked to the discontent within German society itself, means that we also cannot separate him from the events of the Peasants' War. In fact, Luther's interventions during the Peasants' War shocked the rebels, who expected him to side with their struggle.

While Luther acknowledged the root of their discontent, he opposed the rebellion itself and eventually urged the ruling class to violently repress them. "A pious Christian", he wrote, "ought to suffer a hundred deaths rather than give a hairsbreadth of consent to the peasants' cause".[70]

Luther's polemic, *Against the Robbing and Murdering Hordes of Peasants*, can still shock today with its encouragement to the lords to commit violence. Luther encouraged the "dear lords" to "stab, smite, slay" and said, "If you die in doing it, good for you! A more blessed death can never be yours". Indeed, those lords who did not kill the rebels were, in the eyes of Luther, "guilty of all the murder and evil that these people commit." Those who fought the peasants would be a "true martyr in the eyes of God" if they did so as a Christian who "acts in obedience to God's word" whereas anyone who rebelled would be condemned as "an eternal firebrand of hell". Luther continued by condemning all those who sided with the peasants, "Anyone who consorts with them goes to the devil with them and is guilty of all the evil deeds that they commit".[71]

Just a few years beforehand Luther's *Theses* had sided with the poor and condemned the Church for using their donations and tithes to facilitate a luxurious lifestyle rather than helping ordinary people. In point 86 of his *Theses* (above) Luther raged against the great wealth of the Pope, who could have rebuilt St Peter's from his own pocket rather than with donations from the poorest members of the Church.

Stanford points out that "Lutheranism, to all those in Germany who felt downtrodden, abused and unheard, must have sounded remarkably like a creed for their existing situation, rather than for their final destination".[72] Understanding the apparent contradiction between Luther's words criticising the Pope and the Church's wealth and his demand for the destruction of the rebellious peasantry, means we need to look more closely at Luther and the Reformation.

The significance of Martin Luther for the Peasants' War is threefold. Firstly, the Reformation provided ideological backing to the discontent of the peasantry and the urban masses. The Church was the primary ideological wing of the existing European ruling class. Luther's challenge to the Church could not help but become linked with any criticism of the status quo. Secondly, the trajectory of the rebellion meant that Luther became closely linked with the uprising. His angry polemics against the rebellious peasantry were partly about him distancing himself from the uprising, but mostly because he was clarifying his own commitment to a hierarchical society. Finally, the Reformation itself was a response and outcome of the gradual changes that were taking place within European society, and these changes were exacerbating economic and social tensions. Unwittingly, Luther himself fuelled the development of discontent through his ideological attack on the Church's indulgences.

Take the following statement by Luther, published in his *Acta Augustana*, written almost exactly a year after The Ninety-five Theses were printed. It is a response to money being syphoned off by the Church to build St. Peter's in Rome:

> The revenues of all Christendom are being sucked into this insatiable basilica. The Germans laugh at calling this the common treasure of Christendom. Before long all the churches, palaces, walls, and bridges of Rome will be built out of our money. First of all we should rear living temples, next local churches, and only last of all St. Peter's which is not necessary for us. We Germans cannot attend St. Peter's. Better that it should never be built than that our parochial churches should be despoiled... Why doesn't the Pope build the basilica of St. Peter out of his own money? He is richer than Croesus. He would do better to see St. Peter's and give the money to the poor folk who are being fleeced by the hawkers of indulgences. If the pope knew the exactions of these vendors, he would rather that St. Peter's should lie in ashes than that it should be built out of the blood and hide of his sheep.[73]

This polemic would clearly appeal to the poverty-stricken majority of the German population, struggling under tithes and taxes and economic difficulties. But it also appealed to a very different group of people – the rich who wanted to have more control over the use of their wealth and who raged against the way that the Church prevented them using their money how they pleased. As Harman comments, "the feudal economy and feudal society were giving birth to something new, and Protestantism was one of its birth cries".[74]

Chapter 3
The Beginning of the Revolt

Across Germany, in 1524, there was enormous discontent among the peasantry and the lower classes in the towns. This had a number of causes, but the context was a society increasingly fragmented and divided. The Holy Roman Empire, founded in 800 CE when Pope Leo III crowned Charlemagne emperor, had existed for over seven hundred years by the time Charles V was elected emperor in 1519.

At its greatest extent the Empire was a mix of territories and lands, often confusingly organised, and included lands that today form part of Germany, Switzerland, Austria, Slovakia, Slovenia, the Czech Republic and parts of France, Italy and Poland. At the time of the rising, this enormous territory was headed by Charles V but direct rule was down to a bewildering array of dukes, princes, nobles and archbishops who ruled over three hundred different types of territories. Often these were far removed from each other so a ruler might have to travel long distances to visit the lands they controlled. Charles V, for instance, who did not speak German and had never visited the region when he became Emperor, had "possessions" that included "family lands of the Hapsburg at the angle of the Upper Rhine... The landgravate of Alsace...a group of estates in the district now controlled by the strong Swiss Confederation; various countships in Breisgau and Swabia, in Vorarlberg and Tyrol. Innsbruck as the seat of Hapsburg administration in Hither Austria. Last of all there were Austria, Styria, Carinthia, Carniola and the Windish Mark".[75]

Seven "electors", four archbishops and three princes chose the Emperor. One of these princes was Friedrich III, the elector of Saxony, whose land included the small town of Wittenberg. Friedrich had founded the University there, employing Luther and Philipp Melanchthon, which was to become the heart of the Reformation. Such was the power of individuals like Friedrich, that he could refuse to implement the Papal Bull (a public edict issued by the Pope) to excommunicate Luther. Instead, he protected Luther.

Charles V lived in absolute splendour. The princes, dukes, nobles and archbishops who ruled the lands within the Empire were not quite as wealthy, but they were still incredibly rich compared to the vast majority of the population. The lords gained their wealth through the exploitation of the impoverished peasantry, who laboured long and hard in the fields to produce crops. Some peasants were still serfs, who laboured on the land and owed their lords a proportion of the crops they produced. Many more peasants were tenants, producing crops to sell on the market, and paying rents and taxes. This was an economy in slow transition – while the peasant economy was still mostly about feeding the peasants' household, increasingly cash crops were being grown, for instance flax, wool and wine-grapes. But to the enormous disquiet of the peasantry, many feudal obligations, rents, taxes and tithes were still imposed upon them. Anger at these would be at the heart of the rising and the demands of the rebellion. Emerging industries were developing that hinted at a new society. Their workers, miners for instance, were organised as wage labourers and some would play a significant role in the rebellion. While there were some similarities between these miners and modern proletarian workers, there were significant differences. Mines, for instance, were divided into shares, some of which were owned by a lord and some miners had to work for free, much like the obligated work peasants were compelled to do on their feudal lord's demesne land. Indeed, as the historians Tom Scott and Robert Scribner point out, the differing interests that arose between miners who were wage labourers and those who were shareholders undermined at least one local revolt in 1525.[76]

The gradually changing economy was also squeezing landowners, who faced fluctuating prices and rental income and decreasing land values. Rural economies suffered because the harvest was so vulnerable to outside factors – particularly the weather, as well as marauding armies in times of war. While the wealthy could survive fluctuating prices, caused by an abundant harvest (low prices) or a less successful harvest (high prices and shortages), the peasants suffered because their rents remained fixed. Money was not the only problem. Famine regularly stalked the land, with four recent "periods of crisis" in the years 1480-1483, 1490-1492, 1500-1503 and 1516-1519.[77]

The wealthy responded to uncertainty by trying to increase the level of exploitation of the peasants and eroding old rights that had protected the peasant economy from the wealthy. Landowners increased taxes, levied fines and divided land into smaller parcels to increase rental income. Common land that had been reserved for communal use – for grazing or collecting firewood and so on – was enclosed, and rented out depriving the peasantry of income and essential resources. These processes attacked the peasantry, but also subtly changed the agrarian economy in ways that provoked discontent and encouraged resistance. One historian explains what this meant:

> In the south-west, in the valleys of the Tauber and the Neckar, in the Moselle and the middle Rhine districts, the practice of subdividing land had proceeded so far that the ordinary holding of the peasant had shrunk to the quarter of a ploughland; and the effort to check this ruinous development only resulted in the creation of a landless agrarian proletariat. The other process, which was not confined to Germany, was the conversion of land into a speculative market for money. The financial embarrassments of the peasant rendered him an easy prey to the burgher-capitalist who lent him money on the security of his holding, the interest on which was often not forthcoming if the harvest failed, or the plague attacked his cattle; and the traffic in rents, which inevitably bore hard on the tenant, was one of the somewhat numerous evils which Luther at one time or another declared to be the ruin of the German nation.[78]

The division of farms like this led to a large class of people in Germany who had almost nothing. Consider the region of Franconia, which was to play a major part in the revolt. By the beginning of the rebellion, some farms here were an eighth or sixteenth of their original size. Population growth, landowner actions and the division of land among heirs played a role in this. But the consequence was the creation of an extensive class of people with no land, or very little, including "the pettiest tenants, settlers without fields, day-labourers, lodgers and living-in servants...the most varied of village craftsmen and rural migratory workers". In early 1525, "there were about 1,000 casual labourers working in the vineyards around Kitzingen, a town of about 500 households". In Saxony, figures suggest that "one quarter to one half of the total rural population" were immiserated. In Thuringia, up to two thirds (in the poorest villages) of rural taxpayers had no land. Taxes and tithes meant peasants had to give vast amounts to their lords: "30 to 40 per cent of all produce was paid in rents and taxes".[79]

It should be no surprise that these pressures bred discontent. As we have seen, in the years preceding the Peasants' War, Germany had already seen numerous localised risings and rebellions.

In July 1524, before the main risings had begun, discontent broke out in the Upper Rhine. The events demonstrate the interaction between local economic issues and wider political and religious changes. A massive storm in Neunkirch, in the Klettgau, had damaged homes and vineyards and destroyed all the crops. Some people blamed the followers of Luther, others said it was a punishment from God against those who clung to the old religious ideas. One account of the events that followed reported how religious discontent fuelled further anger:

> On 24 June the preacher at St John's in Constance publicly declared from the pulpit that the princes nowadays are greater tyrants than the emperors Nero, Decius, and Diocletian, for they are considering how best to drive out Luther, for which they have no right, reason, or justification. Knights and nobles should nowadays protect the faith! – since they are such raving bloodhounds who arrest and put the common people in the stocks contrary to all justice: there is no fear of God, faith, justice or judgement in them.[80]

This gives a remarkable insight into the bubbling discontent in German society on the eve of the revolt, and how social, religious and even environmental issues shaped it. It also demonstrates that anger at the ruling class was not just frustration at how they treated the lower classes, but also because they were seen to be failing at their traditional role of protecting society and exemplifying Christian beliefs.

Upper Swabia

The revolt began in an area of Germany known as Upper Swabia, a region very roughly bounded by the river Danube, the modern borders of Austria, the German side of Lake Constance and the River Lech, about 50 kilometres west of Munich.[81] The Upper Swabian revolt took place in three distinct areas, whose rebellious peasants came together in three military troops, or bands, and eventually united in a "Christian League". This enormous group eventually involved tens of thousands of rebels, and was the body that produced the Twelve Articles, the most famous and influential declaration of revolutionary demands.

Like all rebellions, it began small, with a specific local trigger in Stühlingen, north-west of Schaffhausen on the modern border between Germany and Switzerland. A rebellion here began, it is believed, on 23 June 1524, when the Countess von Lupfen, whose family owned the estates, demanded that the peasantry stop their work in the fields to collect snail shells which she wanted to use to wind her wool. There is no evidence as to the truth of this, but it is perhaps indicative of the mindset of the local lords towards the peasantry, as illustrated by the demands the Stühlingen peasants produced.

The Stühlingen grievances were listed in Sixty-Two Articles detailing their discontent,[82] including demands and complaints that would become ubiquitous throughout the areas affected by the rising. The articles demonstrate a breadth of complaints, but most focus on the peasants' relationship with the lords, whose power over them was represented by a series of rights to demand their property, labour and wealth seemingly at will. For example, peasants needed permission to marry outside of their community, the lords could ride over fields and damage crops without any risk of punishment and could claim property when one of their peasants died.

The power of the lord to deprive the peasantry from traditional rights caused enormous anger. The poorest were deprived of crucial sources of food and resources. In Stühlingen the peasants complained that even the water on their land had been rented out to fishers. Other demands related to legal rights. The peasants complained that court officials were not elected by the community, that those who formed the court were themselves punished if they made decisions that went against the lords' interests.

The Sixty-Two Articles from Stühlingen are a fascinating insight into the reality of rural class relations in Germany on the eve of the rising. Collectively they represent a rejection of the social and economic relations that formed the basis of existing society, held over from the earlier feudal era. These relations obligated the peasantry to perform labour for their lord. As the Stühlingen peasants explain:

> We are burdened by our lords and their officials with numerous insufferable labor services, and through these we are so hindered from cultivating our holdings, which lie in an inclement district, that we do not know how to nourish our wives and children; also we cannot and may not even perform for our lords that which we are obliged to do. [83]

They continue:

> On one day we have to harvest oats, on another bind hemp, till and sow... fallow and plough again, plough waste land, sow and harrow, cut [corn] and carry it into the barns and when it is threshed carry it from the barns into the castle; mow the meadows, make hay and carry the hay into the barns, item, make fences, hunt, carry nets to catch game, and if any game is caught carry it to the castle.

Their list of labour goes on, detailing obligated labour to transport the lord's wine and crops and manage land and water for the lord's interests, keep hunting dogs for the officials, manure fields and hand over money and crops to the lord. The articles evoke the way that peasant labour constructed the rural economy's infrastructure, such as roads and bridges, but the real beneficiaries were the lords who collected taxes for their use.

Article 23 shows how the peasants in Stühlingen were particularly angered by these arrangements because they did not know the reason for the rents or their levels and what they were supposed to get in return:

> To our great burden, we pay our lord's annual rents, interest, and incomes from our holdings, over and above all military service and other things that we provide and perform for them; but we do not know the origin of these, or for what reason they are paid, or even what they are obliged and liable to do for us in return.

By raising such complaints, the peasants were explicitly challenging the status quo, questioning the basis for their exploitation and demanding a new set of relations. Article 59 of the Stühlingen demands concluded "it is our plea that you adjudge that we should be released from serfdom, and no one else be forced into it."

The Stühlingen Articles are noteworthy for one other reason. Unlike later demands from elsewhere in the rebellion, they contain no reference to religious issues, Martin Luther or the Reformation.

We get an impression of how the peasants at Stühlingen organised from a contemporary account of the start of the revolt in February 1525:

> When the hour was at hand, at which the fire of this revolt was to be lit, it happened in Shrovetide (as it is called), when people are accustomed to visit one another, that about six or seven peasants in a village near Ulm, called Baltringen, came together and discussed many of the current troubles. As was the custom among peasants at that time, they travelled from one village to another as if calling on neighbours, and ate and drank together in convivial fashion; the peasants in the village then also journeyed onwards with them. If anyone asked where they were going or what they were doing, they replied, 'We are fetching Shrovetide cakes from one another'. And in such company they travelled about every Thursday and grew every time in numbers, until they were four hundred men.[84]

After about a week of organising like this, they returned to Baltringen and assembled to discuss their grievances, and, crucially, how to proceed because they worried that the lords would see their numbers and "not take it in the spirit" intended. After discussing their grievances, "each complaining to the other of where the shoe pinched most", they "decided first to complain strongly about their oppression to their lords and superiors, and then to ask for mercy and a reduction in their obligations" but quickly realised they had no one who could represent them.

To solve this, the peasants in Baltringen found a "pious, goodhearted and wise man", Ulrich Schmid, from a nearby village. Interestingly he agreed to represent them, but only on the basis that it was known that he "had no intention of bringing any complaints at all against his own lords concerning himself and his obligations". No doubt Schmid said this publicly so that he could safely mediate and not make himself vulnerable to punishment from the lords he would need to speak with.

In each locality the early stages of the revolt tended to follow a similar pattern, with small groups meeting secretly and then sending out individual representatives and delegations to other areas to spread the message.[85]

In Stühlingen the peasants elected a leader called Hans Müller, who led the negotiations with the lords. Accounts say that the peasants raised a banner which included the colours of Austria, as they hoped for Austrian protection.[86] This connection is significant. Archduke Ferdinand of Austria (who became Holy Roman Emperor in 1556) acted as mediator, but towns nearby to Stühlingen were in dispute with him. In fact, it seems that Ferdinand took on the role of mediator only to play for time: he wrote to the Count of Waldburg suggesting that he "amicably treat with the peasants till he had collected his military forces together".[87]

Müller led a delegation of hundreds of peasants to the nearby town of Waldshut, hoping to win the support of the rebellious population there. According to a chronicle by Heinrich Hug, writing around the time of the rising, the peasants essentially engaged in a strike, refusing to do labour or pay taxes.[88] The size of the rebellion was enough to force authorities to negotiate with the rebels.

But the lords refused to budge, and despite a compromise in September 1524, Count von Lupfen scuppered any agreement by demanding that the peasants kneel and confess their guilt and surrender their banner. The peasants refused, "and every day they marched around, kept watch, and held ready their vanguard; no one knew how to help or console them, and they were seething with rage".[89] By 10 October there were 3,500 rebel peasants organised into three "bands". Columns of peasants marched to villages and towns encouraging them to rise as well.

Hug's account of the rebellion gives a real sense of the dynamism of the revolt. He describes in detail the various places the bands marched to, holding meetings to discuss grievances and courses of action. We also learn that the peasants selected representatives (captains) to negotiate with the authorities. His account illustrates the process through which the rebellion was built:

> The peasants rose and marched… Wherever they came, they had their grievances read out and heard, stating that they wished to do no harm to anyone; they paid for whatever they ate and drank and admonished the peasants to help them gain justice.[90]

Some joined, though others refused:

> They next marched to Tuningen and held a commune there and asked them what their opinion was. Hans Müller from the peasants on the Wutach was also present as their spokesman, for he could speak rather well, similarly Oswalt Meder from Rietheim. Then they marched to Trossingen and held a commune there, but [they] did not want to join them; they remained there overnight on the Wednesday before St Nicholas [30 November], and the peasants who had joined the twenty-five from the Brigach valley up to the Tuesday before St Nicholas numbered around 150. Then they marched to Bräunlingen again…the peasants arrived at Bräunlingen, two hundred in number, and remained there overnight. The Bräunlingers gave them food and drink in return for payment, but otherwise they did not trouble them; but fifteen men from Hüfingen deserted their lords to join the peasants.[91]

This particular part of the rebellion seems to have ended in mid December with a confrontation between two hundred rebels led by Oswalt Meder and a force of five hundred soldiers, including cavalry, and five cannon. During this battle the peasants built a defensive structure by circling carts and wagons, a tactic that would be used regularly later in the rebellion.[92]

At the start of October the villages in the Hegau region, an area east of Schaffhausen that extends towards Lake Constance also rose, followed by villages in the Klettgau region, west of Schaffhausen. In early November, inspired by the Stühlingen rising, hundreds of peasant tenants of the abbey of St Blasien in Hauenstein rebelled, occupying the abbey in protest for several days.[93]

The rising spread through October and November 1524. AF Pollard summarises events:

> There were risings of the peasants all round the Lake of Constance, in the Allgau, the Klettgau, the Hegau, the Thurgau and north-west of Stühlingen at Villingen. Further to the east, on the Iller in Upper Swabia, the tenants of the abbey of Kempten, who had long nursed grievances against their lords, rose, and in February 1525, assembled at Sonthofen; they declared that they would have no more lords, a revolutionary demand which indicates that their treatment by the abbots had been worse than that of the Lupfen tenants. The peasants of the Donauried (NW of Augsburg) had been agitating throughout the winter, and by the first week in February four thousands of them met at Baltringen, some miles to the north of Biberach; before the end of the month their numbers had risen to thirty thousand. They were also joined by bands called the Seehaufen, from the northern shores of Lake Constance, while Hans Müller made an incursion into the Breisgau and raised the peasants of the Black Forest.[94]

The rebellion in the New Year entered a "more overtly revolutionary phase...in which it became a religiously legitimate revolt".[95] Three key rebel forces from Upper Swabia now began to shape events. We have already heard about the rising of Baltringen, who elected Ulrich Schmid as their leader and formed a "band" of rebellious peasants. Two other forces joined this – the Lake Constance band, which came to number twelve thousand rebels and was led by a landowner Dietrich Hurlewagen, and the Allgau band, which developed from the Kempten rebellion and by late February had coalesced into a "Christian Union".[96]

Chapter 4
The Twelve Articles

In March 1525 the rebels of the three key bands of Upper Swabia sent fifty representatives to the town of Memmingen. There they agreed what became the most famous set of rebel demands of the whole rising, the Twelve Articles. These articles present a concise and radical set of demands, which bring together religious and economic discontent, and point towards a radical reworking of the rural feudal world. Historian Henry J Cohn argues that the Twelve Articles "were an outline blueprint for the reform of agrarian society" and that the "net effect of implementing the Twelve Articles would have been a fundamental shift in economic power and social status in favour of the lower orders and at the expense of the lords".[97]

The Twelve Articles themselves were influenced by three hundred sets of demands raised by the rebellious peasants of Baltringen, whose forces made up one of the troops at Memmingen. They were printed, distributed, expanded on and developed by new groups of rebels as the uprising spread. Cohn points out that while the Articles were based on earlier demands, they had a specific focus. Rather than just demanding cuts to the services due to lords, they placed "all the issues at stake between lords and peasants to the touchstone of God's Word as expressed in the Scriptures".[98]

The rebellious peasants who produced the Twelve Articles were keen that those who read them understood that they saw themselves as being good Christians. So they rooted their demands in the Bible, implying that they carried God's authority. This is most clearly shown by the twelfth, concluding, article. This states that should any of the demands be found "not to be in agreement with the Word of God" then the rebels would abandon them, as long as this can be proved the basis of scripture. Furthermore, the rebels included a demand that their lords also submit to the same test – any rights they had that were not supported by scripture should be given up.

The Twelve Articles begin with a demand that was central to

Reformation ideology and went to the heart of the peasants concerns: "it is our humble plea and request...that we should henceforth have the power and authority for the whole community to choose and elect its own pastor, and also to have the power to depose him should he conduct himself improperly".[99] This was not just a demand for democratic control over the priests, it was also a challenge to the feudal order.

Pastors were to restrict themselves to preaching the Word of God, not interpreting it. This was important for two reasons. Firstly, the peasants understood that pastors who were chosen by lords and the Church owed their allegiance to their masters, and thus played a role in oppressing and exploiting them. Secondly, by demanding that scripture was explained without interpretation, the peasants were hoping that they would not be swayed by the interpretation offered by their rulers, instead allowing them to come to their own conclusions. The peasants believed, as they wrote in the first article, that "we can only come to God through true faith", and they needed a pastor that would allow them to do this, rather than use the scripture as a tool of oppression.

The second article is the longest of the demands and concerns the tithes that were imposed on the peasantry. This income, they demanded, should go to the local pastor they had chosen in order that the pastor could complete his services. The rebels suggested an elected Churchwarden who would oversee the distribution of the tithe to the pastor and that anything else over and above the amount needed for the pastor to live would be "distributed to the needy poor present in the same village". Any further surplus above this would be used for the defence of the country if needed. Most of the remainder of the second article explains what should happen to villages where the tithe had been sold to someone else. The final line, however, refers to the small tithe. The large tithe was based on about ten percent of the grain harvested by the peasants and was biblical in origin. The small tithe, however, was a tax on other crops and animals. This, the peasants declared, was "an improper tithe, invented by men." Therefore they said "we will no longer pay it".

The third article was the most radical of the twelve. It called for the abolition of serfdom and bondage. The rebels made clear that they did not dismiss all authority, because the Bible says they should not. But they wanted to live according to God's commandments, "not the free license of the flesh". This meant, they explained, that they should "humble ourselves before everyone, not just authority". The article concludes with the expectant statement that the lords, as Christians would release them from serfdom, and, if not, they should prove from the Bible that they should be serfs.

The fourth and fifth articles are concerned with access to game and other natural resources such as firewood. Here they complained that they were being restricted from hunting, fishing and cutting wood because the lords were taking these resources for themselves. Wood was particularly important for fuel, building materials, and material for tools and fencing for instance. As such the peasants demanded it should be free to whoever needed it.

The sixth article deals with another aspect of serfdom and feudal society, the onerous labour obligation that peasants were expected to do for their lord. These, the peasants complained, were constantly being increased, and they expected these services to be examined to see whether they were fair when compared to those done by previous generations. Crucially any labour that the peasantry was expected to complete had to be judged against scripture.

Related to this, the seventh article was designed to prevent lords breaking agreements and demanding increased services from peasants. It also suggested that the relations between peasant and lord should be more controlled. A peasant should be willing to serve their lord if requested, and before others, but only if it was not disadvantageous, and crucially, for an appropriate wage.

The eighth article was concerned with high and increasing rents, which the peasants could not pay, and demanded a fair rent. The ninth was concerned with crime and punishment, not least the ability of the lords to use the law to arbitrarily punish the peasantry.

The tenth article concerns common lands that had been taken away from the community. These concerns would be key to peasant rebellions across Europe for much of the feudal and early capitalist period as common lands were enclosed and taken out of the hands of the ordinary people. In 1525 the rebels demanded that these common lands were restored to the community.

The eleventh article addressed the hated heriot tax. This feudal tax was supposed to compensate a lord for the death of one of his subjects. It originated in the old feudal relationship between a lord and their serfs whom they had loaned military equipment to, which was supposed to return to the lord on the death of the serf. By the sixteenth century, this had become distorted into a tax on the estate of a dead peasant. It could be horrifically onerous, as this example described by peasants rebelling against the Abbot of Kempten shows:

> Kondrad Fraydinng, serf, had a wife who died; he had to share her inheritance with the abbot and paid him 50 fl. Then he took another wife, who was a free Zinser. She died on him also. But my lord again wanted half the inheritance. He had to give him 30 fl. Then he took a third wife, who died on him also. The abbot then took the half share again, and he had to pay him 20 fl. In the end he died himself. The half share was taken again. His children therefore found these monies paid out in advance. Nothing was left except 18 pounds Heller [a low value coin]. The abbot wanted to have this sum as well… He took everything and some of the children had to go begging.[100]

The eleventh article called for the complete abolition of such taxes.

The final article was not a demand, but a statement. It argued that the articles were written on the basis of scripture and the Word of God, and challenged critics who opposed them to do so on the same basis. It also pledged that further articles might be included if they were found to be justified in scripture. It demonstrated the confidence the rebels had in their demands.

The close linking of the demands of the struggle and scripture is also found elsewhere during the rising. For instance, the authors of the Mühlhausen Articles, published in September 1524 and written by the radicals Thomas Müntzer and Heinrich Pfeiffer, claim that they are based on the Word of God, and would be changed should they be shown to contradict scripture.[101] Both the Mühlhausen Articles and the Twelve Articles, as well as many other similar texts, included references to biblical passages and verses to support the demands. This demonstrates the close interrelation between the religious and economic contexts of the rebellion, which goes beyond the peasants' associating economic oppression with the Church itself.

The Twelve Articles remain inspiring and fascinating. They are an insight into the mind-set of the communities rising up against their rulers. Had they been implemented, it would have been transformative for Germany's agrarian society, which is why they were opposed by the ruling class. The Peasants' War, then, became a battle to implement these, and related, demands. The problem for the peasantry was that implementing the Twelve Articles relied on a beneficent ruling class seeing the error of their ways and granting the changes. This exposes the key weakness of the peasants' strategy. While the Twelve Articles and similar texts were written after the peasants had initially risen, they contained an implicit hope that the lords would implement change in accordance with the Bible. As a result, the peasants found themselves disarmed when their lords refused and instead went on the offensive. The only alternative for the rebels was military action, something the nobility was much better prepared for.

One surprising aspect of the rebellion is how little violence there was from the rebels against their class enemies. Indeed, there was only one significant rebel massacre (at Weinsberg in April 1525) during the whole rebellion. There is no doubt that illusions in the ability of the movement to win over the rulers lay behind a reticence to go too far, at least in the early part of the rebellion. As Friedrich Engels notes, the peasants displayed "a remarkable lack of determination in points relating to the attitude of the armed troops towards the nobility and the governments. Such determination as was shown appeared only in the course of the war, after the peasants had experienced the behaviour of their enemies".[102] Faith that the Twelve Articles would be accepted was, at least, based in some reality. One success in this regard was the way that the archbishop's representative in Mainz, having failed to raise an army to stop the peasants, capitulated and agreed to implement the articles. But this also demonstrates the peasants' weakness. The victory in Mainz arose not because the archbishop's representatives were won to the peasant cause but out of fear of the peasant armies in the wake of the Weinsberg massacre.

In fact the nobility proved adept at using the Articles to slow the rebellion. They formed the basis of negotiations between the rebels and the representatives of the Swabian ruling class, organised in the Swabian League. In other places, such as the revolt in Austria, local rulers were able to string out the rebellion by setting up commissions to discuss the detail of the demands. Unsurprisingly, these discussions went nowhere. But the discussions did allow the rulers space to gather their forces.

Chapter 5
Fear and Loathing at the Peasants' Revolution

"I think there is not a devil left in hell; they have all gone into the peasants" – Martin Luther, 1525 [103]

With the Twelve Articles, the peasants raised their demands. But what really terrified the ruling class was the way that the peasant rebellion was creating new democratic organisations both within their military forces and in the places they captured. As the rebellion spread across southern Germany, authorities and local rulers grew increasingly worried about what might happen. Reports of rebellions elsewhere were reaching them, and many found their military forces and garrisons depleted by conflicts elsewhere. Their letters and reports to their own lords are filled with urgent calls for military intervention.

The rulers' fear was in part about the potential for violence, though this was far from the only cause. That said, the threat of violence was real, as events in April 1525 in Weinsberg, a small town near Heilbronn, about fifty kilometres north of Stuttgart, shows.

Count Ludwig von Helfenstein had led the defence of Stuttgart against Duke Ulrich and was known for his violence against rebels. His act of killing a small group of rebels provoked a violent response. The peasants, encamped outside the town, received a report from a carter who was taking salt into the castle that the nobles and their soldiers had left the castle. So quick did the peasantry move that the Count did not have time to regain the castle and it was quickly captured, along with the Countess and their children. In this the rebels were assisted by the townsfolk who let them in. Then things turned violent, as the parson Johann Herolt recounts:

> Then Lucifer and all his angels were let loose; for they raged and stormed no differently than if they were mad and possessed by every devil. First they seized the count, then the nobility and the cavalry, and

some were stabbed as they resisted. Dietrich von Weiler fled into the church tower, and as he called down to the peasants for mercy, offering them money, someone fired a shot up at him and hit him, then climbed up and threw him out of the window. They then led lord Ludwig… to a field in the direction of Heilbronn and with him thirteen nobles, among whom were two ensigns, Rudolf von Eltershofen and Pleickhart von Ruchzingen. There they made a circle and made the well-born and the noble run the gauntlet with their servants, twenty-four persons in all. The count offered to give them a barrel of money if they would let him live, but there was no way out but to die. When the count saw that, he stood stock still until they stabbed him. Rudolf von Eltershofen went into the ring with his arms crossed and gave himself up willingly to death. Thus, all these were driven through [with] lances contrary to all the rules of war and afterwards dragged out naked and let lie there. May Almighty God have mercy on them and us! After this, they set alight to the castle and burnt it, and then marched off to Würzburg.[104]

The violence in Weinsberg was brutal but was linked to the behaviour of the Count, it was not characteristic of the rebellion. In fact, despite depictions of the peasant rebels as bloodthirsty and violent, murder and massacre were the prerogative of the nobility and their counter-revolution.

For the ruling class, fear of peasant rebellion was exacerbated by the Weinsberg massacre, but there was a deeper fear that the rebellion would lead to the overthrow of the existing order. Numerous articles and demands were published calling for an end to oppressive laws, for property to be held in common and for an end to historic obligations. For authority figures in towns and cities across southern Germany, this raised the real possibility that the peasants would overthrow their rule. So they called, sometimes in vain, for urgent action.

On 23 April 1525, Philip of Hesse wrote to the Duke of Saxony because local peasants had "gathered together in considerable numbers, and have conquered and occupied many of our market towns…with no other intention than to make everything free and to do nothing for, or be obliged to, any authority…if we do not counter such wanton people with seriousness and boldness, then it is a sure and fearful certainty that your grace and all authority must expect the next slap in the face…". The letter was marked "Urgent, urgent" on the outside.[105]

A couple of months earlier, on 12 February 1525, the Bavarian chancellor, Leonhard von Eck, in Ulm, wrote to Duke Ludwig of Bavaria a series of reports that betray the terror of local authorities and their fear that the peasants would introduce radical change:

> I do not know what to write to your princely grace other than that the peasants are increasing in number and no one expects anything other than next Thursday ten thousand peasants will assemble with their weapons. All the nobles to whom these peasants belong are old women and are already dead… I fear that the peasants will achieve something because of the faintheartedness of their lords… So your princely grace should not delay your horsemen. I hope it will not take long… The intention of all the peasants is to pay neither rent nor dues and that all fishing waters, game, and wood should be held in common, and other troublesome articles.[106]

Von Eck clearly thought that the revolution and the radical ideas of the peasantry were due to Lutheran teaching, a conclusion that would have upset Martin Luther. He wrote on 15 February,

> I cannot see or note anything other than that this business has been undertaken to repress the princes and the nobility and has its ultimate source in Lutheran teaching, for the peasants relate the majority of their demands to the Word of God, the Gospel, and brotherly love.

In early March, von Eck makes an interesting point about the class nature of the struggle, and the urban support for the rebellion:

> The peasants' numbers increase from day to day and they have written to some towns, including Ulm, requesting assistance. This has caused a great split within the towns. The Lutherans who are poor think the peasants are right. The non-Lutherans and the Lutherans who are rich think they are wrong.

Echoing many others who thought that the authorities had not acted forcefully enough, and that the peasants would disperse if enough military might was brought against them, von Eck, like others at the time, complained about the lack of initiative and response from the authorities, who he felt would have stopped the peasants in their tracks at even the slightest response.

As we have seen, were the rebellion's demands, as summarised for instance in the Twelve Articles, implemented it would have meant an end to the feudal system and the complete creation of a new society based on local village production. Many historians agree. Peter Blickle, for instance, has argued that the War was a revolution precisely because individuals sought to bring a new order into the countryside using the peasant armies to drive through the change. Blickle writes:

> Godly law and the Gospel, carried from the towns into the countryside by the preachers, made the Peasant War into a Revolution of the Common Man. The limited coincidence of interests between peasants and burghers, in the shape of similar agrarian problems... tax burdens...or encroachments on communal autonomy by territorial lords...was strengthened by a common yearning for a more just, more Christian world.[107]

The revolutionary ideas of some of the peasantry are best described in a revolutionary pamphlet, *To the Assembly of Common Peasantry*, published and printed in Upper Swabia in April/May 1525.[108] While we know little about this pamphlet's origins and authorship, it is according to historian Siegfried Hoyer, the "only known tract from the peasant side which took up the crucial question of the political aim of the revolution and how to accomplish it by military means". Hoyer sums up these aims as being for a "sworn confederation along Swiss lines made up of rural and urban communities who would carry out strictly limited services to feudal lords". It is worth emphasising though, that the pamphlet "polemicised against a fundamental overthrow of feudal property".[109] In other words, the pamphlet called for a restructuring of society along more benevolent and equitable lines. Others, as we will see in the case of Michael Gaismair, would go still further.

To the Assembly of Common Peasantry is an extraordinary piece of revolutionary writing that deserves closer study. We cannot claim it as articulating the revolutionary ambition of the whole peasantry, but we can see in it the sort of ideas that would have been circulating within the most revolutionary elements of the rebel forces.

The pamphlet begins with the question of authority. Here, the opening appears to echo Luther's arguments against the peasantry. Rhetorically, the author argues that since Jesus Christ says that his followers should "render unto Caesar that which is Caesar's" and did so himself by paying tax to the Roman emperor, it is not permissible to rebel, because (and here the author quotes St. Paul), "he who resists the authorities opposes the order of God". It is, concludes the pamphlet's author, "a shocking sacrilege to oppose the authorities". They remind the reader that "disobedience is hated by God to the highest degree".

It is not a particularly encouraging introduction to a revolutionary tract. But the pamphlet's author then continues in a very different direction. Those "blabbering scribes" who argue for obedience to authority have "overextended" the meaning of the word, "making a painted idol out of it". Instead, "true Christian faith needs no human authority". Authority exists for humanity, not because it is needed by Christians, but because of the unchristian. The author quotes St. Paul again, "I know that no law has been ordained for the pious but only for the wicked". God does not care who the pious person is, "shepherd, pope, emperor, or bath-house keeper".

All this theological argument exists to justify the central argument of the author, which is that authority in human society exists only to nurture Christian believers not to hold ordinary people in subjugation. Unlike Luther, then, who was arguing rebellion itself was fundamentally wrong, the author of *To the Assembly of the Peasantry* is arguing that authority has no right to control. This is not to say that the authorities cannot raise taxes, for instance. On the contrary, no Christian would be against the need for towns or areas to raise funds to build bridges or roads. But these should be raised and paid out of brotherly love. The pamphlet rages against those who take up positions of power and declare themselves better than those beneath them. Offices such as those of the rulers should be "heavy burdens" and those that take up those offices for their own sake are "false rulers and not worthy of the lowest office among Christians". Here the pamphlet goes on to denounce the injustice of those false rulers, the taxes, the obligated labour, the poverty and the "terrible Babylonian captivity in which we poor people are driven" to work for the lords. Precisely because these lords are using their position in opposition to God's idea, they have moved so far from God that they are doing the work of Satan. Rebellion against such lords is thus a duty, not a crime.

Here the author points to the Swiss, who, he argues, had lived under tyrannical rule. This authority had to be overthrown, "abolished and rooted out through great war, bloodshed, and use of the sword".

What should replace this authority? Basing their argument on the lives of Roman emperors, the author shows how the fates of each individual were closely linked to their rotten rule, corruption and failings. The problem was that Roman rule went from a "communal government to emperors", which led to abuse and violence. It was the introduction of hereditary rule that had led to serfdom and injustice. "Now to the heart of the matter" says the writer:

> All the lords who issue selfish commands stemming from the desires of their hearts and their willful, unjust heads, and who appropriate for themselves – I will remain silent about their plunder – taxes, customs, payments, and what similarly serves the common fund for the protection and maintenance of the common territory, these lords are in truth the real robbers and the declared enemies of their own territory.

What should happen to them? The Bible offered clear pointers:

> This teaching makes it evident that neither the law nor the authority of the divine order is a true, holy sanction to evil people. It should be commanded that those whom Christ upbraided here as dogs and swine should be thrown from their thrones! This would be most pleasing to God. The rotten tree cannot bring forth good fruit; so it should be cut down and thrown into the fire.[110]

The author is very clear that there are explicit, revolutionary, instructions in the biblical passages for the peasants to follow: "the fourth divine jurist, St. Mark, writes most clearly for us… 'If your eye, hand, or foot offends you, cut it off,' etc. Both kinds of authority are indicated here, the clerical with the eye and the temporal with the hand. And although some say that this refers to spiritual things…I shall say, 'No!'".

There then follows the most extraordinary encouragement to violent revolution against those lords who refuse to back down:

> But if the lords always want to be lords and to treat you poor people in the most arbitrary way, contrary to the divine laws which I have discussed above, then follow Solomon and bravely assemble now! Arm yourselves in the spirit of the bold oxen and steers, who gather together staunchly in a ring with their horns outward, not with the intention of rebelling, but only to defend themselves against the ravaging wolves. In truth, if a wolf is attacking them, he does not get away without cracked ribs, even if he escapes with his life. Thus, you dear brothers, do not engage in this insurrection in order to get rich with other people's property, or your hearts will turn false. Victory will bring you nothing good. You should hate greed as the devil hates the cross! Come together only for the sake of the common peace of the land and to practice Christian freedom! Be united in your goal! Your enemies howl and call miserably for justice. They maintain that they are nonpartisan judges and lovers of God, above all the evangelical preachers. After you have assembled, if your opponents still want to have a war, and they pursue this crazy idea of disputing the gospel with lances, halberds, guns, and armor, then it is God's will. Then let happen what cannot happen differently. Their sacrilegious attacks are hated by God. But you trust in God! Be firm in faith! You are not your own but God's warriors to uphold the gospel and to tear down the Babylonian prison! Each of you should make every effort to deal with the others in all fidelity and love! Do not quarrel among yourselves and be strict with one another! Let each tolerate the others with the greatest discipline and goodness; maintain the fear of God; and do not tolerate any drinkers! In no case allow blasphemers with their damned tongues among you! Then God will surely be your general.

What will happen if the reader does not carry through the rebellion? Then, the author admonishes, having angered the lords already, serfdom will become slavery and oppression will increase until the peasants are completely enslaved. Having encouraged violent revolution, the author moves to the organisation of the rebellion. They suggest the selection of leaders "from your own ranks" to avoid betrayal and while being obedient to the authority within the army, the army should also "hold general assemblies" to strengthen the band.

And what of the future? Here the author returns to the Swiss, whose rebellion abolished lordship and kingly rule, and urges readers to emulate them and build a confederation on similar lines.[111] Though, as Hoyer points out, these "urban communities" would still "carry out strictly limited services to feudal lords".[112]

Everywhere the rebellion spread, mass armies of revolutionary peasants were demanding, and in some cases implementing, radical new ideas about social organisation. Ordinary people were to be empowered, perhaps by giving them the right to select their pastors and other authority figures such as judges. In Salzburg, a "common assembly" published twenty-four articles "intended...to reshape the political order", and in the city, it was proposed that a new council made up of "nobility, burghers and peasants" would run the city "administering the monasteries, filling vacant offices, and managing the finances". The archbishop would keep his position but lose many of his rights and only earn a fixed income. Events in Salzburg offer insight into how the rebels were thinking. They wanted a new way of running society, in this case "a seizure of sovereignty by the common assembly of the rebels".[113] While Salzburg was a particularly developed example, we see similar attempts begun everywhere the revolution spread as declared by countless local proclamations and declarations.

Chapter 6
The Spread of the Rebellion

The movement spread quickly outward from its origins in Upper Swabia. As AF Pollard explains:

> Before the end of April almost the whole of Germany, except the north and east and Bavaria in the South, was in an uproar. From Upper Swabia the movement spread in March to the lower districts of the circle. Round Leipheim on the Danube to the north-east of Ulm the peasants rose under a priest named Jacob Wehe, attacked Leipheim and Weissenhorn, and stormed the castle of Roggenburg.[114]

Pollard reports that sections of the forces of the Swabian League's armies, under General Truchsess Georg von Waldburg, who had marched to fight Ulrich, rebelled out of sympathy with the peasantry. Nevertheless, the League remained strong enough to inflict its first major defeat. An army of three thousand peasants led by Jacob Wehe attempted to reach and capture the town of Ulm, an important bastion of the Swabian League. They were unable to get there so they retreated to Leipheim, about one thousand were lost to the forces of the Swabian League or drowned trying to escape across the Danube.

The Battle of Leipheim was the first major military confrontation of the Peasants' War, and it was a significant victory for the counter-revolutionary forces of the Swabian League. Wehe was beheaded. His last defiant words to his fellow captives were "Be of good cheer, brethren, we shall yet meet each other to-day in Paradise, for when our eyes seem to close, they are really first opening".[115] The destruction of the Leipheim band was, however, only a brief respite for the nobility. Other bands were rising, peasants were flocking to their banners, castles were burning and towns were being captured across the region. At this point the forces of the peasantry numbered perhaps three hundred thousand. Truchsess Georg's forces were strong, but numerically they could not hope to take on these numbers of rebels and there were problems. For instance, his Landsknechts[116] threatened to mutiny a few days after the battle at Leipheim if they did not receive their pay. This was quickly resolved and Truchsess Georg easily defeated a peasant force of seven thousand at Wurzach.[117] But he had to buy himself time to gather more troops and finances in order to defeat the growing rebellion. He decided to do this by negotiating with sections of the peasantry. Pollard explains that the League's forces

> now turned back to crush the contingents from the Lake and the Hegau and the Baltringen band, which had captured Waldsee and was threatening his own castle at Waldburg. He defeated the latter near Wurzach on April 13, but was less successful with the former, who were entrenched near Weingarten. They were double the number of [the] Truchsess' troops, and after a distant cannonade the Swabian general consented to negotiate; the peasants, alarmed perhaps by the fate of the allies, were induced to disband on the concession of some of their demands and the promise of an inquiry into the rest.[118]

A contemporary account by a local clerk to the Territorial Bailiff of Upper Swabia, dated 5 May 1525, gives a real sense of the fears of the nobility:

> In the land of Württemberg the peasants are very strongly united and they first took Weinsberg where there were many nobles. They stabbed them and made count Ludwig von Helfenstein run the gauntlet, and acted quite tyrannically. Subsequently they conquered Stuttgart, Heilbronn, Göppingen, Kirchheim unter Teck and other towns, also [several castles]. It is rumoured that they will march to Balingen. Lord Georg Truchsess will meet them there; God give him good fortune that it may go well, for if the league's army is once defeated, the whole land will fall and the peasants will be the lords. May God prevent it![119]

The account goes on to describe the desperation with which the Swabian League was trying to raise funds to recruit armies to defeat the peasantry, and their real fear that the League would be defeated, leading to "mockery, shame, disadvantage, and total ruin".

But the report also demonstrates that the nobility realised that more than personal ruin was at stake; their very world was under threat. The clerk continues by describing defeats in Bavaria and South Tyrol and worrying that if the uprising spreads, then "no one in these lands would be the peasants' master".[120]

Not everyone was happy with Truchsess Georg's decision to negotiate a treaty with the peasants which had, some thought, given away too much and put those opposed to the peasants at a disadvantage. But, according to the clerk who authored the report, the general made a treaty because:

> The peasants were sixteen thousand strong and the league had no more than one army; if the peasants had been victorious and defeated, they would have gained all they desired and no one would have been able to oppose them; as soon as that happened, the majority of the towns would have gone over to the peasants.

The clerk concludes his report noting that the peasants had not been subdued, though they were weakened. The terms of the treaty, for instance, made them surrender eight cannon. Elsewhere the peasants were not backing down, and in Württemberg some were rallying despite the treaty, so the clerk feared another outbreak of rebellion.

While some were angry at the general's agreement with the rebels, he could redeploy his forces elsewhere and support besieged castles and towns. The scale of the rising remains almost incomprehensible. Bands of tens of thousands of rebellious peasants moved through the land attacking castles and spreading the rebellion. Pollard's summary is authoritative:

> The cardinal archbishop of Salzburg…was soon shut up in his castle by his subjects of the city…while the Archduke Ferdinand himself would not venture outside the walls of Innsbruck. Forty thousand peasants had risen in the Vorarlberg; Tyrol was in ferment from end to end and in Styria [Sigsmund] Dietrichstein's Bohemian troops could not save him from defeat at the hands of the peasants. In the south-west Hans

Müller, the leader of the Stühlingen force, moved through the Black Forest, and raising the Breisgau villagers appeared before Freiburg. The fortress on the neighbouring Schlossberg was unable to protect the city, which admitted the peasants on May 24. Across the Rhine in Elsass twenty thousand insurgents captured Zabern on May 13, and made themselves masters of Weissenburg and most of the other towns in the province; Colmar alone withstood their progress. Further north in the west Rhine districts of the Palatinate, Lauterburg, Landau, and Neustadt fell into the rebels' hands and on the east side of the river they carried all before them. In the Odenwald George Metzler, an innkeeper, had raised the standard of revolt before the end of March, and Jäcklein Rohrbach followed his example in the Neckarthal on the first of April. Florian Geyer headed the Franconian rebels who gathered in the valley of the Tauber, and the Austrian government in Württemberg had barely got rid of Ulrich when it was threatened by a more dangerous enemy in the peasants under Matern Feuerbacher. Further north still, the Thuringian commons broke out under the lead of Thomas Müntzer.[121]

Let's look in a little more detail at events elsewhere in Germany.

Württemberg

In the midst of the growing peasant rebellion, a disgraced member of the nobility, the Duke of Württemberg, moved to try to recapture his lands. The Duke of Württemberg, Ulrich, was an important figure in the history of revolt in Swabia. We have already seen that in 1514, the Poor Conrad revolt broke out against his profligate lifestyle and the taxes he raised on tenants and peasants for a military campaign against his rivals. Ulrich's relations with the Swabian League were further soured by his killing of the husband of his mistress, a knight, which resulted in him losing his lands. After a period of life as a mercenary, Ulrich vowed to regain his position, and, calling himself "Ulrich the Peasant" and posing as a friend of the downtrodden, he invaded Württemberg in February 1525. His forces numbered ten thousand, mainly Swiss mercenaries, and while Ulrich was initially welcomed by the peasants, his previous oppressive rule being forgotten in the rising against the new lords, he was unsuccessful in his attempt to capture Stuttgart, the most important city in Württemberg.

Ulrich's forces melted away before he got close, as most were summoned back to Switzerland following the decisive victory in Italy of the Habsburg Empire over France at the Battle of Pavia. Ulrich fled Württemberg once again, and the Swabian League was free to turn its armies back against the peasantry.[122]

Despite Ulrich's inglorious intervention, the peasantry of Württemberg did rise, inspired by rebellion elsewhere. On 15 April, the revolt began when two hundred peasants from Bottwar assembled on a hill at Wunnenstein and summoned nearby villagers to rally to them. Their leader, an innkeeper called Matern Feuerbacher, led this group to ally with a second band from Zabergäu, led by Hans Wunderer. The combined force then marched around the region, as the bands in Upper Swabia had, gathering forces and uniting with other rebels, eventually numbering twelve thousand. It had significant influence, having won over many areas with many local mayors joining its leading council. The band did what Duke Ulrich was unable to do and took Stuttgart on 25 April.[123]

The story of the Württemberg rising is particularly interesting for the role of Feuerbacher and what this tells us about the rebellion. This innkeeper was not a natural supporter of the peasant cause. In fact he had opposed the previous Poor Conrad rebellion in 1514. But he seems to have placed himself at the head of the Württemberg rising in order to try to restrain it. In 1527 Feuerbacher was placed on trial for his role in the rebellion, and from the minutes of an extraordinary trial which heard from more than seventy witnesses, we learn how the peasants refused to be bought off by the nobility's offer of a "diet", or assembly, to hear their case. However, most interesting is the account that shows how the peasants responded to rumours that Feuerbach was not on their side. The peasants formed a ring, which Feuerbach rode into and circled around giving his side of the story.[124] It seems likely that Feuerbach was very much on the other side, though the peasants did not find him guilty of this "in the ring". Two years later, in 1527, he was acquitted of being a revolutionary leader.

Truchsess Georg was now moving into the Württemberg area and on 2 May he camped at Rottenburg. The Württemberg band marched toward him and captured the city of Herrenberg on 10 May. The peasants then formed a strong defensive position between the nearby towns of Böblingen and Sindelfingen. There they positioned a wagon fort and their artillery on a hill known as the Galgenberg. But the defences on the hill, and the square formed by the peasants' foot soldiers, were not enough to stop the enemy cavalry. The Battle of Böblingen on 12 May 1525 was one of the greatest military defeats of the peasantry during the rebellion. It demonstrated how one sided the military conflict was, with six thousand peasants being killed while the Swabian League only lost a handful of troops. Truchsess Georg also demonstrated his superior tactical experience. Avoiding a frontal attack against the peasants' strong position he used his infantry to capture the town of Böblingen, allowing them to pour fire into the peasant ranks and capture the Galgenberg hill. Once this had taken place, he ordered the cavalry to attack both flanks of the peasant forces. Unsurprisingly the peasants broke and ran, with the cavalry chasing them for ten kilometres.[125]

Franconia

In Franconia, the rebellion was initially centred on the important imperial town of Rothenburg ob der Tauber. The uprising here started later than elsewhere, probably inspired by events in Upper Swabia. From April 1525 onward, a religious revolt in Rothenburg came together with discontented peasants in the rural hinterlands of the town. From Rothenburg, the peasants spread the rebellion along the Tauber. This Tauber Band had perhaps four thousand members. Another band formed in the Odenwald and Neckar valley led by one Georg Metzler, an innkeeper from Ballenberg. A contemporary account describes how this "honorable man" instigated the peasant force:

> The peasants formed mobs and rallied from all the surrounding places, swarmed to the band like bees to the hive, and accepted the Articles at once. Under the pretence of defending and supporting the Word of God, they wanted to overturn all divine, human, and traditionally established laws, governments, ordinances, peaceful order, and unity.

The writer describes the formation of the Tauber Band, with Metzler emerging as the main leader:

> When they had appointed the aforesaid Georg Metzler as their supreme captain (although they already had other junior captains and otherwise such good order that almost anyone could take over command), they armed themselves militarily by occupying the districts and seizing their weaponry, and began to strike out…to take what they could find, to call up and coerce into supporting their deeds others who had not marched to them, with the threat they would fall upon whoever refused to do so. Thus they increased and grew in a short time.[126]

Metzler marched behind his standard, a peasant shoe tied to a pole, a direct invocation of the bundschuh symbol used in earlier peasant rebellions.

The rebellion in Franconia was one of the most successful of the uprising. One aspect of this was that it drew a number of nobles into the movement, who went on to play leading roles. One of those was Florian Geyer. As a contemporary report explains:

> The league could not help the bishop of Würzburg, and almost all the surrounding peasants were in rebellion. There was a Franconian nobleman called Florian Geyer, who at this time had sworn to the peasants and sat in their councils, and who told some of them publicly: 'He and his brothers the peasants had begun the affair in this way, that every prince should have this dance (meaning the rebellion) at his door, so that none could come to the aid of the other.' That made many a person vacillate, who would otherwise have remained steadfast if he had known that the authorities would receive help and rescue.[127]

Geyer is a fascinating figure. He had converted to Protestant ideas before the rebellion. During the Peasants' War, he formed a famous military unit, the Black Troop, which captured many castles. A less honourable role was played here by Götz von Berlichingen, another noble who went over to the peasantry. Unlike Geyer, who was killed after the defeat of the Black Troop, Götz betrayed the peasants as soon as the movement began to decline and towards the end of his life he published a self-justifying account of his actions. Ultimately though it was the power of the mass peasant armies, rather than the involvement of individual members of the nobility in leading troops, that forced the representatives of Franconia's ruling class to negotiate.

Rebels from the Franconia bands captured many towns and castles, many surrendering without a fight following the news of the massacre in Weinsberg. This success meant the rebels could threaten the huge archbishopric of Mainz and demand they accept the Twelve Articles. This led to a remarkable moment in the rebellion when the representative of the archbishop (who was away) was unable to raise any forces to protect the region. The regent surrendered to the rebels on 7 May in Miltenberg and agreed the Twelve Articles as the basis for a settlement.[128] It was a significant, albeit temporary, defeat for the feudal rulers who capitulated to a mass rebellion from below. By accepting the rebellion's most radical demands, the lords encouraged the peasants to turn further outward. The rebellion was now pulling everyone in the region behind it:

> It had even reached the neighbouring free imperial city of Frankfurt-on-the-Main, where the leaders of the city-proletariat had extorted from the council a charter of rights and privileges containing forty-five "articles". An insurrectionary committee, mainly composed of small craftsmen, under the leadership of a shoemaker, had been formed in the town and was in perpetual session, having relations with the peasants of the surrounding territories and with the small towns of the neighbourhood.[129]

From here, the Odenwald and Tauber bands marched on Würzburg. After Mainz it was the next most important bishopric in the region.

A third rebel band in Franconia developed around Bildhausen, north of Würzburg and adjacent to Thuringia, and grew to around seven thousand. This band, however, was less radical and determined than other armies. Despite its size, the force failed to march on Würzburg with the other bands and instead headed north toward Thuringia against Hesse. When Hesse marched off to tackle Thomas

Müntzer's forces, the Bildhausen rebels turned back toward Würzburg, only to change direction again and send the majority of their forces north when they heard that Hesse had arrived at Mühlhausen. They then entered the town of Meiningen and were under siege until 5 June, when they surrendered.[130]

Würzburg was the second most important city in the region and, again, events here demonstrate the strength of the peasant movement and the depth of its reach. The Bishop of Würzburg attempted to defuse the threat by calling a "diet" and offering reforms. But it was the rebels who sent delegates, not the expected nobles. The Bishop gave up and fled. Following a rebel siege, Würzburg fell on 8 May, but the powerful fortress of Marienberg did not surrender and could not be taken.[131] A botched attempt to storm it ended in a massacre. Those assaulting the fortress were inadequately armed, inexperienced and disorganised. Many of those inside the fortress, however, were ready to surrender but prevented from doing so by their commanders. The besiegers might have failed to storm the Marienberg fortress, but they had forced the most powerful rulers in Franconia to submit or flee. In subduing Mainz and Würzburg they had demonstrated their power and implemented radical ideas. But from here events took a turn for the worse.

Alsace

Today Alsace is part of France, but in the sixteenth century, it was part of the Holy Roman Empire.[132] The Peasants' Rebellion here was similar to that elsewhere. Many, but not all, of the peasants came from the wine growing areas of the region. Many of these produced for the market, particularly that in the region's main city, Strasbourg. The area had been prosperous, but in the late fifteenth century, it began to suffer economically and in the run up to the Peasants' War there were three periods of crisis, 1480-1483, 1490-1492 and 1500-1503, as harvests failed. Archival records show that during these crises tenants sank deeper and deeper into debt, taking out loans to survive until better times, or fleeing their leases and their debts.[133] Debt, in fact, became a key issue for the majority of peasants and winegrowers, and it frequently led to creditors demanding their money back and driving people into destitution – or worse. The Church, a big money lender, could excommunicate those who failed to pay back their loans, and often did so. There were other ways to punish the poor. For instance the "monastery of St Marx had all the horses in two villages impounded, because several pounds of rent had not been paid". Creditors also hired "bloodsuckers" to plunder villages with unpaid debts.[134] In the years running up to the Peasants' War, the majority of those living in Alsace were poor and fearful for the future.

Alsace had a tradition of rebellion including the Bundschuh risings of 1493, 1502 and 1513 and the failed uprising in 1517 led by Joss Fritz. By 1525 discontent was again high, with a revolt in Saverne aimed at the church. Local villages also began petitioning for evangelical preachers, including, on 2 April 1525, an armed protest by peasants to free Clemens Ziegler, the leader of the gardeners' guild and a radical preacher.[135] Ziegler was released, but the protest movement grew rapidly and on 14 April, a "band" formed and captured Altorf abbey a couple of days later. A leadership committee was elected, headed by Erasmus Gerber, who invited radical preachers from Strasbourg. Ironically these religious radicals told the peasants to disband and put their faith in the authorities to address their discontent.[136]

Clearly, the peasants did not listen because a few days later they occupied Saverne and the abbey of Ebersmunster, which became a "second major peasants' camp". The revolt spread further, north and south of Alsace. While these rebels had the Twelve Articles, historians Tom Scott and Bob Scribner also emphasise the importance of religious ideas to the revolt in Alsace:

> The importance of the Gospel and the Word of God…in the rebellion, was apparent at several points in the Alsatian revolt. Besides the summons to the Strasbourg preachers, there were banners with religious-evangelical symbols: in the Sundgau [to the south] they bore the simple inscription "Jesus Christ," but in Ebersmunster they carried the motto VDMIE, for Verbum dei manet in eternum ("The Word of God will stand forever"). There were also banners reminiscent of the Bundschuh flag, showing a crucifix flanked by the Virgin and St John, and bearing the imperial eagle, an invocation perhaps of the old Bundschuh programme of having no lords other than God and the Emperor.[137]

They also report antisemitism directed against "Jewish moneylenders in the countryside after the Jews had been expelled from several of the larger Alsatian towns".[138]

The revolt in Alsace would eventually cover a huge area. Its epicentre was around Strasbourg and Ebersmunster, but it spread along the banks of the Rhine, north and south. In the north the rebellion reached as far as the city of Worms, and in the south to Mulhouse (now in France) and almost to Basel in Switzerland, a distance of almost three hundred kilometres. Scott and Scribner note twelve different peasant bands across the region, operating in a highly organised way. The Altorf band was the leading force of the revolt, with a committee of twenty-five and Gerber as its leader. Scott and Scribner describe him as having an "organisational and strategic sense" that placed him alongside Müller, Gaismair and Müntzer.[139] Gerber was elected commander of all the peasants at a meeting of all the bands on 11 May in Molsheim, which also adopted the "Molsheim articles". Tens of thousands of rebels were organised in this impressive force.

In Saverne, Erasmus Gerber and the peasantry seemed keen to make sure the authorities understood that they meant no substantial changes. Indeed, Gerber's proclamation on 13 May, promised that they only wanted to "seize the clergy's goods". He continued,

> we intend no harm in any way to nobles, burghers, or any other subjects of my gracious lord. We intend not to harm the Franciscan friary or the collegiate or parish churches, or anything that belongs to them, as the community has pleaded. Likewise we intend no damage to my gracious lord of Strasbourg's castle or its gardens or outbuildings... We will not injure nobles, burghers, or my gracious lord's subjects, but pay in good coin for any goods handed over. The band requests admittance for one thousand of its men.[140]

Some rebels, however, had more violent intentions, or at least confessed to these following their capture. The confession of Wolf Gerstenwell from Saverne included his belief that "all rents and interest payments should be abolished, the rich become poor and the poor rich". Gerstenwell also confessed, "Those [noblewomen] who wear fine veils must henceforth wear white ones".[141] To "strip [the parsons] of their possessions", and that he and his associates would "share out the property of the rich as soon as the peasants entered the town. They meant to take no action against the peasants or fire on them, for they did not wish to hinder justice." Furthermore, they intended to "attack the chief magistrate and councillors in the council chamber, to breakfast with them the next morning and finally to kill them all because they paid court to the gracious lord on account of their forest and fishing privileges".

Gerstenwell goes on to outline how they had already refused to swear allegiance and would oppose troops being garrisoned in the city against the rebels.[142] These confessions, presumably made during torture or imprisonment, still give a sense of the bravado as well as the ideas of the urban population in support of the peasant rebellion.

But Gerber emphasised that he was in rebellion against the clergy alone, but promising not to attack the persons or property of anyone else was not enough to stop the enemies of the peasantry, who had already begun their response. The rebels were quickly defeated.[143] They were opposed by Duke Antoine of Lorraine, who besieged Saverne on 12 May. Duke Antoine quickly defeated two peasant armies sent to support Saverne, and a third army withdrew. On 16 May the rebels in Saverne surrendered and left their weapons in the city. In the confusion they were attacked and up to eight thousand unarmed peasants were slaughtered.[144] Gerber was captured and executed the following day. A few days later, the duke defeated another army at Scherwiller, which essentially destroyed the revolt here.

News of the violence at Saverne spread quickly. A "Constitutional Draft", associated with Thomas Müntzer, for instance, noted how the nobility "deal with the poor folk as Herod with the innocent children. As the murderous duke of Lorraine has given us a first taste of his princely grace at Saverne and elsewhere. So that this be stopped the people must come together to make an ordinance according to God's word".[145]

The Duke's forces seemed to be little concerned about who was punished. As one complaint made by the Bailiff of Herrenstein Castle to Strasbourg Council on 16 May 1525 makes clear:

> Today the Lorraine cavalry and foot have attacked Dossenheim, where they smashed open the gates of the churchyard, broke open all the chests in the church and the powder tower, burned the powder therein, and caused much distress in the village, ran after the womenfolk and struck some of them, so that whatever man, woman or child could escape…is now lodged with me in the castle. Things are indeed in a sorry state in these parts.

The troops, "headed back to Lorraine with fifteen hundred wagonsful of booty".[146]

South of these events, the rebels in Sundgau agreed to an armistice, but the Austrian government broke this. For two months there was skirmishing and fighting in the region, but rebellion was finally put down on 23 November, though reprisals and punishment carried on into 1526.

North of Strasbourg, in the Palatinate (one of the areas of Germany run by a prince of the Holy Roman Empire), rebellion started in April, around the area of Speyer. One of the rebel bands, from Bruchsal, captured the bishop of Speyer and tried to force him to agree to the Twelve Articles and put rents and taxes on hold. The bishop eventually "agreed only to implement free preaching of the Word of God and to allow the election of pastors".[147] This success, along with agreements from the margrave and the elector were enough to make the Bruchsal band disband.[148] Other bands seemed more radical, such as one in the Kraichgau, which demanded an end to priests and lords, taxes and tithes and government by the peasantry! But this band also disbanded after gaining token agreements from the elector of the Palatine, Ludwig V.[149]

South of Speyer, bands tried to capture the key cities of Wissembourg and Neustadt. The latter was the home of the elector, who met with leaders of the peasant armies nearby. It must have been an extraordinary moment for the peasants, who had forced the foremost member of the local ruling class to negotiate with them. The elector promised to call a diet to discuss grievances and went so far as to consult leading reformers including Philip Melanchthon, on the grievances and the Twelve Articles. Melanchthon supported Luther's approach and called for the suppression of the peasantry, though the other reformer consulted, Johannes Brenz, was more conciliatory. It did not matter. On 23 May, the elector attacked the peasants then continued on to stop the rebellion in Franconia. He returned later in the summer, finally defeating the remaining rebel army of seven thousand, on 26 June at the battle of Pfeddersheim. This was the tragic end of the short-lived Alsace rebellion.

Events in Alsace illuminate one important aspect of the Peasants' War – the links between town and country. Peter Blickle argues that in Alsace, "cooperation between peasants and burghers from imperial cities went much farther than in Upper Swabia". Where there were close links between the lower orders in the towns and the rural rebellion, it was difficult for the towns to aid the repression of the peasantry. Indeed, Blickle shows how some towns, such as Wissembourg, were only able to head off such unity by secularising monasteries within the town, even though they also aided the peasants with cannon. The potential unity between townspeople and local peasants should not be surprising; many of those who lived in towns were "actually farmers" or had close links with rural communities. Breaking these bonds was not easy. Town authorities tried to break such unity by conceding some concessions demanded by the urban population (such as the secularising monasteries) and hoped that this would undermine any alliance.[150]

Chapter 7
The Peasants' War in the Towns

During the rebellion, urban populations often raised demands that related to their desire for increased democratic control over finances and taxation, as well as restrictions on the rights and privileges of the wealthy and clergy. These demands were often in sympathy with those of the peasants, though the movements in and outside urban areas were not completely in agreement. The nature of German towns meant the populations had different interests to rural areas. Nonetheless, the peasants' rebellion opened the space for radical ideas to be discussed, debated and demanded. This chapter will examine the way that urban populations raised radical demands within the wider context of the peasants' rebellion. But it is important to remember that the rebellion began outside of the towns. While the Reformation was, at least initially, an urban phenomenon, the Peasants' War was rural in character, carrying the people of the towns along with it. Though as we shall see, when the radicalism spread to the towns it took on a distinctly urban colouring.

On 22 April 1525, Forty-Six Articles were put to the Frankfurt Town Council, which immediately accepted them. Some of these articles included demands like those raised by the peasantry in the Twelve Articles. For instance, the very first Frankfurt article demands, "the worthy council and commune shall have power to appoint the parish priest in the parish church and other churches, and to depose him". It also insists the priest should only preach the "pure Word of God" and the gospel.

Further articles demand that the clergy return goods that had been taken from the town, as well as insisting that those who wanted to be part of the clergy had to take part in city life by paying taxes and, if required, be tried in secular courts.

The Frankfurt Articles[151] also demonstrate the influence of the

Reformation. They specified that no more monks and nuns would be permitted to enter monasteries or convents and that the Beguine order should be allowed to die out as a result. But most of the articles were attempts to improve the conditions and rights of the poorest. Article seven demands that "corn should henceforth be taken to a free market, and each person allowed to buy two or three bushels or as much as he can pay for". This protection was demanded by the poor because previously the rich had their own grain measures and could buy from farmers before the produce reached market. Such "forestallers", as they were known, bought the grain cheap so they could increase the price at market.[152]

The Frankfurt Articles demand that taxes on essentials such as wine, corn, salt, oil and fish be halved, as should the costs of court fees (and that legal cases should be heard within four weeks). Others demand the removal of restrictions or fees that made it hard for people to rear animals or grow their own food. Running through the Articles is a sense that ordinary people were sick of petty oppressions and being cheated out of the resources provided by nature. For instance, the 17th article reads:

> When the Lord God grants beechmast [beech tree nuts] in the forest, then forest wardens talk to the poor folk as though there were no more beechmast to be had and order them to remove their cattle. Afterwards they sell in the surrounding markets. All this happens at the expense of the poor, and can no longer be endured.

Other things that could no longer be tolerated were the tolls charged for bringing goods across bridges into Frankfurt or for taking goods to the Frankfurt Fair, fees for purchasing goods at market, for people becoming master of guilds without going through the lengthy process of training and proving their skills.

As elsewhere, the encroachment of animal farming onto common land by the wealthy was undermining common rights. The Articles demand an end to the situation where animals, "everywhere infringe the grazing land of the poor commune, to its great harm and to the ruin of the woods. We wish and desire that the shepherding on the Sachsenhausen [river] bank should be abolished and that the shepherding on this side be conducted outside the Landwehr [fortified border] so that the butchers and all fellow citizens might be able to graze their cattle, sows and sheep."

The Articles demand that replacements for deceased members of the town council should be elected not chosen, and that the council had no right to change guild rules. Wages for agricultural workers should be increased by "two hellers' extra pay for each of the three seasons of the year".

These demands were radical, but they were not revolutionary. Indeed, this is no doubt why the Frankfurt Town Council accepted them immediately. They give a sense of a town where the rich and powerful used their wealth and position to enrich themselves and exploit the poor, and that the situation had been getting worse. The Articles give the distinct impression that ordinary people were sick and disgusted at the naked corruption and profiteering. Those putting the articles forward were demanding better recompense in the form of lower, or cancelled taxes and fees, and better remittance in the form of wages. They were also trying to protect their rights, such as ensuring that common grazing land was not overgrazed by animals belonging to the wealthy and extending their democratic control over the council and their guilds.

Had they been implemented, these Articles would have been a major blow to the rich and powerful. But some of them were clearly designed to further the interests of new classes of merchants, traders and manufacturers. So the Articles did not represent, as the peasants' Twelve Articles did, a challenge to existing society. There are also more reactionary ideas. Two of the Frankfurt Articles refer to Jewish people. Article 12 reads:

> No Jew should in any way be allowed to practice such intolerable and great usury in buying and selling, by which they burden the poor man. If any stolen property is found on them, they should be obliged to surrender it without any compensation; but whatever has been pawned to them by way of old clothes of the like may be sold, but only whole and not in lengths.

Article 25 says,

> It is true and well known that many a poor man has had his goods burnt by the Jews, and sometimes had them offered for sale by the Jews, or had them sold elsewhere.

These Articles focus on economic activity and seek to curtail the ability of Jewish people (of which there was a significant population in Frankfurt at the time) to make money by lending or pawnbroking. While Jewish people are attacked for these roles, it is noteworthy that the Articles do not call for the expulsion of the Jewish population. Though elsewhere in the peasant rebellion, rebels did sometimes demand the expulsion of Jews. For instance, in two cases, one in Alsace and another by the Porrentruy Band, rebels added further demands to the Twelve Articles calling for Jews to be expelled from their territories. The Porrentruy Band called on the Emperor to create an area where Jews could "subsist" on their own.[153]

The persecution of Jewish people in this period was two-fold. Religious persecution directed at their faith, and the persecution they experienced because of the social roles they were restricted to in late medieval society. Jewish people were grouped in urban areas, often restricted to living in ghettos and frequently barred from particular jobs and roles. Because Christians were unable to charge interest on loans due to Biblical prohibitions, this left a space in society for people who could loan money, something that was very important for merchants and the nobility. Therefore, some Jews found themselves forced by these restrictions to become moneylenders. Martin Luther himself noted this:

> What good can we do the Jews when we constrain them, malign them, and hate them as dogs? When we deny them work and force them to usury, how can that help? We should use toward the Jews not the pope's but Christ's law of love. If some are stiff-necked, what does that matter? We are not all good Christians.[154]

The restrictions forced on Jewish people resulted in them becoming economically important in feudal society, loaning money to all classes, but often lending very significant sums to the ruling elite. Because of this, they became hated for their role and were frequently targets during periods of popular discontent, though this was not universally true. In his history of the Jewish people and the Reformation, Kenneth Austin notes that many lists of articles do not refer to the Jews at all, which might be because Jewish communities were not very large, but it "equally suggests that they were not widely perceived as a significant threat or high priority". That said, antisemitism was part of the Reformation and German society at the time. Antisemitic myths about "blood libel" were common and led to occasional pogroms against Jewish people. In Wittenberg, the town where Luther was to come to prominence, the parish church where he was married and regularly preached still has a thirteenth-century racist stone mural depicting Jewish people suckling a pig and a rabbi examining underneath the animal's tail. Luther himself wrote admiringly of the statue using offensive and antisemitic language.[155] So the presence of antisemitic phrases in some Articles is a reflection of existing antisemitic ideas in wider society – driven often by persecution from above.[156]

Other cities also raised articles and their contents varied according to local needs. Some of them, such as those raised in Münnerstadt, about 100 km east of Frankfurt, contain detailed demands regarding how and what the clergy could preach. Interestingly, in this case, there is an explicit demand that girls should be taught as well as boys:

> If such preachers and teachers should in time embark upon the estate of marriage, their wives, who will be of upright, honorable, and Christian life, may be directed to teach the girls who are sent there and to instruct them in scripture, so that both the male and female sex, created equal by God, may the better know the laws and faith.[157]

Other demands presented in Münnerstadt relate to tithes, taxes and historic rights, as well as a specific demand that Silvester von Schaumburg, a local noble and supporter of Luther, pay his arrears of tax. Once again, there is also a demand that common lands and resources be given back to those who need it:

The woods and meadows held by the lordship within the boundaries of Münnerstadt once belonged to the town, as we are told; since the citizenry has a great lack of wood and common grazing, which is detrimental to their hereditary plots, we request to be able to use part of such woods and meadows again.

Articles such as those presented in Münnerstadt demonstrate the complex interaction between economic and class issues and the wider religious turmoil of the Reformation. This is most clearly seen with the response to the demands raised by the population of Erfurt.

The Erfurt Articles and Martin Luther's response

Nearly two hundred kilometres away from Frankfurt, the rebellious people of Erfurt and the local peasantry raised another set of demands, which once again reflected particularly urban concerns. Erfurt was, and is, the capital of Thuringia, a state whose rebellion we will examine later as it was closely connected with the leadership of the revolutionary Thomas Müntzer. The Erfurt articles are interesting in and of themselves, but Erfurt's town council sent them to Luther for his comments and his notes give an insight into how the leader of the Reformation reacted to popular radicalism.[158]

Like the Frankfurt articles, those raised in Erfurt were not revolutionary. These twenty-eight articles proposed radical changes that would improve the conditions of the poor, protect their historic rights and improve democracy and accountability from the town's leaders. But Luther's notes indicate his anger and frustration at any implication of popular control from below. Take the first article. This raises the demand, common to Frankfurt and many other places and supported by Luther, that congregations should be able to choose and replace their own pastor. Luther's brief comment only notes: "But the town council should have ultimate authority over who holds office in the town." Here, and in many other of his responses to the Erfurt articles Luther is keen to insist that the Town Council has ultimate authority. For instance, in possibly their most radical demand "on property removed from the commune, such as wood, water, etc", the Erfurt opposition says:

> This should be returned to the use of the commune at once and a control instituted so that nothing further can be done without the consent of the commune.

This clearly implies a desire for communal control over collective resources. But Luther is adamant in his opposition: "That is not to be...the authorities should do it, or purchase it for the common good of the town". Again, when the demand is raised that the council should "present an annual accounting to the guardians on behalf of the quarters and the commune", a basic piece of accountability to the people of the town, Luther dismisses it: "If one does not trust the town council, why set one up? Why have one at all?"

As the driving force behind the Protestant Reformation, Luther was seen by many as a radical for his brave and principled opposition to the Catholic Church. As we have seen, Luther's Reformation helped galvanise and provide encouragement for the revolution. But the radicalism of the movement, plus his shock at the revolutionary demands of many of the movement's leaders, led to Luther turning his back on the movement and demanding it be crushed. In his final comment on the Erfurt documents, Luther notes:

> But one article has been left out, that the council may do nothing, have no power entrusted to it, but must sit there like a ninny and kowtow to the commune like a child, govern with hands and feet tied, and pull the wagon like a horse while the driver reins in and pulls the horses. Thus it would be according to the illustrious model of these articles.[159]

Luther hated the Catholic Church. But one thing he hated more, a hatred shared with the Germany ruling class, was any sense of ordinary people or, as Luther would have it, "the mob", having a say in how society was run.

Events in the towns during the Peasants' War represent very much a differentiation between rich and poor. In general, the towns did not actively support the rural rebellion, though forces within the towns used the opportunity to raise demands of their own and were influenced by peasant radicalism. In many cases the towns allowed the peasants to enter, sometimes because they supported the rebellion but in other cases because they were fearful of a siege or forceful conquest.

Chapter 8
Thomas Müntzer and the Revolt in Thuringia

The revolutionary movement in Thuringia is inseparable from the man whose radical ideas have, for many, become emblematic of the whole revolt itself: Thomas Müntzer. Some of Müntzer's sayings rightly remain inspirational to progressive movements today, as the quote at the start of this book shows. Friedrich Engels saw Müntzer as a revolutionary ahead of his time, a precursor of a proletarian leader, but one who was unable to realise his radical vision of social transformation because of the backward, undeveloped nature of the sixteenth century German economy. Engels writes:

> Müntzer's position at the head of the "eternal council" of Mühlhausen was indeed much more precarious than that of any modern revolutionary regent. Not only the movement of his time, but also the age, were not ripe for the ideas of which he himself had only a faint notion. The class which he represented was still in its birth throes. It was far from developed enough to assume leadership over, and to transform, society. The social changes of his fancy had little root in the then existing economic conditions. What is more, these conditions were paving the way for a social system that was diametrically opposite to what he envisioned. Nevertheless, he was still committed to his early sermons of Christian equality and evangelical community of property, and was compelled at least to attempt their realisation. Community of property, the equal obligation of all to work, and abolition of all authority were proclaimed.[160]

There is no doubt that Müntzer was an impressive radical leader. His ideas were shaped in the early years of the Reformation but saw him eventually break with Luther and other leading figures of the Reformation. Müntzer saw Luther as holding back the possibility of radical, religious emancipation. Despite tragically little of Müntzer's work remaining, we can piece together the ideological route that he took from being a relatively unknown Protestant preacher to the revolutionary leader who led the peasant forces at the Battle of Frankenhausen, and who was to die following horrific torture at the hands of their enemies.

Biographies of Thomas Müntzer are hampered by the limited knowledge we have of his early life.[161] He was likely born in 1489, in Stolberg, in the Harz Mountains, in central Germany, which meant he probably died at just thirty-five years of age.[162] He was likely educated at universities in Leipzig and Frankfurt, finishing in 1516. It is probable that Müntzer was already beginning to engage in debates about the Church by the time that Luther wrote his Ninety-five Theses attacking the sale of indulgences and beginning his criticism of the Church. We know that when this happened, one of Müntzer's friends, Heinrich Hanner, wrote to him to discuss these new ideas, suggesting that they had already had some debates and that Müntzer was already "defending doctrinal positions close to those of Luther in 1517".[163] Over the next few years Müntzer worked in a number of relatively lowly jobs within the Church, but was closely engaged in the debates thrown up in the ideological foment of the Reformation. It seems that he spent at least eighteen months in Wittenberg, where he would have heard Luther's ideas but also "the humanist involvement with ancient philosophy and rhetoric".[164]

In Easter 1519 Müntzer was sent as a stand-in preacher to Jüterbog, near Wittenberg. Jüterbog was infamous as the town where the indulgence seller Tetzel had based himself, angering Luther. At Jüterbog, Müntzer proved himself an able figure in proclaiming the new religious ideas and provoked a local Franciscan priest, Bernhard Dappen, to write a report to his bishop. In it, the priest reports that Müntzer had described bishops as tyrants and adulterers and that Müntzer often claimed that "the Holy Word had lain under a bushel for more than 400 years". [165] In his account of Müntzer's Jüterbog period, Tom Scott argues that Müntzer was, however, going far beyond the standard Lutheran criticism of the Church and was rejecting "the entire apparatus of theological scholarship as a path to faith".[166] From this point onward Müntzer began to develop his own unique and radical understanding of Christian freedom that would shape his later rebellion. The following years were an incredibly febrile period for Müntzer. He read extensively, particularly studying the early Christian church, as well as attending debates involving key Reformation thinkers.[167]

Zwickau and Prague

It was in the town of Zwickau, where Müntzer arrived in May 1520, that he first began to show how far his radical thinking had developed. Zwickau was an important, rapidly expanding town, "a powerhouse of the early capitalist economy" of central Germany, a centre of iron and silver mining and an older textile industry.[168] It was a town where early German capitalism was causing economic tensions and where the new religious ideas were eagerly read. Alongside the wealthier inhabitants were a new class of labourers and workers, men and women whose personal incomes depended increasingly on the wages they could earn from the merchants and manufacturers of the town. This then made Zwickau a microcosm of the economic, political and religious tensions at the heart of the German Reformation. As Drummond points out:

> This busy town and surrounding countryside, then, was subject to the same economic and political pressures that determined the development of the Reformation across Germany, and perhaps more so, due to its advanced stage of economic development. The organisation of industry in Zwickau meant that three sections of society were in conflict: the burghers coveted municipal power, the patrician and rich families wished to retain and increase their monopoly of power and wealth, and the lower artisans and craftspeople – often relegated to lower positions by the influx of the new wealth of the mining magnates – strove for a general improvement in their condition. Sometimes this conflict was sublimated into religious disputes between the followers of Rome and the followers of Wittenberg, or into a three-cornered fight between Hussite-like radicals, Romans and Wittenbergers; at other times it burst out violently in riot with or without political overtones.[169]

It is not hard to imagine Müntzer engaging himself with all these debates, listening, arguing and being influenced by the ideas and arguments being thrown around. But crucially, despite knowing where Müntzer's ideas ended up, we must not see him as simply relating to the poor and oppressed. Müntzer "achieved a lasting rapport with the humbler weavers…[but] his following was never confined to that group alone…he kept support amongst sections of the propertied bourgeoisie, including some rich cloth merchants".[170] This is because Müntzer was framing economic and political questions within his wider religious thinking. Throughout his time in Zwickau, Müntzer continued to attack the existing religion, developing his arguments and making many enemies. His ideas resonated strongly with his congregations and helped encourage mass participation. While this was also true of Luther's sermons, which also inspired crowds to involve themselves, sometimes violently, in church affairs, Müntzer never seemed to discourage people getting involved.

On St. Stephen's Day (26 December) 1520, Müntzer attacked Nikolaus Hofer, a priest visiting from a nearby church, accusing him of being a spy. A crowd kicked Hofer out of the church, throwing mud and stones and chasing him away. Notably the town council did not admonish Müntzer for this, instead criticising Hofer.[171] Despite this support, Müntzer was making enemies. In particular the former preacher at St Mary's Church in Zwickau, Johann Wildenauer, known as Egranus, was a Humanist and supporter of Luther. Luther had recommended Müntzer to Egranus as "the very best of men",[172] and when Egranus took leave, Müntzer was employed as his stand-in. On his return in October 1520, Egranus took up his old post and Müntzer moved to a permanent position as the preacher in St Katherine's Church. Egranus was also moving away from Luther's ideas, and he later took up the opportunity of a new post elsewhere. But Müntzer had developed a growing disagreement with Egranus, and the argument was very public. Egranus wrote to Müntzer complaining that the latter had called him a "devil". According to Drummond, Müntzer

> saw in Egranus not just a weak-willed academic and a dilettante Humanist, but the worst personification of godlessness and blasphemy, both resulting from false doctrine. Yet his opposition to Egranus was not an opposition to Lutheranism; although Müntzer may not have

been defending the doctrines of Luther in this fight, he was still far from consciously opposing them. Instead, Egranus's position, in Müntzer's view, was dangerously close to that of the Franciscans and of the richer citizens.[173]

By February 1521, the town council had to intervene. But Müntzer, never one to let an argument lie, published an attack on his fellow priest. Müntzer compiled a list of twenty-six statements that Egranus was supposed to have made and with which he disagreed. Their value is that they illuminate Müntzer's own views at this time. The key point, Drummond summarises, was that "there are 'Elect' souls, throughout history, who have suffered great pain and torment to come to their faith; that God's law is to be feared; and that human reason and book-learning are of secondary importance in the acquisition of clarification of faith".[174]

These points would become central to Müntzer's worldview. Taken to their logical conclusion they would encourage Müntzer and his followers to reject the very idea that a church, or its clerics, books or institutions, was needed to reach a clearer personal relationship with God. This, in the context of the wider Reformation, was revolutionary and very dangerous to the establishment, even those rulers attracted to Luther's criticism of the Papal Church. At this point Müntzer, while moving away from Luther, had not yet completely broken from the reformer. However, he was unimpressed by the cautious advice that he was receiving from Wittenberg, and this likely fed his own break with Luther.[175]

While in Zwickau, Müntzer was also influenced by the ideas of a weaver called Nikolaus Storch, a leading radical who had built a base for himself in the strong community of clothworkers who were housed in the parish around St Katherine's church. Storch was a "self-taught master of scripture" who claimed to have received divine guidance from God in his dreams.[176] Later, Storch and some of his close associates, dubbed the "Zwickau prophets" by Luther, visited Wittenberg, where they caused a stir within the Lutheran camp while Luther himself was away in hiding.

The extent to which Storch influenced Müntzer is open to debate. There is no doubt that the two shared some ideas, for instance Storch believed in the imminent Second Coming of Christ and also emphasised the importance of a personal route to God, rather than requiring the intervention of the church and its clerics. But these ideas were already ones that Müntzer espoused. More important is perhaps the mystical beliefs of Storch, in particular his "belief in the divine provenance of dreams".[177] This was to become a significant part of Müntzer's thinking.

By now the rift between Egranus and Müntzer was leading to open conflict, with factions from both sides fighting and rioting. By April, "conservative intellectuals and Lutherans began to close ranks against Müntzer, and the town council now joined them, most likely with some encouragement from Wittenberg".[178] On Müntzer's side were the discontented population and most radical religious reformers. Eventually the authorities acted and sacked Müntzer. He was paid his outstanding salary, signing the receipt provocatively, "Thomas Müntzer, who fights for truth in the world", and left town. His leaving Zwickau was the occasion for further protest and a demonstration to support him saw fifty-five weavers arrested.[179]

From Zwickau, Müntzer eventually made his way to Prague in Bohemia. Bohemia had a history of opposition to the Papal Church and was a seat of the radical Hussite tradition. The Bohemian Reformation began in the late fourteenth century, led by the radical Jan Hus. Hus's teaching and rejection of the Pope eventually led to military intervention against the Bohemian Reformation, and nearly fifteen years of warfare. Müntzer may have chosen Prague because of a revival of the movement, under the influence of the German Reformation. Indeed, Müntzer actually preached a sermon in a chapel where Hus had also preached.[180] He was welcomed enthusiastically, but this waned quickly as it became clear that Müntzer was not the representative of Luther's ideas that many expected. The growing gulf between congregations in Prague and Müntzer's ideas was the occasion for one of the most important documents that Müntzer produced, the *Prague Manifesto*. This document is so important that Andrew Drummond has argued we cannot understand Müntzer's life without it.[181] The *Prague Manifesto* is an apocalyptic, intense document, that gives a distinct impression of Müntzer's rage and anger, perhaps reflecting his upset and humiliation in Zwickau and his failure to be accepted in Prague. It begins by attacking the existing church, whose clergy had never been possessed by the "spirit of the fear of God". The elect, by contrast, were "submerged and drowned in an outpouring of this spirit".[182] The *Manifesto* develops a powerful criticism of the Church and its clergy, "these damned parsons who take away the true key"; by contrast the mass of people remain lost and need guidance:

> I do not doubt the people. Oh, you righteous, poor, pitiful little band! How thirsty you still are for the world of God! For now are the days when none, or only a few, know what they should hold or which side they should join. They would gladly do what is best, and yet they do not know what this is. For they do not know how to conform to or comply with the testimony that the holy spirit speaks in their hearts. They are so greatly disturbed by the spirit of the fear of God that in them the prophecy of Jeremiah has indeed become true, "The children have prayed for bread and there was no one there to break it for them".[183]

The Church, with all its personnel, academic discussion, books and institutions had failed, because it was not open to God's message. The elect, however, could "impart knowledge from living experience". Let us be cautious here. Müntzer did not see the elect as some sort of religious vanguard, taking the truth to the masses. Instead, they were a "shepherd" whose job was to lead the sheep "to revelations" and be "revived by the living voice of God, for a master should teach the knowledge of God".[184] But the masses had to open themselves to the voice of God, directly, not mediated through the clergy.

Drummond points out the importance of Müntzer's argument:

> all the accepted doctrines, all the books of the Scholastics, the Canon Law and the Bulls were as nothing beside the living and perpetual experience of the faith. Müntzer, like Luther, created the priesthood of the layman, but went one step further – to the priesthood of the untrained layman, the freedom of opinion for all. And any failure to deal with the old ways, [Müntzer] insisted, would lead to Apocalyptic punishment.[185]

But the elect would have to fight. "The elect must clash with the damned, and the power of the damned must yield before that of the elect. Otherwise you cannot hear what God is." The damned, those that had not "received the holy spirit", which of course included the clergy, were a barrier to the masses receiving God.[186]

The *Prague Manifesto* finishes on a note of hope. Müntzer believed that the time of Christ's second coming was imminent and would allow the elect to fight for a new world:

> In our time God wants to separate the wheat from the chaff, so that one can grasp, as though it were bright midday, who it is that has seduced the church for such a long time. All the villainy, even in the highest places, must come to light. Oh ho, how ripe are the rotten apples! Oh ho, how mushy the elect have become! The time of the harvest is at hand! Thus God himself has appointed me for his harvest. I have made my sickle sharp, for my thoughts are zealous for the truth and my lips, skin, hands, hair, soul, body, and my life all damn the unbelievers.[187]

That hope would not yet be realised. His appeal to the people of Bohemia did not get the response he wanted. Once again, Müntzer was on the move, and he left Prague to return to Germany.

From Prague to Allstedt

After Prague, Müntzer found himself wandering, spending time in towns experiencing growing discontent. The Reformation itself was entering a period of renewal and expansion. Luther was hiding in the Wartburg fortress, protected by his prince, Friedrich III, elector of Saxony from forces of the Emperor and Pope who wanted him arrested. Luther now began to target the practices of the Church, attacking the taking of Mass in private. This was associated with a campaign against the way Mass was celebrated in church, and in Wittenberg there was a move towards celebrating Mass by giving the laity both bread and wine as Holy Communion. One of the prime movers of the more radical actions in Wittenberg was the reformer Andreas Karlstadt. Karlstadt had been a colleague and close collaborator of Luther's. By 1521 he was pushing the boundaries of the Reformation, and at Christmas 1521, performed a German language Mass and gave both bread and wine to worshippers. This practice was known as Utraquism and had its roots in the Bohemian Reformation, a key principle of the Hussites in Prague. In Germany, only clergy received both bread and wine, with the laity just taking bread during Communion. In Wittenberg this led to rioting as rival factions campaigned for different versions of the Communion. Masses celebrated in the traditional way were disrupted; "priests were mocked, threatened and stoned, altars overturned".[188]

Karlstadt married in early 1522, something shocking to the established Church which prevented clergy from marrying, and initiated a number of other radical changes, while also encouraging the destruction of icons and imagery in various of Wittenberg's chapels. Here we see close links between radical Reformation ideas and wider social contexts. The town council introduced various changes, closing a brothel, abolishing begging and offering assistance to the poor. These changes reflected Karlstadt's thinking. He himself preferred to be addressed as "Brother Andreas" and wore the clothes of a peasant. Over the course of the next few years, Luther was to break with Karlstadt, seeing him, unfairly, as a revolutionary in the vein of Müntzer. While Karlstadt certainly did have more radical views than Luther, they were not revolutionary, but in the swirling arguments and debates in Wittenberg in the early years of the Reformation, they went far beyond Luther's own beliefs.

The arrival in Wittenberg of Storch and two others from Zwickau caused a crisis. They took their radical visions, experiences and beliefs to Wittenberg, where, in Luther's absence, they were initially welcomed. They began to preach in public, so called "corner sermons", and were soon to worry Luther's closest allies. The specifics of the debates cannot divert us here, but the presence of the three "prophets" was undermining Luther's supporters and encouraging radicals. Luther returned to Wittenberg from hiding and, supporting Friedrich's position, reversed a number of reforms that had been introduced in January 1522. The Ordinance that was issued by Wittenberg's Council undermined the authority of the prince, and

Luther helped reverse this. Luther was now turning his back on positions he and his followers had advocated a few months before:

> Under Luther's supervision, images were reinstated, Utraquist practices abandoned, and services conducted in the old way with the proper vestments and the use of Latin. In so doing, Luther reversed rapidly away from the very positions he had been promoting only two months earlier.[189]

Here we see the first example of Luther's conservatism in the face of popular movements that were pushing reform forward. His opposition to the "prophets" from Zwickau was rooted in his fear that the Reformation would get out of his control. Luther was finding common cause with the powerful rulers of the German lands. Müntzer, however, was moving in the opposite direction.

Müntzer spent most of 1522 looking for a place to base himself. It is likely that he found some suitable employment, at least temporarily, in several places, visiting Erfurt, Stolberg, Nordhausen, Weimar and Halle for greater or shorter periods. At this point the growing disagreements between Müntzer and Luther led to a final split. In March 1522 he wrote to Luther's closest ally, Philipp Melanchthon.[190] The letter quickly moved into a powerful attack on Melanchthon and, by extension, Luther. Müntzer emphasised his belief that people will find their way to God, not through preachers, or books, but through a personal relationship that sees worshippers open up themselves to the word of God:

> What I disapprove of is this: that it is a dumb God whom you adore, for because of your ignorance about propagation you cannot distinguish between the elect and the reprobate; as a result you totally reject the coming church in which the knowledge of the Lord will dawn in all its fullness. But this error of your, my most beloved, arises wholly from an ignorance of the living word. Look to the Scriptures, on which we rely to trample down the world; they say quite unambiguously: Man does not live by bread alone but by every word which proceeds from the mouth of God; note that it proceeds from the mouth of God and not from books. It is the testimony to the true word which is found

in volumes. For unless it arises from the heart it is the word of man, condemning the turn-coat scribes, who rob the holy oracles, Jeremiah 23.7 The Lord has never spoken to them, yet they usurp his words. O most beloved, see to it that you prophesy, otherwise your theology will not be worth a cent. Think of your God as at hand and not distant; believe that God is more willing to speak than you are prepared to listen.

Müntzer attacks the Lutherans for their caution, directly criticising Luther for his timidity and backsliding and for his concern not to offend the princes:

> Our most beloved Martin acts ignorantly because he does not want to offend the little ones; but those little ones today are just like the boys who lived to be a hundred years old and were damned. But the tribulation of Christians is already at the door; why you should consider that it is still to come, I do not know. Dear brothers, leave your dallying, the time has come! Do not delay, summer is at the door. Do not make peace with the reprobate, for they impede the mighty working of the word. Do not flatter your princes; otherwise you will live to see your undoing, which may the blessed God forfend.

He finishes by warning Melanchthon and Luther that he has no intention of holding back his own struggle:

> Should you wish I will back up all I have said from the Scriptures, from the order of creation, from experience, and from the clear word of God. You delicate biblical scholars, do not hang back. I can do no other.[191]

Drummond concludes that this sees the final split between Müntzer and Luther's Reformation, crucially "on the basis of a profound disagreement on the goal of reform and on the strategy for attaining that goal".[192]

During winter 1522, Müntzer was in Halle, where he had a job preaching at a nearby nunnery. Despite his brave words to Melanchthon, he actually had to hide his true politics, with public preaching "according to the Catholic rite".[193] Eventually, however, he was sacked following a religious riot in January 1523. Müntzer probably had nothing to do with this, but it made his position untenable. Now he made his way to Allstedt, a small town, where he was given a permanent position preaching at the Johanniskirche and where he was to spend a year and a half.

In Allstedt, Müntzer finally found the space he needed to develop his ideas into practical examples of how religion should be run. He spent time reforming how Mass was celebrated creating a radical new liturgy including the "first German version of the Mass with music, and a book of common prayer, or order of service".[194] This took time and money, but it transformed ordinary worshipers' experience of religious service, so that "the congregation actually participated and understood what was going on".[195] The use of German rather than Latin is notable, not least because Luther had deliberately reversed this in Wittenberg the previous year. Müntzer also translated key texts himself, using the words to drive through his vision of a Christianity where ordinary people fought to transform their spiritual and secular world:

Drummond argues:

> The dominant tone of almost all these texts is one of strength through pain, ultimately promising victory over the heathen; this is particularly evident in the offices of the Passion, where the number of references to suffering is quite overwhelming. Even in the Advent and Christmas offices, where you might expect the tone to be one of cheer and festive positivity, there are prayers quite openly calling for the destruction of the godless and the raising up of the poor. It was, indeed, quite extraordinary that the common people of Allstedt and its environs were every week standing up in church and singing songs about the overthrow of the oppressors.[196]

Müntzer's transformation of the liturgy was immensely popular, though it quickly brought him into conflict with the local authorities. Some reports have up to two thousand people coming from surrounding towns and villages to take part in his Sunday service. One local prince, Count von Mansfeld, attempted to prevent his population going to Allstedt by erecting roadblocks. Predictably,

Müntzer reacted with polemical anger in letters in September 1523. Müntzer begins with a blistering attack on the Count:

> I am accused of using the words "heretical rascal" and "scourge of the people" about you. Now this much is true; I know for a fact – because it is notorious – that you have issued a public edict stringently forbidding your subjects to come to my heretical mass and sermons. This led me to say – and I mean to complain to all believers in Christ about it – that you have had the effrontery to ban the holy gospel, and that should you persist (which God forfend) in such senseless banning and raging then I must continue to censure and denounce you and blot you out on paper as long as the blood flows in my veins, and not only to the Christian people, either, but I will have my books accusing you translated into many tongues, and let Turks, pagans and Jews know you for the unbalanced, insane person that you are.

Next, he emphasises how the Count's physical barriers had become a religious barrier for those wanting to hear Müntzer's sermons because it stopped them accessing God's word:

> But the key to the knowledge of God is this: to rule the people so that they learn to fear God alone Romans 13, for the beginning of true Christian wisdom is the fear of the Lord. Now that you, however, want to be feared more than God, as I can prove from your deeds and your edict, you are the one who takes away the key to the knowledge of God and forbids the people to go into the churches, for you can never change for the better.

And he warns the Count that he will not let up:

> If you drive me to the printers I will deal with you a thousand times more drastically than Luther with the pope. Be my gracious lord, if you are ready to suffer and show it, but if not, then let God's will be done.[197]

Given the power of such authority figures, it is extraordinary that Müntzer was willing to send such an insulting letter. It demonstrates how little he cared about earthly positions and how fearless he was in fighting for his beliefs – and how far he had gone in breaking with those, such as Luther, who were concerned not to offend the princes. Surprisingly Müntzer's actions did not lead to any direct problems, though the Count did complain to Friedrich the Wise, elector of Saxony.

Over the course of 1523, Müntzer spent his time strengthening his position in Allstedt. He also found time to engage in dialogue and polemic with his critics. In November 1523, he learnt that Luther had suggested that the authorities should question Müntzer closely through a list of eleven questions. While this did lead to a meeting between Müntzer and representatives of Friedrich, Müntzer was keen not to fall into the trap of debating with his opponents behind closed doors. He wrote a public defence of his position, *The Protestation or Proposition of Thomas Müntzer*, a lengthy exposition.[198] It is the first document that shows Müntzer opposing infant baptism, something to become important later in his adoption by some of the Anabaptist movement. As we shall see, infant baptism was a significant point of contention for some religious figures in the Reformation, as it did not allow for an individual to come to the Church as a result of their own relationship with God but by being entered into Church when they were baptised. Müntzer was at his most prolific in 1523, publishing multiple works and reorganising the church in Allstedt, and marrying Ottilie von Gersen, a former nun. The following year was to be even busier as Germany tipped into revolution.

The Sermon to the Princes

Allstedt was moving closer to open conflict with the local authorities. Much of this discontent centred on a local nunnery. In the new year, the people of Allstedt refused to pay the tithe, "using the revenues instead to establish a poor chest in the town".[199] In March this discontent spilled over into open rebellion as a crowd of Allstedt's citizens burnt a chapel associated with the nunnery to the ground. Those responsible were not found, though it is clear that Müntzer's sermons had encouraged such attacks, and he was a witness to the fire. The town authorities were unsure how to proceed, fearing a response from the ordinary people but also feeling pressure from the abbess, who had complained to the local duke. What takes place in the aftermath of the fire is complicated.

On several occasions, as different factions in the town and regional ruling class tried to find those responsible, the masses of Allstedt and its surroundings took to the streets. It is an example of the way the Reformation, or rather the ideas unleashed by the Reformation, were manifesting themselves as concrete issues for ordinary people. On one occasion, a deputation of Mansfeld miners turned up to support Müntzer and those implicated in the fire. On another night, the duke's representative tried to take control of the town, the whole population of which came out at night to protect the town council. Müntzer himself is supposed to have rung the alarm, and "even the women were told to arm themselves with pitchforks and stand to the town's defences".[200]

Allstedt was clearly at the centre of a major social and religious rebellion. In July 1524 the local ruler, Duke Johann, and his son Johann Friedrich visited Allstedt and Müntzer to preach to them. The resultant Sermon to the Princes is one of Müntzer's most famous polemics. It is remarkable but complex, as it is steeped in biblical reference and allusion. It takes as its starting point the second chapter of the Book of Daniel, where Daniel describes and interprets a dream of King Nebuchadnezzar. After troubling dreams, the King had wise men brought to him, asking them to both tell him what these dreams involved and what it meant. It is a test of their powers, but none of the magicians and sorcerers can tell the King what he dreamt. Instead they declare that "no one can reveal it to the king except the gods".[201] Daniel however, is able to recount the dream. It involved a huge statue, a head of gold, chest and arms of silver, thighs of bronze, legs of iron and feet of iron and clay. In the dream, the statue falls apart and the fragments are dispersed by the wind except for a stone that becomes an enormous mountain.[202] Daniel interprets each part of the statue as representing different, successive kingdoms, with the head representing Nebuchadnezzar, and each later kingdom being successively less powerful. The stone, however, represented the growing strength of God's kingdom.[203]

Because Daniel has the dream revealed to him by God and is thus able to interpret it, Nebuchadnezzar ends up "worshipping" and rewarding Daniel.[204] It is not hard to see how Müntzer was using this story to argue his belief that religious knowledge would come from a direct relationship with God, not passed through interpreters and academics.

> Oh, you beloved lords, how well the Lord will smash down the old pots of clay with his rod of iron, Psalm 2. Therefore, you most true and beloved regents, learn your knowledge directly from the mouth of God and do not let yourselves be seduced by your flattering priests and restrained by false patience and indulgence. For the stone torn from the mountain without human touch has become great.[205]

Here Müntzer appears to be telling the duke and his son that they have to choose which side they are on and break from the old Church and take up arms to defend the elect against their, and God's, enemies. More than that, they must accept that the world had to be turned upside down. Princes like them had a new role – the defence of the elect, the active engagement in the struggle for religion:

> Now, should you want to be true rulers, then you must begin government at the roots, as Christ commanded. Drive his enemies away from the elect, for that is your appointed task. Beloved ones, do not offer us any stale posturing about how the power of God should do it without your application of the sword. Otherwise, may the sword rust away in its scabbard on you. May God grant this![206]

And for those who won't follow?

> Nebuchadnezzar perceived this divine wisdom through Daniel. He fell down before him after the mighty truth had overpowered him. He was blown like a straw in the wind… Similarly, there are now innumerable people who accept the gospel with great joy as long as everything is going well for them in a pleasing way. But when God wants to put such people in the crucible or when he puts them into the fire of a crucial test…oh, then they are angered by the smallest word of the gospel… By the same token, without a doubt many untested people will be angered by this booklet, because I say with Christ…and with the instruction of the whole of divine law, that godless rulers, especially the priests and monks, should be killed.[207]

The Allstedt League

At almost the same time as Müntzer was delivering the Sermon, his supporters in the nearby town of Sangerhausen and other areas around Allstedt were attacked, with many fleeing to Allstedt. Travel to Allstedt was then stopped to prevent people hearing Müntzer, and the Sangerhausen priest, a follower of Müntzer, was arrested. Müntzer's response was to send letters supporting his followers, promising to stand up for them and encouraging them to resist:[208]

> If your prince or one of his people order you not to go to this place or that to hear the word of God...then you should not obey them, for then the fear of Man is being put in place of the fear of God... The dangerous time is upon us, a time when a bloodbath will be unleashed upon this poor obstinate world because of its lack of faith.[209]

More concretely, on July 25 1524, Müntzer formed a "defence organisation", the Allstedter Bund, or Allstedt League, to protect and organise his followers:

> There must be organised a simple league, so that the common man may unite with pious administrators only for the sake of the gospel... [It] should only be a warning to the godless that they should cease their raging so that the Elect may learn the knowledge and wisdom of God with all proofs.[210]

While he had raised the ideas of such organisations earlier in the summer, this was the first time that Müntzer had actually pulled together any sort of group that would actively organise to defend his followers and ideas. It was a step beyond the passive congregations that he would preach to, or even the disorganised groups that might, under Müntzer's encouragement, go out and attack buildings and commit iconoclasm. Drummond cautions that this was not the precursor to a revolutionary group or organisation, but rather the "vanguard pursuing God's will" linking the "preachers and administrators" and wider people. Crucially it was not to raise social issues.[211] It flowed naturally from Müntzer's own belief in the elect as the chosen of God and the wider masses who had not yet been won to this vision.

Müntzer's Allstedt League grew to an impressive size with five hundred members, but it did not actually engage in any direct action. Notably the town council joined, though on condition that "the league would not promote the withholding of taxes".[212]

It is worth noting what Müntzer was arguing at this point in his life, a few months before the peasants rose up. In a letter to the "persecuted Christians of Sangerhausen" on 20 July 1524, he includes this direction:

> A prince and sovereign lord is put there to have authority over temporal goods, and his power extends no further than that, and this is also the view of St Peter and St Paul when they write about man's powers. Hence you should speak up boldly and say this: "My dear lord, my dear master! If our lord the prince has not enough income from the dues and rents which we give him each year then let him take all our goods as well; we will gladly grant him these. But he shall have no authority at all over our souls, for in such matters one has to be more obedient to God than to men; make of that what you want. If you make us suffer on this account, we will denounce this and let the whole world know, and then it will realise why we are suffering, for as far as temporal things are concerned we are willing to do or leave undone whatever is well pleasing in your eyes. What more can we do?"[213]

In other words, Müntzer is still telling his followers to obey their lords in temporal matters, but if they are persecuted for their religious beliefs and actions, then they have the right to speak out. It is, one should note, far from the revolutionary urging in the anonymous pamphlet *To the Assembly of the Common Peasantry* that appeared in May the following year. But nor is it the automatic obedience being preached by Martin Luther. Consider the next section of Müntzer's letter:

> Therefore, my very dearest brothers, if they demand this you should enter prison or confinement again and stick to these words. If, however, they want to fine you, then pay the devil whatever he wants, but keep

your conscience free and clear and do not get it ensnared in the commands of the tyrants...let the tyrants have their pleasure with you for a little while, for this unbelieving world has not deserved any better lords and princes. So let them plague you as long as God permits and until you come to recognise your guilt.

Müntzer now argues that the "guilt" of the people lies precisely in their adulation of earthly lords and the concern for their earthly needs, which has distracted them from their part to God:

For the whole Christian people is becoming a whore with its adulation of man. It is adulation of man – one sees that clearly now – when fear of their lords and princes leads men to deny God's word and his holy name completely for the sake of their pathetic food and of their stomachs... The devil is a really wily rascal, always luring men with food and security, for he knows that fleshly men are fond of that. And so for the sake of it they are forced to deny God.

Müntzer goes on to argue, with reference to scripture, that his followers have to renounce their earthly desires and needs in favour of a struggle for God – one where the lords were part of the problem:

So why are you letting yourselves be led around by the nose? For it is common knowledge, and can be proved from the holy bible, that the lords and princes as they behave today are no Christians. Likewise your priests and monks pray to the devil and are still further removed from being Christians. Likewise all your preachers are hypocrites who bow down before men. How much longer will you go on with false expectations? Precious little can be expected of the princes. So anyone who wants to fight the Turks does not need to go far afield; the Turk is in our midst.[214]

Müntzer's enemies could not finger him for urging the destruction of the lords and princes; he was not arguing for social revolution yet, but he was arguing that the princes and lords were a barrier. It was a potent and powerful argument to those won to his theology.

Luther responds

In the midst of this turmoil and growing radicalism in Allstedt, Martin Luther intervenes with a long open letter to the princes of Saxony, *Concerning the Rebellious Spirit*.[215] The spirit is of course Müntzer, and Luther makes his concerns clear:

> I have written this letter to Your Princely Graces for this reason only, that I have understood from their writings that this same Spirit does not simply want to stick to words alone, but wants to threaten with his fist and set up a power against secular authority and straight away start a worldly rebellion… What might the spirit unleash if he wins the support of the common people?

Luther asserts his belief in the God given right of the lords and princes to rule and maintain the status quo, and it is worth contrasting his words with those of Müntzer we have just looked at:

> Your Princely Graces most humbly to take a serious view of this, and from your responsibility and duty to exercise reasonable force to defend yourselves against such mischief and prevent rebellion. For Your Princely Graces know well that your power and worldly sovereignty are given to you by God with the command that they should be used to keep the peace and punish the unruly, as St Paul taught in Romans 13. So Your Princely Graces should neither slumber nor miss this opportunity. God will demand an answer of you if you neglect to use the sword which has solemnly been entrusted to you.[216]

Luther's demand put even more pressure on the authorities and in early August they finally acted. Müntzer and other representatives from Allstedt were summoned to appear before a panel of representatives of the princes of Saxony. Inevitably, it did not go Müntzer's way, and he was instructed to close down his printshop, sack the printer, stop his preaching and disband the League. Müntzer faced a choice to either shut up or defy the princes. He could not surrender. Instead, he decided to find somewhere else to put forward his revolutionary ideas. On the night of 7 August, Müntzer climbed the Allstedt town wall and, leaving behind his family and his belongings, he headed toward Mühlhausen. It was here that Müntzer's revolutionary radicalism would finally crystallise and from where he would take it into the Peasants' War.

Mühlhausen

Both geographically and theologically, Müntzer's path to revolution was convoluted. Friedrich Engels says that Müntzer was the first to put down "communist notions" and was the "first to formulate them with certain definiteness", and he argues that Müntzer was the figure who "forcefully" set out the "demands and doctrines" of the only group that formed a "revolutionary party" during the Peasants' War, the "peasants and plebeians".[217]

When he arrived in Mühlhausen, the town from where his revolutionary politics exploded into the public arena, he drew radical conclusions from his previous experiences. In a letter to the people of Allstedt, he is at pains to justify his actions: "perhaps I am supposed to keep quiet…like a dumb dog", but he demonstrates a growing radicalism:

> In my preaching to you I was moved to rebuke very sharply those tyrants over the Christian faith who, under the pretence of governing, put the people in chains and fetters to make them deny the Gospel. It was impossible for me to refrain from doing this, and now I have found it imperative to attack that other group which dared to defend such godless, abandoned men. Truly I had no option but to howl out a warning against these ravenous wolves; it was my duty as a true servant of God, John 10, Isaiah 56, Psalm 76. Yet all I really did was, to put it briefly, to say that a Christian should not offer himself up so pitifully to the butcher's block, and that if the big wigs do not stop this, one should take the reins of government away from them.[218]

As Drummond points out, the letter sent was far less abusive and angry than the two surviving drafts, because Müntzer was still in need of help from the people of Allstedt. He asks for assistance for his wife and for the printer's type for the liturgies he had prepared to be sent on to Mühlhausen.[219]

Müntzer's arrival in Mühlhausen provokes Luther to another poisonous polemic against him in which he tries to get the town council to expel him immediately. Müntzer, Luther says, "brings forth no other fruit than murder and rebellion, and calls for the shedding of blood, all of which he openly preached, wrote and sang in Allstedt". It is not difficult to detect a note of desperation in Luther's ranting about Müntzer and his followers: "Anyone who listens to them or follows them will be named the chosen son of God; whoever does not listen will be called godless and will be killed".[220] But the town council did not follow Luther's advice. They were in no position to do so.[221]

In this breathing space, Müntzer was busy at work, writing and finishing two polemical pieces. One of these, *An Explicit Exposure of False Faith, Presented to the Faithless World*, opens with another example of the growing openness of Müntzer's revolutionary beliefs:

> Dear fellows, it is now our turn to make the hole in the wall wider, so that the whole world might understand who these great bigwigs are who have thus blasphemously turned God into a painted figure, Jeremiah 23. Thomas Müntzer with the Hammer…Jeremiah 1: "I have set up an iron wall against the kings, princes and priests, and against the people. Try as they might to fight against you, a wonderful victory is prepared for the downfall of the strong and godless tyrants".[222]

Drummond points out that this article also has "something new", a "direct appeal to the common man to break away from the Lutherans".[223] It is a remarkable pamphlet in which Müntzer openly extols his revolutionary vision.[224] As Drummond explains:

> Here we approach the essence of Müntzer's revolutionary ideas, in passages positively blazing with anger: the existing political, economic and social structures constituted a wall between the common people and their God. This wall was shored up by the doctrines of both Papists and Lutherans. The only solution was for this entire structure to be overthrown, so that the true belief might be passed on to the illiterate and the poor.[225]

The pamphlet attacks almost everyone, Luther and his followers, false preachers who are only interested in money and the princes, who are a barrier to the true understanding of God. What is needed, Müntzer says, is not preachers who can talk about faith and religion – anyone can do that. Instead, preachers are needed who "know who sends them out to the harvest, for which, like a fine strong scythe or sickle, we have been sharpened by God from the beginning of our lives".[226] increasingly here, Müntzer is also seeing the elect as a core revolutionary group, steeled by a lifetime of preaching God's word – and one that can lead others. The symbol of the scythe and sickle was no doubt chosen because of its familiarity – not least to the peasants whom Müntzer was coming to see as those who could bring through his revolution. But the symbol of the harvest has a deeper meaning, and Müntzer is referencing a Biblical passage in which Jesus urges his followers to go out, as "labourers into his [the Lord's] harvest" and find converts.[227] This is then linked by Müntzer to another favourite reference of his, that of tares or weeds:

> The present church is a real old whore by comparison, which can still be put right, though, by burning zeal. The tares will first have to suffer the attentions of the winnowing-shovel. But the time of harvest is certainly with us, Matthew 9. Dear brothers, from all sides we hear the tares crying out that the time of harvest has not yet come. O, the traitor betrays himself: A true Christianity for our days will soon be in full swing despite all the previous corruption, Matthew 18.[228]

The reference to tares is a nod to a parable of Jesus, told in the Gospel of Matthew, which tells the story of an enemy who sows weeds among a crop. The slaves offer to dig up these weeds when they grow, but their Master warns them not to, as they will damage the wider crop. Instead, they should wait until the harvest and then cut the weeds separately, protecting the wider crop.[229] Later the symbolism is made explicit, the weeds are the followers of Satan, and "the harvest is the end of the age, and the reapers are angels".[230] For Müntzer the story of the harvest and the select few bringing in the good crop, while destroying the weeds, has an obvious analogy with the needs of the time.

Müntzer now turns all his fire on Martin Luther, authoring *A Highly Provoked Vindication and a Refutation of the Unspiritual Soft-Living Flesh in Wittenberg*.[231] Space precludes a detailed discussion, though the polemic is a no-holds barred, abusive, attack on Luther. It concludes,

> O Doctor Liar, you wily fox. With your lies you have saddened the heart of the just man, whom God did not cause to grieve. For you have strengthened the power of the godless evil-doers, so that they could continue on in their old way. Therefore your fate will be that of the fox that has been hunted down; the people will go free and God alone will be their Lord.[232]

Müntzer had now completely broken with his former ally Luther and was openly calling for him to be destroyed alongside the princes that he protected. The time of the harvest was coming.

Müntzer's presence in Mühlhausen meant that the town "effectively became the centre for the radical Reformation in central Germany".[233] Here he was surrounded by many other radical reformists, but the town was also home to an angry and militant population who had protested and rioted, both against clergy and priests and over social issues. In May 1523 the people elected fifty-six representatives to the town council, who put forward a list of demands which called for what Drummond describes as "a statement of early bourgeois democracy",[234] focusing on demands to improve democracy, justice, finance. As we saw earlier, the demands of people of the towns tended to be much less radical than those the rural population would call for during the Revolution and reflected the interests of the emerging bourgeoisie. Nonetheless, this radical context meant that when Müntzer arrived, he was able to join an energised movement, alongside the radical preacher Heinrich Pfeiffer.

In September 1524, just a month after Müntzer had arrived, more rioting led to Pfeiffer and Müntzer proposing eleven Mühlhausen Articles, which called for the election of an "eternal council".[235] When compared to other sets of articles produced in this period of rebellion, the Mühlhausen eleven seem somewhat at odds. The eternal council, for instance, was to have "no fixed term of office". The articles themselves contain no real economic or political demands, focusing on the need for the council to govern according to religious principles. These, Müntzer and Pfeiffer seemed to think, would be enough to keep the eternal council on track. While the articles were popular among the population of Mühlhausen and surrounding towns, they failed to win over the peasants. The discredited Council was able to get two hundred peasants to enter Mühlhausen and use them to expel Pfeiffer and Müntzer. Pfeiffer returned quite quickly, but Müntzer was away until February 1525, when the peasants' uprising was well and truly underway.

Before returning to Mühlhausen, Müntzer travelled around, spending some time in Nürnberg (Nuremberg), where he attempted to publish more polemical writings. But in December he left and travelled widely throughout south-west Germany, then in the midst of the uprising. Tragically we know nothing about his travels, but the experience radically changed Müntzer.[236] As Drummond speculates:

> Living amongst the rebels for a few weeks, he would have acquired valuable insights into the mind and motivations of the common man. This was a completely new period in his life, and a totally new experience: he was well outside of his comfort zone, which had until then been largely defined by church services, preaching and study in an urban environment; he was now immersed in large gatherings of country people with little or no learning, who were engaged in a tangible struggle for social and economic justice.[237]

Returning to Mühlhausen in February 1525 and re-joining Pfeiffer, Müntzer found himself in a city where the radical movement was growing and becoming much more confident. This included attacks on religious buildings and, interestingly, one event in which we know women were involved when a group of women, including Müntzer's wife Ottilie, invaded a convent and interrupted prayers.[238] Appointed by "three of Mühlhausen's poorer districts" as a preacher, Müntzer set about developing revolutionary forces. Müntzer was undoubtedly influenced by the peasants' rebel organisations he had witnessed over the previous winter.

In early March, an armed muster of the town's people brought out over two thousand armed men to rally just outside the town. Here Müntzer began to make a speech "render unto Caesar the things that are Caesar's. And come to a proper accord with monks and priests". He then went on to call for the overthrow of the princes, but his preaching was interrupted by a captain who said, "Dear citizens, have you not already had your fill of oaths?", whereupon the crowd refused to support Müntzer and swear an oath and returned to town. This, alongside another notable episode when Müntzer's call on his congregation to remove idols and expensive items from their homes was ignored, show that while Müntzer's preaching was popular, his listeners were not entirely won to his revolutionary vision.[239]

Müntzer clearly hoped that he would be able to use the militia's muster to begin a new League, like that he had set up in Allstedt, and similar to the peasant organisations he had seen elsewhere in Germany. Tom Scott argues that Müntzer could not do what he had done in Allstedt precisely because Mühlhausen was not the small community that Müntzer had formerly lived in, rather a larger town which had a number of different, competing radical traditions and leaders.[240]

While there were other leading figures, including Müntzer's compatriot Pfeiffer, Müntzer was, nonetheless, a well-known and important figure in Mühlhausen's radical reformist movement. A week after he had failed to turn the town's muster into a rebellious army, they were able to get rid of the town council and elect another "Eternal" council. In the election for the council, six hundred voted for a new council and only 204 for the old leadership. Out of this, sixteen people were elected "subject to recall at any time by the citizens of the town".[241] Drummond highlights this "recallability", which brings to mind the revolutionary democracy of the (much later) Paris Commune and the Soviets of the early years of the Russian Revolution. However, he cautions that the council was "not exactly a nest of revolutionaries". Indeed, it represented a cross section of Mühlhausen's (male) population, with some very rich members, though the majority were poorer artisans. Nonetheless this was a radical step, and the town's magistrate said of the new council that God had "cast down the mighty from their thrones and raised up the mean; what a wonderful God this is!".[242]

The new council set about reforming Mühlhausen along religious lines. The Church was transformed, so that the "last vestiges of Catholicism were finally swept aside and the seal was set on Mühlhausen's formal conversion into a Protestant city". A sheep farm, owned by the Teutonic Order, was expropriated, but the radical reforms remained religious – the new Council, elected out of rage with the old order, did not make any social changes.[243]

It is possibly out of frustration at the failure of the council to enact more thorough-going change that Müntzer created another body, organised along military lines, called the Eternal League. We do not know when exactly he did this, it might have been as early as September 1524 or in March 1525. But we do know that 219 people were part of it, their names are listed in a surviving copy of the membership list. Of these only Pfeiffer was given a named role – Chaplain. Müntzer is known to have organised an impressive banner, displayed in St Mary's at Mühlhausen, inscribed with the Latin words "verbum domini manet in aeternum" ("May the word of God endure forever" [Peter 1:24])[244] and the slogan, "this is the emblem of the Eternal League of God: let all those who will stand by the league assemble hereunder." The silk banner would have been costly and an arresting sight; it was about thirteen metres long and painted with a rainbow. Müntzer's Eternal League was made up of "poorer and plebeian elements of the city and its suburbs", and he stated he wanted to increase its membership to two thousand men.[245]

By now, the peasant rebellion was growing fast, expanding into areas near Mühlhausen. Müntzer threw himself into agitating for the revolution. On April 26/27 1525, he wrote a letter to his former supporters at Allstedt. The Letter to the League at Allstedt is Müntzer at his most agitational, urging his supporters to join the rebellion, pressing on them the urgent need for action and reporting on events, with only some exaggeration, that he thought would encourage them. He names his former closest collaborators and calls them "first to the dance". The Letter opens with the rhetorical question, "How long are you going to sleep?" and warns against hesitancy:

> Get going and fight the battle of the Lord! It is high time. Make sure that all your brothers do not mock the divine witness, otherwise they are all lost. All of Germany, France and Italy is in motion.

He urges:

> Even if there are only three of you who are firm in God and who seek only his name and honor, you need not fear a hundred thousand. Now, at them, at them, at them! It is time.

He encourages the recipients of the Letter to pass it onward, and makes it clear he expects further propaganda and material to follow in a more organised form:

> Pass this letter on to the miners. I have received word that my printer will come in a few days. Right now I can do nothing else. Otherwise I would give the brothers enough instruction for their hearts to become greater than all the castles and armour of the godless evildoers on earth.

His rhetoric is vintage Müntzer, referencing the biblical story of the fall of the tower of Babel, and the downfall of the ruler who supposedly built it, Nimrod:

> At them, at them, while the fire is hot! Do not let your sword get cold, do not let your arms go lame! Strike – cling, clang! – on the anvils of Nimrod. Throw their towers to the ground! As long as they live, it is not possible for you to be emptied of human fear… At them, at them, while you have daylight! God leads you – follow, follow![246]

It is not hard to imagine Müntzer thundering out these words from the pulpit or speaking to a crowd of armed revolutionaries. We know he also wrote to other communities to spread the revolution. Following the defeat of the revolution, captured peasants from Merxleben, ten kilometres from Mühlhausen, referred to a letter that was sent at the same time as that to Allstedt, which also urged rebellion.[247] We know of two further letters sent by Müntzer at the end of April, both written "from the field", offering aid and guidance to other revolutionary communities.[248] By now he was on the move.

On 27 April Pfeiffer and the Eternal League set out from Mühlhausen with their banner and about four hundred men.[249] They first went to Salza (now known as Bad Langensalza), where they had heard that a rising had taken place. When they arrived, they found that the people of Salza were already in control, were thanked for coming and given a huge barrel of beer in gratitude. But they were told they were no longer needed. Events in Salza show that local revolutionary risings were taking place, and that Müntzer and Pfeiffer were at the centre of a network of communication about the risings and were attempting to assist other towns. Müntzer actually mentions in his letter to Allstedt that he had just received news of events in Salza, and this likely prompted the Eternal League to march out of Mühlhausen. Finding themselves not needed, and having drunk all the beer, some of the army proceeded to sack a nearby abbey while Pfeiffer and the remaining rebels returned to Mühlhausen, no doubt to report on events in Salza and gather further support.

A short time later, bands of peasants began to descend on Mühlhausen. On 28 April the forces began to gather at the nearby village of Görmar and on 29 April Müntzer replied to a letter from Frankenhausen asking for two hundred men to support them. Müntzer promised his whole force, and they marched off. On the way they sacked some castles and captured several knights, pressing them into roles and questioning them about how they treated their peasants. The knights had to promise to give up their titles and treat their peasants better.[250]

On 29 April the army arrived in the town of Ebeleben and here there appears to have been a difference of opinion. Müntzer wanted to continue onward to settle scores with Ernst von Mansfeld, but Pfeiffer wanted to divert to the area of Eichsfeld, where many of the army's peasant forces had come from. No doubt they wanted to tackle their own lords, including destroying the castle near Heiligenstadt. It seems that Müntzer did not prevail, and the army diverted toward Heiligenstadt. Further destruction and looting took place on the way. The army did not simply burn the lords' buildings and castles; they systematically dismantled them: "Buildings were literally taken apart, tile by tile, stone by stone...fish ponds were cleared, livestock removed".[251] This systematic destruction is reminiscent of the way that peasant rebels in other risings destroyed buildings and records that represented their own repression. It is as though the peasantry felt that their liberation would coincide with the destruction of these buildings. It was not just the army that did this, but "a supporting role was played by local people".[252] But in all this destruction, not one person was killed by the rebels.

From Heiligenstadt six thousand armed rebels headed out, and though contemporary reports suggest they were "unskilled", they did bring with them several guns.[253] But suddenly, and historians do not know why, the army decided not to continue on to attack further strongpoints but to head back to Mühlhausen. Drummond suggests, plausibly, that they were short of provisions – armies in this era were rarely able to carry much food and survived from plunder. Within a couple of days of leaving Heiligenstadt, Müntzer was back in Mühlhausen. But there was no real pause in the campaign.

On 6 May 1525, the Peasants of Sangerhausen wrote to Müntzer appealing for help. It is worth reproducing their letter in full, because it represents the voice of a people in rebellion, calling on the man they saw as their revolutionary leader, for guidance, but above all assistance:

> Reverend sir, our father in God, dear master Thomas Müntzer! We poor country folk from the villages of the whole district of Sangerhausen want you to know that we country folk, together with the town of Sangerhausen, the council and the bailiff, have vowed and sworn a divine covenant, in the love of God and the holy gospel, being ready to offer up our bodies and lives for it. The Naumburg district has done the same. Further some of us have returned home honourably and with due leave, but some have also deserted us dishonourably and without our knowledge etc. Further they were all forced to go to the castle at Sangerhausen and had to leave all their weapons in the castle. Further they had to take pledges that they would devote their lives and goods to helping to pursue us. Moreover, the bailiff took away from the men of Riestedt and Blankenheim all the cattle, sheep, cows, pigs and horses which they had captured at Caldenborn and intended to add to our booty. We trust that you will give this your best attention and beg you

for the sake of God to recognise that we have stuck it out here for a long time under great difficulties, that our poor wives and children have to spend their days and nights in the fields and in the woods because of their great fear of the authorities.

We also got a message today that some folk from the Mansfeld territories wanted to flee here because of their fear of the tyrants and were cut to pieces on the way — may God have mercy on them. In haste on the Saturday after Misericordia domini [the second Sunday after Easter] at Frankenhausen. The whole district of Sangerhausen begs for help as soon as humanly possible to get rid of the [lords] of Sangerhausen because of their ruthlessness. Beg in the name of God for a godly answer, which we will gladly and whole-heartedly accept.[254]

The very next day came another letter, this time from Frankenhausen, requesting urgent support from the "Christian fathers and brothers, gathered at Mühlhausen". The letter warned that there were considerable military forces ranged against them, which they lacked the resources to "counter". The letter continued:

> spare no effort to fulfil your promise and your kind written undertaking by speeding on your way to us with all the artillery, people and resources at your disposal. Unless you do so our Christian blood will be shed in great quantities, which will be a great scandal and detrimental to the holy gospel, since we would never have presumed [to act] without the help of God and yourselves. So again we beg you to show your Christian and brotherly hearts to us. Come to our help with all the resources at your disposal, within two days at the latest, in order to save innocent Christian blood from the devilish jaws of the wolf. In the oneness of faith and Christian love we will always be in your debt, our dear fathers and brothers. God's will be done, then. Jubilate Sunday [The third Sunday after Easter] in the year 1525.[255]

The letter was signed: "The whole Christian community and assembly at Frankenhausen". At least one other letter came requesting help, because we know that Müntzer wrote to the "Christian brothers of Schmalkalden, now encamped at Eisenach" asking them to be patient.

Interestingly he tells them that while they have "become conscious of what it is that oppresses you" he has not "been able to make our folk here aware of this in any whole-hearted way". But things were moving in this regard, "because God is driving them forcibly".[256]

By now the revolt in Thuringia was coming to a climax and moving in directions that Müntzer did not always support. A letter Müntzer wrote to the people of Eisenach on 9 May admonished them for taking a money-chest and capturing a commander, warning them that their struggle should focus on God rather than worldly possessions, probably arrived just before Philip of Hesse arrived outside the city gates with his massive army.[257] Philip of Hesse was a convinced Lutheran, having been converted by Philip Melanchthon, but was working closely in arms with Heinrich of Braunschweig, a convinced Catholic. These two's loyalty to their class and the protection of its wealth overrode their differences of opinion on religious matters. They marched together across Thuringia, putting down rebellion and massacring rebels. Philip of Hesse particularly saw Mühlhausen as the centre of rebellion and was determined to subdue it:

> If Mühlhausen is not punished this rebellion will not be able to be quelled for some time, because that city is the font and origin of all these violent rebellions... If it is not now seriously punished...it may stir itself to even greater rebellion and continue to inflict manifold harm, especially considering that the Franconian band has not yet been punished and might come to their aid... So it is his princely grace's definitive advice that one should attack and coerce the city of Mühlhausen because it has initiated an evil rebellion, in order that it may be punished, or at least brought and forced to serious negotiations which may redound to the princes' glory and honour.[258]

But it was to be at Frankenhausen where the final confrontation would take place. A muster of troops willing to go to the town's aid from Mühlhausen brought together a disappointing number of just one thousand. About a third of these were put under Müntzer's command to go with eight guns to Frankenhausen's aid, and a third remained under Pfeiffer to protect Mühlhausen.[259]

Frankenhausen was a small town, based around salt works, with a population of one thousand eight hundred or so people. It had risen in April and, by May, thousands of peasants and miners had come to the town, mustering in a force of four thousand.[260] The movement was strong enough to force several nobles to join the armies, and there is a record of the articles that Count Botho von Stolberg was forced to agree to. These required him to allow free use of the commons (fishing, wood, water, hunting, fuel, shelter etc) "for each to use according to his need" (surely one of the earliest usages of this phrase). All castles were to be destroyed; nobles were to give up their titles and in exchange the peasants would give the count the property belonging to the monasteries on the lord's land.[261] But most nobles were not captured and were able to organise with other armies to confront the rebels, attacking and harassing their forces. East of Frankenhausen, Philipp of Hesse was marching toward the city, commanding a formidable force of one thousand seven hundred cavalry and three thousand infantry. In Thuringia the nobles were having difficulties uniting. As Drummond explains:

> Duke Georg himself was not having much luck; his attempts to persuade his cousin, Friedrich the Wise, to raise a united Saxon army against the rebels had not been greeted with much warmth. The Lutheran Friedrich was dithering. His great fear was that Georg would gain military victory over the rebel armies and then use this as an opportunity to reverse the progress made by the reformed religion in towns across Saxony.[262]

Nonetheless, when Müntzer's forces arrived in Frankenhausen on 11 May, it was clear to everyone that a major confrontation was coming. Over the next couple of days, letters from Müntzer to nearby communities called for more. Müntzer also wrote to his old opponent Count Ernst of Mansfeld, whom he addressed as a "wretched sack of worms" and threatened that unless he stopped his attacks on rebels, they would "descend on you in the name of God… [and] execute without delay what God has commanded".[263] Similar threats were sent to Ernst's brother Albert. Perhaps Müntzer really believed that the counts would listen to him and pull back. But this attempt to weaken Frankenhausen's opponents failed. Hesse diverted his forces toward the city in response to Müntzer moving his force there. The Duke of Saxony arrived a day later, with a large force. Both sides now numbered about eight thousand, but the advantage was with the nobility, whose troops were well experienced, heavily armed with many of them having recent experience putting down rebellion elsewhere.[264] Nonetheless, on Sunday 14 May, a small skirmish between an advance patrol of Philipp of Hesse's army saw the attackers pushed back toward the main force, which was setting up camp at the village of Rottleben, a few kilometres to the west of Frankenhausen.[265] Perhaps emboldened by this minor victory, the Frankenhausen rebels moved their forces to the top of the hill immediately to the north of the town. There they fortified their position with guns from Frankenhausen's walls and a circle of wagons.

On the morning of the following day, Monday 15 May 1525, Duke Georg's forces arrived outside the city. The Battle of Frankenhausen was about to begin, a battle that would seal the fate of the Peasants' War in Thuringia and set the tone for the nobles' response elsewhere.

Chapter 9
Military Organisation

Before we look at the outcome of the Battle of Frankenhausen and other confrontations towards the end of the peasants' rising, it is worth looking at how the rebels organised themselves, which was very different from traditional armies. Peasant rebellions of the Middle Ages were often characterised by the creation of mass armies of thousands of armed rebels who marched on capital cities or locations that represented local authority and power, such as castles, and frequently engaged in military style confrontations with the enemy forces. Such mass confrontations characterised risings such as the English Uprising of 1381 and Jack Cade's rebellion, which marched on London and captured the capital in 1450. These revolts from below should not be confused with the military confrontations that characterised elite revolts, when sections of the feudal nobility rebelled against their lords or kings resulting in confrontations between armies funded and represented by different sections of the aristocracy. Examples of this type include the Wars of the Roses (1455-87), which saw two aristocratic families in England vying for the crown.

Nor should they be confused with revolts that saw a mix of elite rebellion and popular discontent that manifested themselves through military confrontation. One example of this is the Revolt of the Comuneros, or the War of the Communities of Castile, a rebellion against the Crown of Castile which manifested itself in a battle over who should rule. This also saw simultaneous struggles from below, with risings in local communities, towns and cities.[266]

The popular name of the German Peasants' War comes in part from the military armies or "bands" of armed peasants and their confrontations with the counter-revolutionary armies of the ruling class. The peasant bands took on the form of armies, emulating the forces they opposed, but they had a particular characterisation that showed their origins in a mass rebellion. Specifically, this saw hierarchical organisation with elements of democratic control and selection of leaders, plus participatory democracy that allowed members of the band to shape decisions.

In sixteenth century Europe, there were no standing armies – these would have been far too expensive to maintain for any length of time. Indeed, a crucial factor in the warfare of this period was how long kings or lords could afford to keep armies in the field. Mercenary troops were common. The Landsknechts were mercenaries recruited from the mass underemployment in rural Germany.[267] Landsknechts would serve in both peasant and noble armies, with the balance of these forces usually proving decisive. Forces like these were often recruited in bands to fight specific wars, and, at the outbreak of the peasant rebellion in 1524, many were already fighting in northern Italy for the Holy Roman Emperor. It was not uncommon for peasants to have had experience in these forces, and when they came to set up their own military forces, they often emulated the Landsknechts' military organisation.

Not only would many peasants be aware of military organisation and know others who were serving in or who had served in mercenary units, they were also part of an informal military structure linked to the feudal system. As part of their obligations to their local lords and the feudal state, the peasants had to be ready to muster for the defence of their locality or region if required by their lords. They were expected to maintain weapons and protective gear (their harness) at home, which, in England, is famously why peasants were able to use a longbow. In Germany, most peasants would have a short sword, though their weapon of choice, and that of the Landsknechts, was the pike. By the time of the German Peasants' War, cannon and guns were also available, though these were very much concentrated in urban areas and castles. The peasant bands did capture some of these, though they were not able to deploy and use them as effectively as the nobility.

The main defensive tactic of the German peasant armies was a temporary fort, made with a circle of wagons within which baggage, animals and stores could be protected. Given enough time the defenders could deploy guns outward from the circle and block gaps between the wagons as well as dig protective trenches to hamper cavalry charges. This tactic had been learnt during the earlier Hussite wars, but it was only defensive and required time. In some cases, such as at the battle of Leipheim, peasants had little time to deploy arms and were only able to move a few wagons or simply form a circle.[268]

The German peasantry had two great military weaknesses. They lacked cavalry capable of confronting the mounted forces of the nobility, and their forces had to periodically return home to work their land. The peasant armies operated a rotation system that allowed some to return to their farms to tend the fields or bring in the crops. In Alsace, for instance, peasants organised on a rota of eight days with their band and three weeks back at their farms.[269] This was also the case for silver miners in some bands who were sent back to continue extracting the precious metal so the revolutionaries could pay their mercenaries.

Landsknecht units were often recruited from the same village, and thus retained a link to their place of birth. This meant that when the rebellion exploded, whole units joined particular peasant bands and operated within those armies. Most importantly, however, the Landsknechts had a particular type of semi-democratic organisation that meant they had a different collective spirit to traditional armies. Modern armies are characterised by highly authoritarian, centralised, hierarchical organisation. Those at the top select the officers below them, which creates a loyal structure that will cascade decisions downwards so a general can expect orders to be obeyed without question. While mediaeval armies were also hierarchical, the Landsknechts organised differently, as did the revolutionary armies of the peasants.

The Landsknechts operated under "extensive disciplinary power of their superiors" but "possessed in certain matters an autonomous communal administration". This meant that the troops elected a spokesman and "had the right to receive information on certain questions from the commander before the battle".[270] They also had the right to discipline their own men for some offences. Elite Landsknecht troops were, foremost, loyal to their comrades before their commander and the person paying their wages. The loyalty of mercenary units, however, is never guaranteed. The history of mediaeval warfare is littered with examples of mercenaries who switched sides at crucial points because they received a better offer or found themselves on the losing (hence, unlikely to pay) side.

The Landsknecht in the German Peasants' War, however, switched sides sometimes for different reasons. In 1525 thousands of Landsknechts returned from Italy and many of them joined the peasant bands at the same time as many others were being paid to fight for the nobles. While not all the peasant bands agreed with recruiting mercenary forces for cash, it was recognised as unavoidable. On at least one occasion, whole regiments of Landsknechts deserted rather than attack the peasants. A mutiny in Dagersheim saw Landsknecht regiments from Memmingen, Lake Constance and Augsburg, all centres of the rebellion, refuse to attack the peasants at Ulm.[271]

The revolutionary peasant armies organised on a very different basis to traditional military hierarchies. Take the suggestion in the political pamphlet, *To the Assembly of Common Peasantry*.[272]

> Always set a platoon leader in charge of ten men, and have a centurion over ten platoon leaders, and have a captain over ten centurions, and above ten captains have a general, etc. Indeed, such an order has in the past often caused common bands to thrive. All those in your ranks should be of the same kind...everyone should be diligent and obedient towards his authority... Hold communal assemblies often, for nothing confirms and upholds the common band more cordially together. Offer to subject yourselves to the Emperor in the name of Christian order, just as other pious imperial cities. Do not soil your hands with other people's goods unless forced by need.[273]

In April 1525, the rebellious peasantry in Franconia, who made up the "Bright Band", issued Field Ordinances, which give further insights into the self-organisation of the revolutionary armies,[274] including various regulations designed to ensure the force was self-disciplined, such as limitations on disorderly behaviour like "superfluous" eating and drinking, gambling, swearing and blasphemy and a ban on "unchaste women" at the camp. But most of the ordinances are concerned with democracy within the army. Point 6 reads:

> The supreme commander is to be elected by the common bright band, to exercise power over all the people. Each person is to be subject and obedient to him, but with the proviso that the same supreme

commander shall not undertake or negotiate anything personally without the will and knowledge of the appointed captains and councillors who have been appointed by the entire band.

Follow up points made it clear that this commander could not even open communications from anyone or reply without the knowledge and presence of the appointed officers. The commander and his elected lieutenant would even have to camp in a designated place so that they could be located at any time. This democracy went down to the lower parts of the army too. Ordinance 13 reads:

> A captain is to be elected by each troop, to whom those in the troop may reveal their needs and grievances. Afterwards, the same captains shall present these grievances to the supreme commander in the presence of the appointed captains and councillors, which will be discussed by them, and so all disorder and trouble will be kept in check.

Also elected by the companies of troops or the common assembly were colour sergeants and judges and the "provost marshal". These last two were part of the discipline and punishment sections of the army, with the marshal having powers to erect a gallows and arrest "all evildoers and transgressors" and imprison them until they could be tried. Interestingly the marshal had "no power of his own to do violence…to anyone, be they clerical or lay, Christian or Jew" but only on the orders of the other elected officers. The marshal also had to assess provisions brought to the camp and had the right to take fees from each delivery. Other officials were to be elected to manage the camps and organise marching, but two other more general points are worth reproducing in full as they relate to the wider politics of the band's aims. The first relates to non-military personnel who were sworn into the brotherhood of the band:

> Item, in this brotherhood and union all women, maidens, widows, and orphans, young children, the old and the invalid, the sick, and women in childbirth shall be protected, defended, left unharmed and free, and shall so remain. Likewise, all millers shall be protected and

left unharmed and no plough shall be stolen, but preserved for the common good. No one shall undertake by force or criminal act to attack or to harm any convent, church, chapter, or like ecclesiastical property without the command and order of the supreme commander and the councillors.

The other ordinance which is worth noting relates to the question of those nobles who wanted to join the band:

> Whatever nobleman desires to join this Christian brotherhood shall and must accept that his castle and fortifications be broken up, or shall have the power to do it himself at a suitable time. But whatever movable property he has, he shall have power to retain in his own custody. The cannon that he has in the castle should be turned over to the bright band; likewise refugee property, such as that belonging to the clergy, monks, nuns, priests, or other nobles shall be handed over to this assembly, on pain of loss of life and property. He shall henceforth keep no armored horse while this business remains unresolved.

Finally, those in the band, or brotherhood, had to abide by "common law" and "until a reformation has been established", no one should "demand rents, annuities, interest, entry-fines…until the establishment of the reformation."

Taken together the 38 points of the Field Ordinances of the Franconian peasants are a remarkable insight into the ideas and organisation that the rebellious peasants felt that they should abide by. They demonstrate that the peasants understood that to maximise participation, while maintaining an effective military force, they had to combine democracy with subordination to elected leadership. At the same time, they understood that leaders were not infallible and that accountability and oversight were essential.

Chapter 10
The End of the Rising

Thuringia

On 15 May 1525, the revolt in Thuringia ended at the Battle of Frankenhausen. This, however, was no battle. It was a bloody, one-sided slaughter by an army that was far more experienced and heavily outgunned its peasant opponents. Despite this, the rebels' side began the day confidently. They arrayed themselves on the top of a hill just outside the town of Frankenhausen. Their few cannons were protected within a circle of wagons. But whatever advantages their position gave them, the rebels were simply outclassed.

Müntzer must have known that the rebels could not win militarily, so he tried to inspire confidence and encouragement with a powerful sermon. He reminded his troops that they were fighting a war for God's word. An account, written shortly after the battle by Johann Rühl and sent to Luther, included a report from two miners who were with the peasant forces. They told Rühl that Müntzer "admonished the people to stand firm... He continually rode around the camp shouting that they should all think of the power of God, which was in those who were coming to their aid... When they came to Heldrungen, no stone would be left standing and all who were within would yield to them, even the very stones themselves".[275] Perhaps fearing their opponents and hoping to divide them, the rebels wrote to the princes:

> We are not here to harm anyone, John 2, but to see that divine justice is maintained. We are not here to shed blood, either. If your aims are the same, then we have no desire to harm you. Everyone should be guided by that.

The rebels had also discussed, and rejected, an ultimatum from the princes – it called on them to give up Müntzer, though still promised to punish them for rebellion.[276]

The enemy troops formed up on the other side of the town, below the hill numbering about two thousand eight hundred cavalry and four thousand foot soldiers. The first shots were fired by the peasantry and demonstrated their inexperience. The range was far too great, firing over the town at the enemy beyond, and they caused no damage. The more experienced enemy forces moved into position on two sides of the rebels and began their attack.

The peasants had painted rainbows on their banners, and it is likely that Müntzer had brought his own massive banner with them. Hope had been raised by the appearance of a rainbow, or halo, around the sun, and its similarity to the peasants' symbol was taken as divine intervention.[277] According to an eyewitness, the Anabaptist Hans Hut, Müntzer told them, "you see now the rainbow, the league, the sign that God is on your side. You must fight valiantly and be bold!"[278]

But Müntzer's exhortations, the seemingly divine appearance of a halo, and the belief that God was on their side was not enough. Rühl's miners reported that the first enemy cannon fired missed and Müntzer called out "I told you, no shots will harm you". But these were just ranging shots. As cannon balls began to land among the peasants' defences, the rebels immediately broke and fled towards the town.

Count Philipp von Solms described what happened in a message to his son the following day:

> We gave pursuit and killed the majority of them between the hill and the town, but many got inside. We began to storm the town at once and conquered it speedily, and killed everyone caught there. Many of them were found in the drainage canal of the saltworks or else in the houses, and goodly numbers were not captured by the soldiers and horsemen until the evening, last night, and this morning, and their lives were spared. The pastor of Allstedt, called Müntzer, was also captured… He was turned over to count Ernst by our gracious lords, the princes, to deal with him at his pleasure. He had him sent to Heldrungen within the hour and he will have received his just deserts there. Over five thousand peasants were slain and left for dead, others were captured as mentioned above, some are still in hiding, and others have escaped, but not many.[279]

Up to seven thousand of the eight thousand or so rebels in the peasant army were killed on the day, thousands of them on the hill and many more in the town itself. Half of Frankenhausen's population were killed and only a few hundred peasants were taken prisoner. Müntzer was captured after being found hiding in a bed, pretending to be sick and immobile. He might have got away with things, but his habit of carrying copies of his correspondence with him was his undoing. He was recognised and taken to the fortress at Heldrungen.

Nonetheless, Müntzer's spirit was not entirely crushed. On 17 May he dictated a letter to the people of Mühlhausen, which touchingly asked for them to look after his wife, but the main thrust of which was to urge them to avoid further bloodshed and risings:

> it is quite crucial that the sort of disaster which befell the men at Frankenhausen should not be your lot, too; there is no doubt of its root cause: that everyone was more concerned with his own self-interest than in bringing justice to the Christian people. Therefore make a clear distinction between these; see to it that you bring no further harm on yourselves. It is for your good that I refer to the Frankenhausen affair, which ended in great bloodshed, that of more than four thousand people in fact. Step forward with the clear, unwavering righteousness of God, and this will not happen to you… I have often warned you that the only way to escape the punishment of God – which the authorities execute – is to recognise what harm will ensue, and it always can be recognised… For I know that most of you never had anything to do with this rebellious and self-seeking insurrection, but used every means to oppose and prevent it. To avoid innocent people like yourselves being drawn into grave trouble, as happened to some people at Frankenhausen, you should now shun all gatherings and disturbances and seek the mercy of the princes. I trust that you will find the princes disposed to show you mercy. I wanted to declare this at my departure, to relieve my soul of the weighty burden of conniving at further insurrection, so that innocent blood can cease to be spilt.[280]

The letter repeats his argument that those who put personal material gains before spiritual interests will suffer God's punishment. This,

Müntzer believed, was the reason for the defeat at Frankenhausen, and it was the lesson that had to be learnt. The previous day's massacre was foremost in Müntzer's mind. But he did not abandon his hope that people could find their way to enlightenment. Drummond also adds that this letter shows Müntzer's leadership, even in defeat, tactically calling for the rebellion to stand down to avoid further killing, and he points out that Müntzer expected this from both sides.[281]

The slaughter on the day, and the execution of Müntzer, was followed by heavy repression, and the victors encouraged further violence, as described in Johann Rühl's letter to Luther:

> At Heldrungen they have beheaded five priests. After the greater part of the citizens in Frankenhausen was slain and others taken prisoner, those who remained alive were released at the plea of the women of the town, but on condition that the women should punish the two priests who were still there. Both priests were beaten with cudgels by all the women in the marketplace, it is said, for half an hour after they were dead... There is so much punishment that I fear that Thuringia and the country will only gradually recover. The princes are marching to Mühlhausen with a great train of foot and horse, and over 300,000 florins are said to have been plundered at Frankenhausen. Robbery and murder are the order of the day here.[282]

It is difficult to imagine the barbarity associated with these events. The massacre was completely one-sided. The violence did not stop there though. On 25 May 1525, the princes captured Mühlhausen, Müntzer's base. Fearing for their lives, the population of the town met to discuss what to do. Many of the rebel leaders had already fled, knowing that they faced execution if captured. Those who remained decided to beg for mercy. According to the *Mühlhausen Chronicle*, about one thousand seven hundred women, plus the men who were still able to walk, went to the princes' military camp. They were surrounded and guns trained on them, but were reprieved. The princes and their troops entered the city and captured it. The following day, the population had to surrender all their weapons and one person, Jacob Schulz, a cobbler, was publicly beheaded. The princes forced everyone to swear their allegiance, and a new town council was appointed.[283]

With his letter to Luther, which was sent on 26 May, Rühl also enclosed Müntzer's confession, which had been extracted a few days previously. This document is often used as an uncritical declaration of Müntzer's beliefs. It is from this confession, extracted under torture in Heldrungen, that the famous quote "Omnia sunt communia" (All things are to be held in common) is taken and attributed to Müntzer by generations of radical historians of the Peasants' War, including Friedrich Engels. It is the main source of the argument that Müntzer was an early communist. The problem is that this phrase is unique in Müntzer's known writings. It does not really fit with the essence of his thinking and reads like a slogan attributed to him by his torturers as a way of discrediting his ideas and legacy. Ironically, the opposite may have happened - generations of radicals have subsequently associated Müntzer with this early communist vision.

Müntzer's *Confession* is an unreliable document. It probably tells us more about his interrogators and torturers, and those who were paying them, than Müntzer. It tries to link Müntzer to various events during the Peasants' War, perhaps with the aim of scapegoating him for the whole rising. It certainly attempts to paint the darkest possible picture of his activity, linking him to the risings in south-west Germany.

The *Confession* repeatedly paints Müntzer as a bloodthirsty revolutionary, whose organising had taken him around Germany and begun many years prior to the uprising, and who was willing to destroy and murder. He is supposed, for instance, to have admitted that if "he had taken the castle at Heldrungen, he and all his followers had intended to cut off the head of Count Ernst, and that he had often talked of doing this".[284]

His torturers were keen to highlight that Müntzer wanted to end the rule of the rich: "He had launched the rising with the aim of making all Christians equal and of expelling and doing to death the princes and gentry who refused to support the Gospel" and that anyone opposed to him would face dire consequences. When placed in context, the most famous slogan, "All things are to be held in common" sounds distinctly unlike Müntzer:

All things are to be held in common and distribution should be to each according to his need, as occasion arises. Any prince, count, or gentleman who refused to do this should first be given a warning, but then one should cut off his head or hang him.

Finally, the *Confession* was used to target others. Pfeiffer was named, as were contacts and acquaintances of Müntzer from all around the areas he had travelled and organised in. These individuals were linked to him precisely so the vengeful ruling class could target them next. As the *Confession* continues:

If things had turned out as he had hoped and planned he had meant – and that had been common knowledge among all the members of his covenant – to appropriate all the land within a forty-six mile radius of Mühlhausen and the land in Hesse, and to deal with the princes and gentry as described above. About this all of them were pretty well informed.

Of course it is impossible to know what Müntzer actually confessed to, or what he said. In the *Confession*, however, we can hear the voice of the ruling class, who had been terrorised by the revolution and wanted an opportunity to place the blame. When comparing these words, demands and slogans to Müntzer's writings, it is difficult to see the same person. Nonetheless, as the rebellion developed, Müntzer was becoming increasingly radical and his vision of a society based on equality and faith was a direct challenge to the rule of the princes. While we must be wary of claiming Müntzer as a full-rounded proto-communist, it is entirely fair to say that he was fighting for a world of equality and freedom, based on the participation of ordinary people in democratic and communal life.

On 27 May 1525, Müntzer was executed for daring to challenge the rule of the princes, and scapegoated as a revolutionary leader of the peasant rising. Also murdered on that day was his fellow radical, Heinrich Pfeiffer, who had left Mühlhausen and was captured in Eisenach, alongside dozens of other rebel leaders. Both Müntzer and Pfeiffer's heads were displayed on spikes to deter the population from further rebellion.

The rising in Germany did not end with the defeat at Frankenhausen and the death of its best leaders. Elsewhere in Germany the rising had already seen major defeats, and more were to come with further slaughter and massacre of rebels.

Franconia

At the end of April the majority of the peasant forces in Franconia concentrated on the city of Würzburg, which they finally captured in early May. The failure to take the city's fortress, known as the Marienberg, was a major problem as the continuing siege there used up rebel troops that could usefully have been deployed elsewhere in Germany to support forces under pressure from the nobility's counter-attacks. In fact the failed storming of the Marienberg fortress took place on the same day as the defeat at Frankenhausen, barely three days after the peasants had been slaughtered at Böblingen. The close timing of these events is more than coincidence as it shows that in the various regions in revolt, following the initial shock of the rising the nobility had managed to coordinate and marshal their forces. The failure in Würzburg threw the rebels into confusion. Truchsess Georg, fresh from defeating the peasants at Böblingen, was now marching on the city. Götz von Berlichingen deserted with about a quarter of the rebels also heading home.[285]

Franconia now became the location for a gathering of forces loyal to the nobility that would be able to take on the rebels wherever they gathered. Forces of the Swabian League under Truchsess Georg and the Elector Palatine now numbered thirteen thousand troops, on foot and horse, and forty-two cannon. There followed a series of battles between these forces and various bands of rebels, but it was on 2 June 1525 that the peasants experienced their first significant defeat, which enabled the nobility to break through and begin the complete defeat of the rising in Franconia.

Königshofen is a town south-west of Würzburg. Rebel forces under Wendel Hipler and Georg Metzler had set up a defence on a hill known as the Turmberg. They had a wagon fort protecting their rear and cannon aimed downhill towards the League forces lined up behind Königshofen to the peasants' south-west. The peasants might have expected Truchsess Georg to send in his infantry first, using cavalry to break the flanks of their defences. Instead, the League cavalry charged, dodging a bombardment from the peasant cannon and attacking the left flank of the peasant defences. From there they broke through to the rear of the peasant army, scattering the rebels. It must have been terrifying. As the armoured horses smashed through the scant defences, the peasants broke and ran. An eyewitness account from the time described the cavalry charge, which led to some four thousand peasants being killed. Others, who survived the initial assault hid themselves in a wood and fought back until the evening when they surrendered and were taken to the parish church where they were ransomed. Those who could pay were freed, and the remainder imprisoned.[286]

In the immediate aftermath of the battle, an event took place that gives us an insight into how the counter-revolutionary forces were organised, and what their leaders thought about their troops. Because the battle had been won by the cavalry, the League's commanders refused to pay the mercenary foot soldiers. The next day the soldiers went on strike and refused to march. This can only have been a temporary setback, and, presumably, cash was quickly found for the troops were used quickly in the next setback for the peasantry.

The peasant forces at Würzburg initially marched out to confront the League. But reports filtered through of the massacre at Königshofen and they returned to the town, after issuing a call for villagers in the nearby towns and villages to come to support the rebellion in Heidingsfeld, a suburb of Würzburg.[287] On 4 June, the peasants assembled there – the forces from Würzburg and those who responded to the call. Interestingly it seems that the mayor and other officials of Würzburg decided over the same couple of days to surrender and "excuse themselves for rebelling and to ask for mercy". The peasants marched towards Königshofen planning to massacre the League, "hang the horsemen and cut the throats of the footsoldiers". Their confidence came, because they had received false information that the peasant army at Königshofen was not actually beaten, but besieged on top of the Turmberg. The opposite was true and this new peasant force came face to face with the League's forces, including the now paid mercenaries. Seeing the enemy, the peasantry fled as soon as the League attacked. Lorenz Fries, the eyewitness whose chronicle reports the battles of Königshofen and Ingolstadt two days later, describes the massacre:

> Since the ground on which they stood was broad and flat, the horse gave chase and dealt with them until around five thousand were slain. The field all around was full of them. Someone also said that the roads towards Ochsenfurt up to a quarter of a mile from the town were strewn with dead peasants.[288]

The peasants' plan to slaughter their own enemies was turned against them. No mercy was given to those surrendering, who were killed in cold blood on the orders of the League commander who had heard of the peasants' boast. The peasants took a brave stand, including some survivors from Geyer's Black Troop[289] who

> had fled into the church in Ingolstadt; some got up onto the roof where they broke off the tiles and hurled them at the enemy. But it was in vain, for they were slain, and those who had fled into the church were not spared.[290]

Florian Geyer's Ingolstadt castle was nearby, or at least the remains of it were – it had been burnt earlier in the rising by the peasants – but now it proved a temporary refuge for some two hundred rebels, led by Geyer, who hid in the ruins and built makeshift defences. Despite the limited defences, the peasants held out for some days, and Lorenz Fries tells us that eventually the besiegers became "heated with shame and anger" at their failure to capture the ruin. They stormed it and killed all the defenders. Again, this was a massacre. Some rebels tried to surrender, then hid in a cellar. The League's soldiers burnt them out with few survivors. The next day an eyewitness counted 206 bodies.[291] Other rebels fled to Giebelstadt where they were burnt out of hiding and allegedly turned against each other on the promise that they would be spared. The League burnt local towns and villages, mopping up remaining rebel forces. Florian Geyer and the remnants of his Black Troop were finally caught a few days later, and Geyer was killed.

The League forces now marched on Würzburg, where they gave punishing terms of surrender to the town, including demanding heavy compensation, the punishment of the rebellion's leaders and the turning over of arms and armour. When Würzburg's negotiators asked to be allowed time to discuss the terms, they were told that if they did not surrender, the town would be attacked and everyone over twelve killed. Despite the pressure the town leaders must have been under, the terms were written out and distributed throughout Würzburg to all the wards, and each resident was summoned so that their opinions could be gauged. Not everyone was keen to give up but others were despondent, and, according to the City Secretary Martin Cronthal, some "did not mind that all should be lost, since they had no security of body or goods, and would have nothing and be as poor as before".[292] But the majority did accept and the League forces rode in the next day, whereupon Cronthal and the rest of the town's leading figures prostrated themselves in front of the princes begging their forgiveness.

The ordinary people of Würzburg did not do so well. The victors read out names of rebels they wanted captured. They executed leading figures of the rebellion. It is worth naming some of the individuals we know were killed, as it gives us some insight into who fought on the rebel side, and as the names of rebel figures are often lost to history. A prisoner Jakob Köhl, of Eibelstadt, who had been a captain of the peasants, was executed as were "Bernhard Wissner, a pewterer; Philip Dietmar, a painter; Hans Schieler, a coppersmith and a council servant; and Hans Leininger, a barber". The famous woodcarver Tilman Riemenschneider was imprisoned and tortured, alongside other members of the town council. Cronthal recalls that many were robbed. A further, unnamed, fifty-four people were beheaded "guilty or innocent".

One final element to the defeat of the peasantry at Würzburg is worth mentioning. As a result of the peace treaty the town was forced to pay compensation to the landowners and aristocrats who had lost property. Cronthal tells us that many of the rich lied about what had happened, over-valued their property and even increased the damage. Many, says Cronthal, "overvalued their old, dilapidated rat's nests" and "became rich, built handsome new castles and mansions in place of old tumbledown residences". Some of the "bigwigs" who had sided with the peasants now "when the shoe was on the other foot" became the most vocal in condemning the peasants and claiming compensation.[293]

The horror did not finish there. After the League's forces left Würzburg, they suppressed the rebellion as they marched. The Elector Palatine separated from Truchsess Georg, headed homeward, pausing only to destroy a peasant army at Pfeddersheim, killing one thousand five hundred and shelling the town until it surrendered.[294] Towns like Bamberg were subdued, with ringleaders executed and fines imposed. But in the wake of the League armies, there was a reign of terror on the surrounding villages with mass executions, torture and punishments, including blinding or having fingers or limbs cut off. This was led by the Margrave Casimir (or Kasimir), who is supposed to have taken two hundred thousand gulden over the next two years from his own subjects in compensation.[295] Dozens of villages and towns were punished by Casimir and his forces, with brutal repression taking place. We need not detail here the massacres and violence, which included the suppression of the rebellion in Rothenburg, but the report of the margrave's commander is horrific. It finishes with an appalling invoice from the margrave's executioner, Master Augustin, known as Master Ouch. He charged "a florin for each person beheaded, and a half-florin for cutting off fingers or putting out eyes". His total bill was 118 and a half florins.[296]

After capturing Würzburg, Truchsess Georg returned to Ulm, the headquarters of the Swabian League, from where he was sent to Allgäu in Upper Swabia. There the revolt had been rekindled and peasants were laying siege to the city of Memmingen, the city where the *Twelve Articles* were first agreed. With the approach of the League's forces, which numbered one thousand five hundred cavalry and six thousand foot soldiers, the peasants found a strongly defensive location near the village of Leubas. Some eight thousand rebels, strengthened by the leadership of experienced Landsknecht officers, had an excellent position between the river and a wood. Truchsess Georg understood he was not in a strong position, so sent a request for reinforcements, calling on General Georg von Frundsberg who had some three thousand additional troops.

The battle of Leubas began with both sides bombarding each other, followed by a peasant attack on Truchsess Georg's position. The arrival of Frundsberg on 21 July changed the odds, and overnight the peasants fled. One explanation for this is the plausible suggestion that Landsknecht officers who had previously served under Truchsess Georg decided that their loyalty, and presumably financial interests, lay with him again. Another is that the peasants had run out of gunpowder. Whatever the reason, a small group of peasants fought a last stand on a nearby hill. They were defeated not by military storm, but because the League burnt two hundred villages about the region so the rebels would starve. The surrender of the rebels led to their execution. Thus ended the revolt in Upper Swabia.[297]

Freiburg im Breisgau

In the Black Forest, in south-western Germany, the peasant rising broke out in April 1525. This rebellion built on years of discontent and religious radicalism. The background to the rebellion in the Black Forest was chronicled by one Heinrich Hug, a town councillor in Villingen. His contemporary account is a fascinating explanation of the causes of the rebellion. We have already looked at Hans Müller, the peasant leader elected in Stühlingen who led a march to spread the rebellion in the area. Hug's account describes this process in detail, and one of the events he reports on, presumably from personal experience, is what happened when the Villingen town council met to discuss the rebellion. The council sent to nearby towns for military assistance, and one of the places that responded was Freiburg, which, on 6 December 1524, sent a hundred men to Villingen. Other forces also joined them, and the troops set out to put down the rebellion. While there were some skirmishes, the main body of the peasants was not engaged, and by mid-December, it looked like things had calmed down.[298] The town of Freiburg, however, found itself at the heart of resistance to the rising. It sent forces to protect the village, stocked up for a siege and building defences. It was clear that the spring of 1525 would bring renewed rebellion. By April, Hans Müller's forces were marching to the Breisgau, the area around Freiburg, where the rebels had summoned him. The intention was to capture the region and Freiburg itself. Freiburg was an important target. A wealthy trading city that was at the junction of trade routes and the River Rhine, it was also, in April 1525, directly between the revolt in Upper Swabia and the Upper Rhine. Tom Scott argues that Müller would have understood the strategic importance of the city for the peasants:

> Its capture held the key to linking the revolt in Upper Swabia and the Black Forest uplands with rebellion on the Upper Rhine, the breeding-ground of the Bundschuh. Furthermore, its size and wealth made it the rebels' main prize: if Freiburg capitulated the whole of South-West Germany was within their grasp.[299]

Thousands upon thousands of peasants were now in revolt in the region, having captured villages and towns across the area. Freiburg was surrounded, cut off from support and desperate. A message to the Truchsess did not bring relief. Instead, the town council met with a rebel delegation. Following this, the town council tried to buy time but eventually the peasant armies of the Black Forest and the Upper Rhine laid siege to the town.[300] The peasants captured the town's castle and used it as a platform to bombard the town. They dammed the water supply, leaving Freiburg unable to power the mills to grind corn. In classic divide and rule tactics, Freiburg tried to "negotiate separately with the individual troops" of the peasants, but this failed and after six days, on 23 May the town surrendered.[301]

The town council agreed to join the Evangelical Brotherhood, or Christian Union, the organisation of the peasant rebels, and promised to pay a three thousand florin tribute, in respect of the various clergy and nobles who had hidden in the town. The city's surrender was agreed by the mayor and council members, who were, however, keen to make it clear that any commitments made to the rebels did not negate their existing obligations to the Emperor. The final agreement was that the peasants agreed that they would work with the town's leaders to "punish and dissolve…and share" the property of the associated "convents and ecclesiastical foundations" linked to Freiburg.

The Treaty of Surrender was signed by Müller describing himself as "commander-in-chief of the four companies".[302]

It was probably Müller's greatest moment. Certainly, it was a massive defeat for the nobility, who realised that their own peasants and the poor of Freiburg had sided with the rebels and undermined their defence by opening the town gates during the siege. One of these, Jakob Ziler, said after the rebellion that had the council not joined the Christian Union, "all prelates, priests, nobles and the town magistrates" would have been killed.[303] But despite the scale of the victory, Müller and the rebels failed to utilise it fully to their advantage. Despite a small garrison being left in the town, it was allowed to stay neutral. In fact Freiburg refused to send reinforcements after the main body of the rebels had left and only four old light cannons were handed over. As the rebels were beginning to be pushed back, they failed to use the victory at Freiburg to develop their position.

Discontent inside Freiburg grew after this, with unrest in the city developing during the summer election of the guildmaster for the winegrowers. This unrest illuminates a little the way that the peasant rebellion was driving deep wedges between classes within all areas of German society. The outgoing guildmaster asked the winegrowers for nominations, "reminding them that the serfs of foreign lords were not eligible to stand". One winegrower, Blasi Bomer, put forward a candidate who was ruled out of order, and Bomer said that they "should acknowledge no lord but God and the emperor: why should a serf be held inferior to a free man". He was arrested, which led to a protest to release him. The disturbances continued for several days and the winegrowers planned to call on the peasants from nearby villages to support them. In response Bomer was exiled and four leaders were executed. Dozens more received fines. The repression gives us a sense of how worried the town rulers were that the peasants' rebellion would inspire further revolt. However, it is notable that "support was confined to the wine-growers themselves" and did not draw in other guilds. But it was the links between the guild and the peasants that scared the town council. As Scott concludes, this could have been disastrous if it had happened during the siege. As it was, Freiburg weathered the storm. By mid-July they would renounce the Christian Union.[304]

After the capture of Freiburg, Hans Müller took some of the peasants to join the siege of Radolfzell. On the way, they captured the town of Breisach, but this was Müller's last victory. In early July 1525, he was captured and executed near Laufenburg, while on a mission to unite the Hegau and Swiss peasantry. He was a formidable opponent. Andreas Lettsch described him as "most eloquent and forward of speech – he had no equal as an orator: God had clearly provided them with a capable man. Everyone feared Hans Müller. I too knew him well myself. He was a well-proportioned man of full stature who had previously served as a mercenary in France."[305]

With Müller's death, the rebellion came to an end in the place it had begun, Upper Swabia. But the ruling classes' retribution had only just begun. Consider what took place in Freiburg. The authorities there made sure that those who had supported the rebels were punished. Scott and Scribner have produced a list of dozens of peasants who lost property as punishment. They included Hans Fry, who lost four head of cattle, Hans Thoma, who had sixty small linen cloths, household goods and clothing confiscated. Diepolt Metzger's wife and daughters had their "beds, windows and stoves smashed". Thenius Müller lost everything he had to a value of sixteen florins. Heinrich Mentz and Severinus Mentz also lost everything. Hans Ackermann lost his clothes, his wife lost all her money.[306]

These punishments would have left the poorest in crisis. Some among the nobility were cautious, however, but not because they were concerned about the lower orders and their wellbeing, but, instead, as the Margrave Georg wrote to his brother Casimir, "if all the peasants are killed where shall we get other peasants to make provision for us?"[307]

As well as robbing, blinding and murdering thousands of peasants, the ruling class also had to try to restore order. While punishment and violence went some way, they also tried to cow the peasantry into submission. Remember that the revolt had begun with the Stühlingen peasantry, who had, according to the Bernese Chronicler, Valerius Anshelm, a great deal of complaints:

> The peasants of the counts of Lupfen and Stühlingen...first began the rebellion, complaining in many points that they were so severely oppressed that they had neither peace nor rest, and that even on feast days they had to collect snail shells for winding yarn, and pick strawberries, cherries and barberries, etc; do labour service for the lords and their ladies in good weather, and in bad weather to let game and hunting dogs [on their land] without regard for their own harm.[308]

The peasants were violently repressed, but afterwards those that survived were forced to recommit to the old social relationships that served the ruling princes so well. On the 12 July, the surviving Stühlingen peasants were forced to swear their allegiance to lord Georg, count of Lupfen and landgrave of Stühlingen, and others. *The Articles of Allegiance* are worth quoting in full for the insight they give into the nature of the counter-revolution and the concerns of the ruling classes.

The Articles of Allegiance of the Stühlingen Peasantry, 12 July 1525, at Ewattingen

1) That each serf, dependant, resident, villein, and servant of the aforesaid lords… has sworn to be loyal and obedient to their graces, to advance their good and avert harm, and to perform all that which their forefathers have performed, excepting three articles concerning labour services and rights of forest and chase, which shall be observed henceforth [this refers to an agreement made in 1524]…

2) Second, that they shall settle speedily with their lords about inflicted damage and on suitable conditions, but where that cannot be amicably agreed, it shall fall to the decision of his Highness or his appointed councillors, and remain so without protest.

3) Henceforth they shall observe in their churches all Christian ordinances as were observed of old and allow no change to take place. The subjects shall pay for whatever was taken from the churches or churchwardens.

4) Henceforth they shall have no brotherhood or hold any commune contrary to their authorities, nor take any other counsel, on pain of loss of life.

5) The churchyard and the fortified tower shall be torn down and broken up by the subjects...

6) Since the peasants sounded the alarm with the great bell, this shall be removed from the tower at the command of the commander-in-chief to prevent it happening in future.

7) Each village shall pay his Highness six florins from each house as punishment and compensation, but the rich shall come to the aid of the poor therein; half the money is to be paid on Michaelmas, and the other three florins to be paid off annually, one florin on each Michaelmas until they are paid and settled. And whatever village does not pay its sum by the due date will be plundered and burnt.

8) Widows and orphans shall not be assessed for this penalty.

9) Those who were not in the brotherhood with the peasants will not be burdened by this levy, but if they suffered damage, they will be reimbursed by the subjects.

10) The wives and children of refugees will be sent to join them and all their goods seized. This confiscated property will fall half to the prince [Archduke Ferdinand] and half to the lords.

11) Whoever wounds or kills a refugee shall be held to have committed no crime.

12) When a refugee is captured, he shall be punished in life and limb by the local authority, although his Highness reserves the right to pardon refugees.

13) The subjects are obliged by their oath to seize refugees where they can and to turn them in at Stühlingen.[309]

The lords were ensuring several things with this post-rebellion agreement. Firstly, they were reaffirming old relations and agreements. Any gains that the peasants had made during the rebellion were voided, and even symbols of the rebellion – such as the church bell – were to be destroyed. The victorious lords were keen to ensure that they were compensated for their losses through heavy fines. But the lords also understood that they could not punish the peasants too harshly without the risk of undermining their own wealth, which depended on the peasants' labour – thus the fines were spread over a period of years. Notably the lords also wanted to ensure that the new religion was excluded. Finally, those who had fled the repression were still to be punished, as was anyone who helped them.

The emboldened ruling class could not ignore the discontent that had bred rebellion. In 1526 the Diet of Speyer met "in obedience to the emperor's directive".[310] It elected a "Large Committee" to investigate the peasants' grievances. Those who took part in the Committee were mostly concerned with religious implications, but they also took account of the *Twelve Articles* and other demands. Their recommendations were mostly concerned with religious reform, recommending for instance that various fees for religious practices were abolished. More radical demands, such as the election of local pastors, were not supported. This was far too dangerous, but the Committee did recommend that such choices were now placed in the hand of "ecclesiastical and lay princes". This was a major rebuke to Rome and should be understood as reflecting the impact of the Reformation and the differences between the interests of those in the Holy Roman Empire and the wider church.

In other areas, though, the Committee did suggest changes. It recommended, for instance, that the small tithe was abolished and made other suggestions to reform the large tithe. Other significant recommendations were included. Taxes should be reformed, particularly the most egregious, such as the death tax. Over concerns around issues like loss of common land and rights to hunt game, the Committee sided less with the peasantry, though they suggested reforms. There was no desire at all to allow democratic control over these, but provisions were suggested so that the peasantry could try to prove their historic rights. The Large Committee "did not propose legislation" to deal with the "bewildering variety of legal customs in the empire", but it did want to clarify confusion over jurisdiction. It also hoped that the lords would treat their subjects "in a manner consonant with their 'consciences,' the 'law of God and of nature,' and 'fairness'."

Little of the Large Committee's recommendations made it into the Diet's final agreement. This is not surprising. There is a long tradition of governments and ruling classes responding to rebellion by promising to set up a committee or inquiry to look into a dispute or source of grievance and then burying the outcome after many months or years of discussion. But the pure fact that representatives of the Emperor had to sit down and examine the *Twelve Articles* and other rebel documents and respond to them reflected a recognition that existing laws and organisation of society bred rebellion. Some of the recommendations, such as the Committee's acknowledgement of the limitations caused by multiple, incompatible legal systems throughout the Empire and criticism at the level of fines and taxes imposed on the peasantry, came from a recognition that these were a barrier to economic development within the Empire. But as Peter Blickle points out, the main thrust of the Diet was not to end discontent through reform, but to prevent rebellion by moving "conflict to the arena of judicial compromise". He also notes, however, that this was not successful, "as the numerous revolts throughout the empire in the seventeenth and eighteenth centuries make plain".[311]

Chapter 11
Michael Gaismair's Unchristian, Horrible Order against the Royal Domain of Tyrol[312]

One other part of the Peasants' War should be looked at, though it had a slightly different trajectory to the rebellion elsewhere in the Empire. Despite defeat elsewhere, the peasantry in parts of Austria remained strong as rebellion here began later in May 1525. The revolt began in several different places, but key was the victory of the peasants in Salzburg.

In the Austrian region of Styria, the nobleman Sigismund Dietrichstein was captured by a peasant army numbering four thousand. Dietrichstein's troops were known for their barbaric violence against the rebels earlier in the rebellion, including "impaling, flaying and quartering" rebels and "cutting off the breasts of the peasant women and ripping open the abdomens of those about to become mothers".[313] He had headed to the town of Schladming, near Salzburg, to prevent it going over to the rebellion, but on 3 July 1525 the rebels stormed the town killing some three thousand of Dietrichstein's troops. It was a significant military victory for the peasantry, but came too late to change the course of events elsewhere in the Empire.

Dietrichstein was forced to surrender to his own mercenary forces who had mutinied and gone over to the peasants. An interesting event now took place, with the peasants collectively voting on the fate of Dietrichstein and other nobles. They voted to execute them, but when Dietrichstein "pleaded the promise of knightly treatment he had obtained from the free-lances" the decision was passed on to the peasant council in Salzburg. They decided that some "foreign" nobles would be executed, but others, including Dietrichstein, were "stripped of their knightly raiment and dressed in peasant clothes… and they were led away on waggon-horses to the castle of Werfen." The peasants in and around Salzburg were not defeated immediately. Salzburg was relieved after a two-week siege by forces of the Swabian League who promised, again, a diet to consider the peasants' grievances. The failure of this diet to make any changes led to a resurgence of the revolt in Austria in May 1526 which saw it joined by Michael Gaismair, a rebel leader from Tyrol.[314]

In May 1525, rebellion erupted in Tyrol, part of the Empire and located in the mountainous area between contemporary Austria and Italy. One fascinating aspect to the rebellion here is the far-reaching vision of a new society developed by its leader, Gaismair. One historian has described the rebellion in Tyrol as an attempt to create an "Alpine workers' commonwealth" which was "radically egalitarian".[315]

Gaismair usually receives only passing mention in accounts of the German Peasants' War. Engels describes him as "the only one of the peasant chiefs to possess any military talent"[316] and gives a brief account of the rebellion and aftermath. Despite the few lines that Engels devotes to Gaismair, the rebel leader has been celebrated as a revolutionary precursor to modern socialists. This is in most part due to the radical constitution, the *Landesordnung*, written by Gaismair in 1526 as a model for a new egalitarian Tyrol. This was, according to Walter Klaassen's biography of Gaismair, nothing less than an attempt to plan a "completely new and different social order".[317] We will look at the *Landesordnung* in more detail later. Before exploring the revolutionary events in Tyrol, let us get a picture of the rebel whose leadership of the rebellion was to make him one of the greatest enemies of the nobility.

Michael Gaismair

Tragically, we know very little about Gaismair's life and ideas. In contrast to Thomas Müntzer, whose writings and letters fill a large collection, we only have a few pages of Gaismair's writings, some notes he made and the *Landesordnung*. Despite, or perhaps because of, the sparsity of information, Gaismair's name has been adopted by many different people since. Bizarrely, given Gaismair's commitment to democratic and egalitarian society, even the Nazis tried to co-opt him. In 1944 a Nazi SS regiment was given his name, and Joseph Goebbels commissioned an (unmade) film about his life.[318]

We do not even know precisely when Gaismair was born, but it was probably between 1485 and 1490.[319] He came from a relatively privileged background – his grandfather was a farmer and his father had grown wealthy from the mining industry before buying a farm. Klaassen points out that Gaismair will have had little personal experience of poverty; rather his education and career would have been that of a well-off member of the prosperous Austrian middle classes. What was it that drove Gaismair towards the radical ideas that characterised his life?[320] The first influence was likely the reality of life in Tyrol for the poorest people, something that we will look at shortly and which Gaismair encountered throughout his working life. The second influence were the radical religious ideas that were beginning to gain traction in Tyrol. These were, firstly, radical Catholic ideas and then, gradually, the ideas of the Reformation, which were slowly penetrating the relatively isolated Tyrol. Finally, and most importantly, Gaismair was driven to radicalism by the experience of the Peasants' War itself, which saw him take a leading position in the revolt and shattered his illusions in the region's benevolent ruler.

We know that Gaismair was secretary to the vice-regent of Tyrol, Leonhard von Völs. One of the roles of the vice-regent was supposedly to defend the liberties of the people, something that he failed to do. Unsurprisingly, one of the demands of the 1525 rebellion was that he be replaced.[321] We know many of the complaints made by the peasantry to von Völs and, as his secretary, Gaismair would have read and followed many of these cases of oppression. One example, found by a biographer, is a poem written in Gaismair's handwriting in the margins of the minutes of one case:

> I suffer in silence and wait,
> As I remember their innocence,
> No good remains unrewarded,
> No evil unavenged,
> One can get far by going slow[322]

In April 1521, Sebastian Sprentz was elected bishop of Brixen (today Brixen Bressanone) supported by von Völs. It seems likely that this relationship was how Gaismair ended up working for Sprentz. The bishop's role brought together two crucial aspects of late feudal society

– religious and secular lordship. But this was contradictory. No one could simultaneously rule through force and offer religious guidance. Klaassen argues that it was seeing how this played out in reality that led Gaismair to some of his radical conclusions.[323]

While this contradiction would become highly influential on Gaismair's radical thinking, it was the progress of the peasants' rising and the ruling class response to it that was finally to transform Gaismair into a revolutionary.

The Rising in Tyrol

As with the risings elsewhere, the rebellion in Tyrol had a number of direct causes. Chief among these was the economic oppression of the peasantry and the lower orders. As we shall see, the demands produced out of the rising in Tyrol highlighted many examples of oppression and inequality – from heavy tithes and taxes to unfair treatment by the legal system and greedy clerics and officials. All of these contributed to the pressure on the peasantry.

This all took place in the context of growing economic problems for the nobility, whose extravagant spending and frequent creation of new knights was squeezing their wealth. At the same time, the position of the nobility was threatened by the erosion of their military power, which was being replaced by Landsknecht infantry. As a consequence, the nobility demanded more and more from those below them.[324] This feudal exploitation manifested itself with extraordinarily heavy and extensive taxation and obligated labour, as well as growing intrusions on historic rights to use land and natural resources.

A further concern for the peasants was the proposed introduction of "Roman law", designed by King Ferdinand I to strengthen his position and improve management of the kingdom. This would, it was thought, further remove ancient rights and make it harder for the peasants to defend themselves legally.[325] Also of concern was the growing wealth and power of banking and merchant "corporations", such as the Fugger bank, which was driving up costs of basic goods. Finally, critical ideas directed at the Church were gaining traction, though Tyrol's relative isolation meant that few Protestant ideas or preachers had penetrated the region. Some had, however; one priest imprisoned for preaching criticisms of the Church was freed by a "mob".[326]

Anger at the Church was directed at the corrupt and greedy behaviour of vast numbers of the clergy. In 1524 and 1525, when peasant discontent began to move towards open rebellion, Bishop Sprentz repressed them violently, torturing and executing forty-seven people.[327] In September 1524 a peasant, Peter Pässler, was arrested for rebellion and, after a lengthy trial, sentenced to death by burning. Pässler was a peasant rebel whose father had been "deprived of his living by the bishop of Brixen" and subsequently failed by the legal system. He had subsequently taken to the hills with a small band, becoming, according to Klaassen, a Robin Hood figure.[328] The extended trial of Pässler lasted from summer 1524 to May 1525. It came after Bishop Sprentz's execution of dozens of other rebels, but the death penalty for Pässler was the final straw. As he was led out to be burnt to death on 9 May 1525, a protest by a crowd of peasants separated him from his guards and spirited him away to freedom.

The next day, the people of Brixen, together with the local peasantry, rose up and took control of the town. The rich and powerful were expelled, their homes and wealth appropriated. Bishop Sprentz hid in his castle. Over the following days, the rebels captured, plundered and took over towns and villages throughout the region. They expelled clergy, elected new officials and appropriated the wealth and gold of religious buildings and, in one case, a Fugger bank. One noteworthy person expelled was Gabriel Salamanca, a hated Spanish noble who was treasurer and a close friend and adviser to Archduke Ferdinand, who provided a link between the royal treasury and the Fugger bank. On 13 May Gaismair was elected leader of the Brixen rebels.[329]

On 30 May, the rebel delegates from across Tyrol met in Merano (Meran). This assembly produced a massive set of peasant demands numbering sixty-two articles. These articles were the "product of a special situation reflecting relative remoteness from Reformation influences and the higher level of political participation and sophistication of the Tyrolian peasants".[330]

Space prevents a detailed analysis of the Merano Articles. But along with the many other similar sets of peasant demands from the 1525 rising, they represent a general discontent with conditions.

This was summed up by the introduction to the Articles, where they complain that

> many evil abuses have arisen in the secular and spiritual Estates for some time now, through which the Kingdom of God is hindered, the love of Christ, and good neighbourliness are forgotten, and all matters turn on self-interest and not the common good… [W]e desire your Highness to establish the following articles…to make a new territorial ordinance.[331]

The first article continues by demanding that the whole of Tyrol becomes subject solely to the territorial prince, Archduke Ferdinand, not local lords and bishops. The income from these lands should be given to him rather than local lords and clergy, and excessive interest on mortgages and loans should be reduced. The number of clergy and convents should be controlled, and their income managed to levels enough to cover their needs. Neither "spiritual nor secular nobles should have towns or jurisdictions or legal rights subject to them, nor should they exercise any secular rule, which should fall to his Highness alone."

The subsequent articles that challenge the existence and power of local lords and clergy can be seen as an expression of massive discontent at the corruption and waste of the Church and nobility. As elsewhere, the rebels wanted to elect their local parish priest and control their income, and they saw the Archduke as the figure who would oversee this justly.

The next section of the articles demanded equality in the law, especially in terms of access to legal rights and easy access to appeals. The rebels also wanted towns to choose their own judges "of honourable birth, of good morals…dependent on the court for his income, and have the language of the court as his native tongue".

With these articles, we get a sense of how the majority of peasantry wanted to reform society to reduce injustice and inequality. This was not a revolutionary program, but it was a militant one that saw participation, democracy and a just leadership as prerequisites for a better society. Much faith was placed in the Archduke as arbiter of the law, but the peasants also wanted to change the laws that they saw as unjust. For instance, the peasants wanted a standardised system of weights and measures introduced.

The peasants also demanded that "all running water and streams, all man-made lakes, and all game and wildfowl should be free for all to enjoy…also weirs which cause the streams to overflow should be removed…all commons, woods, grazing and meadows which each person has removed from the community without permission or behind its back should be returned".

Interestingly, the rebels tried to ensure that private property was not affected by this, "if anyone has made or bought a fishpond on his own land and property, he should be left undisturbed by the community." The appropriation of land and resources was directed against those who were seen to have stolen it, or deprived others of its use.

The Merano Articles also contained restrictions on outsiders, such as "Savoyards, Scots, Netherlanders, and other hawkers", who were exempt from taxation and regulation. Non-resident hawkers would have to leave, and, before being allowed to settle, strangers had to pledge that they would not break the law. There was also a strong rejection of the wealth and activities of the growing capitalist banking and mercantile corporations:

> So many companies have grown up, from whom we must purchase our necessities, so that the common land is ruined we request that such companies, be they great or small, should be abolished, so that all goods and commercial wares shall once again be sold at the same price; especially that the Fuggers, Höstetters, Welsers, and all the companies be allowed no purchases of silver in the land.[332]

At the same time the peasants wanted to reduce the burdens from feudal oppression, such as the death taxes. In addition:

> The common man is quite overburdened by landlords and their stewards to whom he must give his grape harvest, hay, straw, food, and drink, etc. the peasant is always forced to harvest his grapes not when it suits him but the landlord, so that many peasants who do not have their own winepress find that part of their wine is spoiled… Such abuses should

be abolished and all lords should pay the appropriate share of wages for harvesting the vines, guarding the vineyards, carrying the grape-hods and treading the grapes.

The Merano Articles covered every aspect of life in Tyrol, from wine production to the use of woodland, the selling of goods in markets, the maintenance of roads, the control of foreigners as well as the right to justice, election of officials and rules about inheritance. They reflected all aspects of peasant discontent, and the rebels who gathered in Merano and produced the Articles at the end of May 1525 had every hope that Archduke Ferdinand would implement the changes, as they concluded:

> We request his Highness graciously to receive and confirm all the above articles for the good of his Highness's commons and the furtherance of the common good; furthermore, to hear the grievances and requests of individual towns, jurisdictions and person, and to remedy them.

Ferdinand dashed their hopes, and Gaismair was driven to far more radical conclusions.

Revolutionary Conclusions: The Landesordnung

As rebel leader between May and June, Gaismair oversaw the appropriation of wealth, land and buildings, but it is also likely that he did not see the rebellion as being a direct challenge to the existing order. Despite the radical demands of the Merano Articles, they left the structures of feudalism intact.[333] In fact, in common with many peasant rebellions, Gaismair and the other peasants did not initially see the rebellion as being against Tyrol's ruler or the Emperor.[334] But following his experiences in the revolt, and as the nobility failed to deliver anything to the peasantry, Gaismair arrived at a more radical position.

Archduke Ferdinand quickly moved to regain some control. Unable to stop the peasants meeting at the Diet of Meran, he brought forward a proposed general Diet at Innsbruck, which he could control and use to "crush the revolt". As Gaismair's biographer makes clear, Ferdinand understood this clearly, to the shock of the peasant delegates in

Innsbruck. The peasant delegates had gathered in large numbers, they made up the largest grouping in the Diet, and had every expectation that their discontent would be sorted.[335]

Ferdinand used a number of subterfuges to win the day. Hopelessly outnumbered in terms of delegates, he was in a weak position. There were few noble delegates because they would not risk leaving their castles, and the peasants made sure the clergy weren't represented.[336] Despite the scepticism of some attendees, Ferdinand was able to rely on the fact that most delegates, including the peasants, trusted him. By turning the peasant delegates representing richer areas against those from poorer areas he was able to divide his opponents, but the biggest problem for the rebels was events elsewhere in Germany. On 14 June news arrived that the peasants had been heavily defeated at the Battle of Würzburg. Committees were set up to discuss the Merano Articles, but as the discussions dragged on, the more radical delegates drifted away. The crux of the discussions hung on a constitutional point. Ferdinand argued that implementing the peasants' demands required a change to the constitution, which he argued he was powerless to do. The peasant delegates denied this, saying they just wanted their grievances addressed. But their position in the Diet was becoming weaker.

Ferdinand was able to use the conference to defeat the radicals. Their faith in Ferdinand meant they were unable to recognise that his manoeuvres were undermining their position. Firstly, he made a concession by agreeing to take over some of the secular roles of the Church, taking control of the prince-bishopric of Brixen. This looked superficially like Ferdinand had given in to one of the rebels' biggest demands and the rebels celebrated that one of their biggest foes was defeated. This reform would only last for a few months, but it enabled Ferdinand to get the revolutionaries to surrender.[337]

The defeat in the Diet of Innsbruck was not total, though, as Klaassen concludes, most of the benefits went to the better off peasants. Both sides could claim some victory, though it is clear the real victors were the nobility who had disarmed and divided their opponents and bought themselves valuable time, while elsewhere the peasant rebels were being massacred. Tragically, it seems that even the most revolutionary and best organised of the peasants were still not able to see past their illusions in Ferdinand. But Gaismair himself went to Innsbruck to watch events first hand, and there his illusions were shaken. He told his friends back in Brixen not to start a further uprising, fearing further violence.[338] According to Klaassen, when Gaismair finally realised that he had been betrayed, he threatened to assassinate Ferdinand himself. It was a betrayal that was to drive Gaismair to even greater radicalism. Some of this was religious – Gaismair brought radical preachers to Tyrol. But it was also social. Divisions within the peasant camp meant that the better off peasants wanted an end to the revolt, but the poorer still hoped for change. Radical protest continued, with refusals to pay taxes to Ferdinand and radical preaching, but the countryside was increasingly subdued. Perhaps, however, Gaismair retained illusions in the Archduke, or supreme belief in his own ability to raise rebellion, for he made a classic mistake in continuing to trust the authorities to uphold their side of the bargain made at the Diet. In early August, he received an invitation to appear in Innsbruck to discuss the situation; on arrival, he was immediately arrested.[339]

Ferdinand himself was now in a stronger position. He had received a huge loan from some princes and the Fugger bank. Hiring a mercenary army numbering two thousand, he was able to put down the remaining rebels. The reprisals were violent.[340] Many rebels fled, including Gaismair, who escaped prison and fled to Zurich. His letters at this time demonstrate his anger, growing radicalism and a desire for revenge.[341]

In the aftermath of the peasants' defeat, Gaismair, partly in conjunction with the radical Swiss theologian Ulrich Zwingli, developed a plan to invade Tyrol. By now, Gaismair had moved from Zurich to the Grisons region of Switzerland. While Ferdinand had signed a note promising Gaismair safe passage, there is no doubt that the rebel leader was worried for his safety. The plan concocted between Gaismair and Zwingli called for a coalition of forces from various Swiss cities, as well as a Tyrolean army raised by Gaismair. This would attack Tyrol, at the same time as France and Venice started a war against the Emperor. Gaismair had already gathered seven hundred sympathetic men.[342] What would they do when victorious?

It is with his invasion plan that Gaismair's radicalism reached its apogee. Alongside his military preparations, in 1526 Gaismair produced a revolutionary new constitution for Tyrol based on the needs and demands of the peasant rebellion.

The *Landesordnung* was a twenty-four-point radical reimagining of how Tyrol could be reorganised in favour of ordinary people. It is the most radical document of its time, arguing for the overthrow of the existing order and the creation of a new Tyrolean society based on democracy and equality.

The text begins with a call that inhabitants of Tyrol swear to look after each other and act together through collective decision making. Gaismair hoped that inhabitants would join in a communal society and not live selfishly while accepting the authority of those chosen to rule. Crucially, everyone would firstly live to honour God, and secondly, they would seek to improve the common good. This opening on its own demonstrates Gaismair's radicalism. But he quickly goes further. He argued next in the *Landesordnung* that people would have to get rid of their enemies, which included those who attack religion and oppress ordinary people and the "common good".

Society would be reorganised to ensure that the rich and powerful had no special privileges, which Gaismair claimed were against the word of God. No one, he wrote, should "have an advantage over anyone else". The equality that Gaismair insisted on was necessary because inequality led to "dissension, arrogance and rebellion". Running through the *Landesordnung* is class struggle – that used against the poor by the rich – and the need for a struggle to overthrow this order.

To ensure this happened, Gaismair called for the destruction of castles, fortresses and city walls, which would mean everyone living in villages and with no class differences.

At the core of Gaismair's vision is a more democratic Tyrolean society. Every parish would elect judges and jurors annually and their expenses would be paid by the state. Gaismair also called for weekly court sittings and that cases would not take longer than a fortnight. This addressed peasant discontent with long delays caused by the infrequency of legal hearings, resulting in cases going unresolved for years. This was particularly an issue over questions of land ownership or access.

The government, to whose authority Tyroleans would pledge, would meet in Brixen, and regents would be elected regionally including from the mining areas – the miners, a considerable economic force, would get their own representative. Gaismair, no doubt under the growing influence of Protestantism, called for images and crucifixes to be removed from churches. He also wanted a university, not to develop new ideas or philosophy, but to study and teach the word of God. Three "learned men" from this university were to be permanently part of the new government to ensure that no rules or laws were made that were contrary to God's will.

Gaismair's economic programme was less detailed.[343] Taxes, tolls and tithes were of concern to the poorest producers, and Gaismair was concerned that taxes should be placed under democratic control. Their abolishment, or at least a year without them, would be decided collectively. Tolls, on the other hand, would be abolished in Tyrol, making imports toll-free – though exports would be charged. Here, Gaismair is concerned with ensuring that Tyrol's wealth remain within its borders. He was specifically concerned that taxes might need to be raised temporarily for defence – no doubt because he expected that Tyrol would only be won to its new constitution by military conquest, which would be open to counter-attack. Tithes would be paid, as they were seen as ordered by God in the Bible, but they would be used to support a priest with any excess used to help the poorest and prevent vagrancy and, interestingly, reduce the number of unemployed.

The next part of the *Landesordnung* is concerned with protecting and helping the poorest and gives a clear sense of Gaismair's thinking about the sort of society he wanted to create:

> The monasteries and the houses of the Teutonic Knights are to be converted into hospitals. Some will be for the sick where together they can be given proper care and medical treatment. Others will accommodate the aged who can no longer work, as well as indigent orphans who can be taught and honourably brought up. The very poor are to be aided... Wherever the tithe is not sufficient for the support of the pastor and the poor, people are to give alms faithfully according to their ability... Every hospital is to have a manager, and beyond that a general administrator over all the hospitals and welfare is to be appointed. It will be his duty to supply the hospitals regularly with whatever they

need, and to oversee the care of the poor. The local magistrates are to assist him in their jurisdictions with the tithe and alms, and also with the identification of the very poor and all the information pertaining to them. The poor are to be given not only food and drink but also clothing and everything else they need.[344]

This outlines a caring, equal society, where the common good begins from the needs of individuals, and officials are appointed to ensure this takes place. The wealth and property of the rich would be taken from them and redistributed to facilitate and organise this process.

Gaismair was next concerned with how the land was used and organised. Officials would be appointed with duties including the maintenance of roads, bridges and infrastructure, as well as woodland and waterways. Unproductive areas would be converted to arable land upon agreement by the government. Gaismair was explicit about some land changes, presumably drawing on his own personal knowledge. He called for the swamps of Tyrol to be drained and converted to pastureland, as well creating land for other crops like olives and saffron. A shortage of grain was to be solved by growing it among vineyards for producing red wine. Draining the swamps and the better red wine would, Gaismair thought, improve the health of the population at only a small cost.[345] However, the community as a whole was to take responsibility for the maintenance of communal land.

Production of non-agricultural products was to be strictly controlled. Gaismair was concerned about usury and so private business was to be banned. Instead, manufacturing was to be concentrated in one place – Gaismair suggested Trent – to ensure that goods produced were at a sufficient standard, quality and price. Prices would be controlled and goods would be distributed via centres established in convenient locations throughout Tyrol, where they would be sold at cost.[346]

Gaismair seems to have been at great pains to prove that the new order he planned for Tyrol was viable. He included, for instance, plans to stabilise the currency. He also suggested that precious metals confiscated from the rich and from places of worship should be made into coins to be used for the benefit of all.

While some of Gaismair's vision was insular, removing the rights of foreigners to trade, for instance, he was keen that a new Tyrol would maintain good relations with neighbouring states with special markets set up to facilitate trade. But a reserve of currency was to be kept in case of war.

Finally, it is notable that Gaismair included a section devoted to the future of the mining industry. Here, Gaismair sounds most like a modern revolutionary, declaring that all the mines and buildings belonging to the rich nobles, merchants and companies like the Fugger bank would be confiscated. These owners have, he says

> Forfeited their right to them for they [bought] them with money acquired by unjust usury in order to shed human blood. Thus also they deceived the common man and worker by paying his wages in defective goods…raised the price of spices and other products by buying up and hoarding stocks. They are to blame for the devaluation of the coinage, and the mints have to pay their inflated price for silver. They have made the poor pay for it, their wages have been lowered in order that the smelters can make some profit after buying the ore. They have raised the prices of all consumer goods after they gained a monopoly, and thus burdened the whole world with their unchristian usury. By this they have amassed their princely fortunes. They are now justly punished and their activities prohibited.[347]

In contrast to the profiteering practices of Fugger bank and other corporations, Gaismair wanted democratic control of the mining industry. A manager was to be elected to oversee the whole mining industry and report annually on the state of it. All mining was to be under the manager's control, and no private industry was to be allowed. Mineworkers would be paid in cash. It was a radical idea to place a national industry under collective control.[348]

Gaismair's Tyrolean constitution was a masterpiece of radical thought, dressed up to be as popular as it could be to a discontented population. Its vision of democratic oversight of key parts of the economy, the expropriation of the wealth of nobles, bankers and the Church and the way that Gaismair constantly returned to the need to use this wealth for the common benefit, describes a radical new way of running society. Walter Klaassen is right to say that Gaismair's constitution has "no parallel in the sixteenth century for its radicalism in calling for the sweeping away of the whole ancient order".[349] The following century saw a handful of similar ideas begin to take shape – the most famous being Gerrard Winstanley's vision of a commonwealth that arose out of the radicalism associated with the English Revolution and Civil War.

The *Landesordnung* was a direct challenge to the existing system where the masses were exploited for the wealth of a minority, a minority that included a growing number of capitalist interests. In contrast, Gaismair imagined a society where production was organised for the benefit of all, the old order was swept away, and laws and rules were based on a radical, democratic, reading of the Bible.[350] Gaismair deliberately rooted his vision for a future society in the discontent at the old – witness his consideration given to practicalities such as standardised weights and measurements, or ending the payment in kind for mineworkers. But drawing on these inequalities and oppressions, Gaismair constructs a vision of a new order – one that was a threat to nobles, the Church and capitalists alike. They would not let it come to be.

Despite his promise of safe conduct, Ferdinand knew that Gaismair was a threat as long as he was alive. With a high bounty offered for his capture or death, there were at least one hundred attempts to assassinate him. On 2 May 1526, Gaismair set out with his army to support the renewed revolt in Austria, crossing the mountains in a remarkable feat of military leadership. Once in Austria, Gaismair joined the revolt, taking command of the siege of Radstadt. But the revolt's wider defeat saw this abandoned. Now, however, Gaismair saw his opportunity to invade Tyrol. It looked like sections of central Europe's nobility, organised in the League of Cognac, were moving against the Holy Roman Emperor, Charles V, who was in a remarkably weak position. In early July 1526, Gaismair took a peasant army of about two thousand over the mountains towards Lienz. There, they collectively decided to march on Tyrol, capturing several strongpoints on the way. However, as his army approached, the communities he had expected to join them did not rise up. Once again, a collective discussion took place among Gaismair's rebels as to what to do next. They decided to go to Venice, saying "they would stay together and commit all they had to plunder and kill all the clergy and the nobility". Arriving in Venice, Gaismair hired himself and his troops out as mercenaries.[351]

Gaismair found himself a ready commander, and his forces did well. Ironically, in taking this route, Gaismair now found himself fighting with allies of the Pope. He did not immediately give up hope of his army sparking a revolution in Tyrol, but increasingly it faded away. Ruling class fear of Gaismair's radicalism did not disappear. In August 1527, the price on his head reached one thousand guilders together with an annual pension of four hundred more. Gaismair managed to survive until 1532, when he was finally assassinated in Padua, where he was living with his family on a pension from the Venetian government.[352]

It is pointless to speculate what might have happened had the population of Tyrol risen with Gaismair's army in 1526. Certainly, both Gaismair and his enemies, particularly Archduke Ferdinand, thought this was possible, even likely. But this did not happen and Gaismair's *Landesordnung* was never put to the test. Ferdinand's obsession with killing Gaismair is testament to the fear his class had of his ideas – though it is likely that Gaismair had long since abandoned any hope of revolutionary change.

In the history of the German Peasants' War, Gaismair's ideas have often been forgotten and neglected in favour of better-known figures such as Thomas Müntzer. If Müntzer has been seen as a proto-communist, this has been to the detriment of Gaismair, whose vision was far more radical and farsighted. Gaismair's attempt to implement a new revolutionary society was foiled precisely because those he hoped would form the basis of the new order were not willing to rally to his flag. Nonetheless, we should not forget the radical vision that Michael Gaismair outlined, one that still speaks to us today.

Part Two
Causes and Consequences

Chapter 12
The Reformation, the German Peasants' War and the Bourgeois Revolution

In 1976, in the aftermath of the 450th anniversary of the German Peasants' War, the East German government commissioned an enormous panoramic painting by the artist Werner Tübke. In 1989 the completed painting, measuring over 120 metres in length, was unveiled in the Panorama Museum at the site of the Peasants' defeat in Frankenhausen in 1525. The museum opened ready to mark the 500th anniversary of Thomas Müntzer's birth and just a few months before the Stalinist state of East Germany ceased to exist.

Visitors today may be slightly perplexed by the painting's title; "Early Bourgeois Revolution in Germany". The phrase originated with Friedrich Engels. His conception of the Peasants' War as an "Early Bourgeois Revolution" is often quoted and appears regularly throughout the literature relating to events in 1524-5, particularly that produced in East Germany for the 450th anniversary. The East German historian Max Steinmetz, for instance, wrote that Engels

> [p]roved that the years between the beginning of the Reformation (1517) and the end of the Peasant War formed the early bourgeois revolution in Germany. He showed further that in the course of these years the characteristic stages of development of a bourgeois revolution emerged with full clarity.[353]

In July 1893 Engels wrote to Franz Mehring, referring to the "failure of the bourgeois revolution in Germany during the sixteenth century".[354]

Steinmetz, however, took this much further than Engels. He, and others like him, who were writing from a viewpoint shaped by East European politics and interpretation of Marxism, saw within the German Peasants' War and the "early bourgeois revolution" an expression of much more contemporary ideas. In fact, the Peasants' War was to become a sort of origin story for the German working class's revolutionary ambitions.

Steinmetz, for instance, believed that the "early bourgeois revolution" was "precipitated" by Luther's *Theses*, which he said "unified all classes and strata – with the exception of most spiritual princes and prelates…under the leadership of the middling bourgeoisie" against the Catholic Church. This unity, argues Steinmetz, was shattered by Luther's actions at the Diet of Worms, which led to four different camps, including radical and moderate bourgeois wings and a "revolutionary" wing characterised by Müntzer's and Gaismair's politics. The most radical programmes of the peasantry in 1524 and 1525 expressed, for Steinmetz, the argument of the bourgeoisie that what was needed was the "destruction of the feudal system, handing over power to the people and setting up a democratic republic". The Peasants' War, then, was the culmination of this movement for a bourgeois revolution and an attempt to "create a unified national state from below". But when Müntzer, who was for Steinmetz the "most prominent leader of the early bourgeois revolution", was executed, there was no longer effective opposition to those forces that wanted to hold back the bourgeois revolution. This meant that the bourgeoisie was exposed – they were not prepared to carry through a revolution that could unify Germany and create a nation state. Müntzer, by contrast, had a vision of the "development of Germany (as a democratic republic)". This, Steinmetz argues, was "immature" and "utopian" for the time but was "an inspired anticipation of the truly national policy of the German working class".[355]

Here, in 1979, Steinmetz was twisting Marxist ideas into something which Engels himself had not believed. He was arguing that within the German Peasants' War existed ideas and social forces that were an early expression of the workers' movements of the 20th century. In contrast, Engels wrote about the German Peasants' War because he was trying to understand the cowardice of the German bourgeoisie in his own time, during the revolutions of 1848. Then, mass revolutionary movements exploded across Europe, seeking to sweep away the remnants of the old aristocratic feudal order. But in Germany in 1848 the bourgeoisie backed down from a final confrontation, fearful of revolt from below. There are obvious parallels with the Peasants' War, but Engels did not believe that 1848 was a direct copy of events three hundred years previously.

At that time, in 1525, the German bourgeoisie was not yet powerful enough to make its interests known collectively, although there were some small, hesitant steps in this direction. No bourgeois class, as a distinct, capitalist strata existed in early sixteenth century Germany. Nonetheless, there were individuals and groups of individuals whose economic interests required a break with existing, feudal, social relations. They were the nascent bourgeoisie whose wealth arose from trading and was increasingly associated with manufacturing and industrial processes. These individuals dominated inside the towns and cities of the Empire. Remember that in 1525 some rebellious towns and cities produced articles inspired by peasant demands, but further shaped by urban interests. Chief among these were demands that made it easier for merchants to profit from trade.

As Engels noted, the only class that gained from the 1525 revolution was the princes,[356] since sixteenth century German society was too fragmented for a united movement against feudalism to emerge. By 1848, however, Engels argued that things had developed much further:

> The Revolution of 1848…was not a domestic German affair, and was an episode in a great European event. Its motive forces throughout its duration transcended the narrow limits of one country, and even those of one part of the world.[357]

In fact, Engels was explicit that 1525 and 1848 were not the same. The two revolutions (note that Engels did refer to 1525 as a revolution) were "in spite of all analogies, essentially different".[358] So what was the Peasants' War?

One of the most influential historians of the Peasants' War, Peter Blickle, saw it as a "revolution of the common man", an "attempt to overcome the crisis of feudalism through a revolutionary reshaping of social and seigneurial relations on the basis of 'the Gospel'"[359]. Despite being known as the Peasants' War, Blickle continued by arguing that the revolution was carried forward, not by the peasantry, but by the "common man", which included, "peasants, miners, the citizens of territorial towns, the politically disenfranchised citizens of imperial cities".[360]

Blickle's description is useful, if a little nebulous. It captures the spirit of the Peasants' War, as a mass movement of disenfranchised people from the bottom layers of German society in conflict with those at the top and demanding a reworking of society in the common interests of the population. In fact, Blickle defines the "common man" not in itself as a class but in reference to other classes. For instance, in his discussion of the "Communal Reformation", which we will return to, Blickle wrote that the "common man"

> definitely did not include male and female servants, mercenaries, beggars, and vagrants...above the common man were the lords, lay and clerical, and below him were the lower social classes and those groups entirely outside the hierarchy of social estates.[361]

Lyndal Roper has criticised Blickle and other historians for their use of the term Common Man, as it obscures "its sexual and social partiality".[362] She argues that while women were part of political protests and actions, they were constrained by a "framework which constituted them as non-political".[363] In the towns, women "could not be councillors, could not vote in elections to office, and appear, even as widows, to have had neither a formal say in the conduct of guild affairs or a place in the social life of the guild. Though non-citizen males could be incorporated into this vision of community, women, it seems, could not".[364] That said, women did often play a central role in the urban economy. In her study of women and production in the late mediaeval period, historian Martha C Howell notes that "women held high status jobs in all economic sectors of Cologne" and identifies three women's guilds related to gold spinners and yarn and silk makers. These guilds all "organised import-export businesses run by families, not individuals; all drew their principal membership from Cologne's new merchant capitalist class; none had power in Cologne's government". She continues: "The mistresses in all of these three guilds, then, were part of family businesses, but these were, indeed, special businesses. Although artisans themselves, these women did not belong to the artisanal sector disappearing from Cologne but to the capitalist class then emerging in the city".[365]

So, to say that women were excluded from the political sphere is not to say that women did not participate in the Reformation or the German Peasants' War. As Roper says, in the city of Augsburg, for instance, we know that women disrupted church services:

> A girl threw blessed salt in the font; women made sure they were in church when they knew "something was going to happen" and women are frequently named as the sources of rumour or the channels of information about action against urban Councils, in favour of the Reformation.[366]

In this account of the Peasants' War, we have seen a number of examples of the roles played by women – as participants in protests, such as the storming of a convent, or attempting to prevent the execution of captured rebels. We have also seen how the ideas of women's work and role in society were being changed by Reformation ideas and emerging notions of gendered labour.

In other words, the communal reformation and the Peasants' War was fought out in a highly gendered way, within the context of a society that saw women as property and subordinate to men at all levels. This is not to say that women did not participate, or were not victims, or that their concerns and demands were not expressed through the articles and the rebellion of the lower orders, but women were not able to participate fully in the rebellion because of their subordinate role within existing society and, in consequence, there was no attempt to imagine how this might be transformed. This must be borne in mind when we hear the term "communal", either in contemporary history or in accounts from the sixteenth century.

In his discussion of a "Communal Reformation" and a "Revolution of the Common Man", Peter Blickle saw both the Reformation and the Peasants' War as being closely linked. Indeed, he makes a strong argument that the Reformation could not have taken place without the class struggle that characterised German society in the late Middle Ages and into the sixteenth century which culminated in the events of 1524 and 1525.

Indeed, it was the struggle of "communal organisation" for self-identity and emancipation that led the lowest orders to drive forward change in town and country. As Blickle writes, "with the help of communal organisation – and only in this way – did peasants and the burghers learn to say no, to protest, to question the demands of lordship and the claims of the authorities. The protest of the faithful against the church in Rome was rehearsed in the protest of the subjects against their lords".[367]

This is an important insight. Some of the demands of the Reformation and the criticisms put forward in 1517 by Luther were not new. What was different was the way that they were taken up by thousands of people, propagated and then further developed. The people of Germany did not merely repeat the ideas of reformers like Luther, but they expanded upon them in ways that were "identical in their basic principles". Of the reformers' concept of the church, commoners in towns and the countryside insisted "that it imposed an obligation for concrete action".[368] In the hands of ordinary people, the Reformation became a tool to recreate their communities in their own way. Before Luther, many thinkers had made criticisms of the Church and its practices. Luther's Reformation, however, "would not have made it beyond the monastic walls and the university lecture halls had its theology and ethics not been so highly compatible with the concrete reality of communalism".[369] Tens of thousands of people took reformation ideas and developed them further shaping them to reflect their own interests. The rapid spread of the Reformation cannot simply be reduced to the skills of Luther's oratory, or the availability of the printing press, though both of these were important. It was also the way these ideas connected directly with the discontent felt in different layers of society.

As Blickle summarises:

> Their struggle for the Christian Republic was the qualitative leap from the theory of the intellectuals, who shied away from responsibility, to the concrete, day-to-day practice of the common people. And this practice was not nourished by religious faith; rather, its explanation

lies in the actual living conditions, in the village and the city, in the political culture of the late Middle Ages.[370]

This political culture reflected concrete reality, which included the changing interests and desires of many people in German society. Take one example used by Blickle himself. This is the instructions given by the community of the Franconian village of Wendelstein in late 1524 to their new priest:

> Thus we shall not recognise you as a lord, but simply as a servant of the parish. You do not command us, but we command you. And we order you henceforth faithfully to preach to us the gospel and the Word of God, pure and honest in accordance with the truth (untarnished and unobscured by human doctrine).[371]

Here we see a key demand of the Reformation playing out in practice among the villagers, who, together with their mayor, were telling their new priest that his role was not to transfer instruction from above to the people through his interpretation of the Bible, but simply to preach the gospel. The idea that communities could elect their own priests was central to Protestant belief, which held that every Christian was a priest and all had equal authority. As Luther said, "if we are all priests…and all have one faith, one gospel, one sacrament, why should we not also have the power to test and judge what is right or wrong in matters of faith?"[372]

But in the minds of discontented peasants and town citizens, these ideas easily became a call for democratic control over religion, and then over society, and inspired a sense of equality among people trapped in a rigidly hierarchical society. Crucially, the ideas of the Reformation became inseparable from wider economic concerns. For instance, opposition to tithes, essentially a religious tax, raised the principle of opposing all taxes and then the whole social order. As a result, under the impact of the Peasants' War, with armies of thousands of peasants demanding radical change, equality and an end to lordship, Luther changed his position on communities choosing their priests. In his direct response to the rebels' Twelve Articles, Luther now argued that while communities had the right to decide on their own priest, they had to do it by petitioning the authorities. If this was refused, then they could choose one themselves, but must "support him from its own resources".[373]

The Peasants' War was thus an extension of the Reformation into open class war. Again, this is a point made very well by Blickle:

> Peasants and burghers voiced the demand – an uncompromising demand – that authority submit itself to the gospel. All incidents of rebelliousness in city and countryside, from the sacking of monasteries by the peasants to the expulsion of recalcitrantly Catholic councillors by the burghers, had no other purpose than to push through this demand. Submission to the gospel became the stamp of legitimacy. Lordship as such meant nothing... The communal reformation posed a fundamental challenge to the legitimacy of political authority... This was a significant by-product of the communal reformation...the rebellions in city and countryside were also much more fundamental and deep reaching than ever before... Where the authorities were deaf to the gospel, peasants' and burghers' reformations could merge into a revolutionary movement.[374]

This was not to say that the Peasants' War can simply be narrowed down to the Reformation. The demands of the peasants and urban commons, particularly those around economic issues, make it clear that religious radicalism was intertwined with wider economic discontent. How this manifested through the Peasants' War depended on specific circumstances, though it is notable that the Twelve Articles were almost universally accepted in many different areas of rebellious Germany. But there were some significant differences. We have already noted the difference between the demands of rebels in the countryside and towns. Blickle argues that because the countryside was a more "authoritative political structure", Reformation demands there were "politically far more explosive" than in urban areas.[375]

In particular, and most threatening to the existing order, was the way that Reformation ideas fuelled wider concepts of freedom. In particular, this manifested itself in growing calls for the abolition of serfdom – something that was common in many different peasant demands. "Serfdom should be abolished for bondsmen in the entire county of Tirol" read one of the Merano Articles of May 1525, or, most influentially, the third of the Twelve Articles:

> It has hitherto been the custom for the lords to treat us as their serfs, which is pitiable since Christ has redeemed and bought us all by the shedding of his precious blood, the shepherd just as the highest, no one excepted. Therefore it is demonstrated by Scripture that we are free and wish to be free. Not that we wish to be completely free and to have no authority, for God does not teach us that. We should live according to his commandments, not the free licence of the flesh... Therefore we ought to live according to his commandment, which does not show and teach us not to obey authority, but rather that we should humble ourselves before everyone, not just authority, so that in this way we will gladly obey our elected and appointed rulers (whom God has ordained over us) in all reasonable and Christian matters. We have no doubt that, as true and genuine Christians, you will gladly release us from serfdom, or else show us from the Gospel that we are serfs.[376]

This is why Luther, and other Reformation thinkers like him, were so horrified by the Peasants' War itself. Within it they could see that ideas of freedom and equality were a direct challenge to the existing social order. While Luther was keen to repudiate the insurgents, the Peasants' War had grown out of the Reformation because it had landed on fertile territory – the desire to end the old feudal order. It was precisely to defend the existing social order, indeed the very concept of hierarchical authority, that Luther urged the repression of the peasantry in such a bloody way. It was also why nobles on both sides of the Reformation debate united to massacre the rebels on battlefields such as those at Frankenhausen and Böblingen.

The Peasants' War was a class struggle that encapsulated the anger and frustrations of the common people against existing society and its rulers. The people who rebelled had a variety of reasons and justifications for doing so. These were rooted in a rejection of the old, feudal order, that remained a hangover from the Middle Ages and its theological representation in the Catholic Church. But there was also a new, emerging group of people whose interests somewhat coincided with the commoners. This nascent bourgeoisie found the existing order a barrier to their ability to make money. They were particularly organised in the towns and cities and were interested in fighting for a reorganisation of society but one organised in their own image. Struggles to do this, that overthrew the vestiges of the old feudal order and left in place a world where capitalist relations could develop and flourish, are known as bourgeois revolutions. As discussed above, many thinkers, following Engels, have argued that the Peasants' War was an early example of this.

Attempts to explain what Marxists mean by bourgeois revolution have been extensive.[377] For Marx and Engels, the bourgeois revolution was the process by which the old feudal order was replaced by a bourgeois society that opened the door for capitalist development. The classic case was the French Revolution of 1789, which saw a mass movement of small producers, led by the most radical elements of the bourgeoisie, overthrow and execute the French monarchy and place power in the hands of a National Assembly. Driving this revolution through required the mobilisation and participation of the great mass of the French lower orders; it was the ordinary peasants and artisans of Paris who stormed the Bastille for instance. But despite their reliance on the peasantry to drive through the Revolution, it was the emerging capitalist class who were the beneficiaries of it, even if this meant they had to make some compromises. As Alex Callinicos comments, "This outcome does not invalidate the view of the revolution as bourgeois, since it undoubtedly benefited the "really existing" capitalist class in France".[378]

While France provided the classic example, the problem for those studying the transition from feudalism to capitalism is that there were a number of different paths that the bourgeoisie could take in order to overthrow feudal relations and institute a new society. England had, perhaps, the next closest series of events to those in France, but the English Revolution took place over a century before the French when English society was far less developed than in France. Nonetheless, Oliver Cromwell, using the mass power of the "middling sort" as represented by the New Model Army, was able to defeat the Royalist forces, which led to the execution of the king in 1649. While the Restoration of the monarchy in 1660 superficially appears to have reversed the English Revolution, the Stuart Restoration led, in fact, to a monarchy in thrall to bourgeois power. Elsewhere on the European continent, the path from feudalism to capitalism was less straightforward. In particular, the German bourgeoisie in 1848 proved too cowardly to drive through its revolution against the old aristocratic order, fearful of the power of the workers' revolt from below that would accompany it.

But things were very different in Germany in the sixteenth century. Then there was no working class. While there were small numbers of people who lived by selling their labour to others, they had yet to become a class in itself. As we have seen, the vast majority of people in Germany in 1525 were either peasants or part of the peasant economy. They suffered enormously from high rents, taxes and tithes. The whole system of feudalism was geared toward squeezing as much from the peasantry as possible. While some of the peasantry were motivated to rebel purely to improve their lot without imagining any fundamental change, others drew more radical conclusions. But what that radical alternative looked like was shaped by the peasants' class position in society.

The changes taking place in the European economy during the Middle Ages were gradually transforming society, creating individuals and groups of individuals whose interests were hindered by the existing order. These individuals found in the Reformation ideas that helped lubricate their rebellion – giving them ideological tools to challenge the status quo.

Revolutionary peasants imagined a world where the products of peasant production were fairly used and distributed. Many of those people, inspired by ideas of equality and freedom that grew out of Reformation criticisms of the Church, were commoners, whose struggle in the Peasants' War centred on the fight to make a more equitable communal society and saw the overthrow of serfdom as key to establishing this. This was different to the alternative to feudalism imagined by the most radical merchants and traders.

For wealthier individuals, particularly the merchants who made money from trading goods between towns and cities, the nascent capitalist class, the Reformation offered an opportunity to criticise a society that supported feudal power, diverted wealth towards the Church and limited their ability to make profits.

Whether the Peasants' War can be classed as a bourgeois revolution has been the subject of much debate. The historian Rainer Wohlfeil, writing on Engels' book on the Peasants' War, expresses frustration that the rebellion is referred to as a bourgeois revolution precisely because he cannot see the "movements as actions of the bourgeoisie". He criticises those "Marxist-Leninists" who saw the movement as being "bourgeois in character", i.e. without the existence of a significant bourgeois class.[379] But this is to misunderstand the nature of the rebellion itself. Engels argues that "the Reformation was a bourgeois movement". In fact, he emphasises that there were three "decisive battles" in the "long fight of the bourgeoisie against feudalism" – the Protestant Reformation in Germany, followed by the English and French Revolutions.[380] Therefore, Engels clearly sees the German Reformation as a significant part of the long struggle of the bourgeoisie for a new order. Indeed, in notes he made at the end of 1884 for a revised edition of his book on the German Peasants' War, Engels emphasises that the Peasants' War was "the critical episode" in "bourgeois revolution No.1":

> Reformation – Lutheran and Calvinist – bourgeoisie's revolution No.1, in which Peasant War is the critical episode. Dissolution of feudalism, along with the development of towns, both decentralising, absolute monarchy therefore a virtual necessity for holding together the nationalities. Had to be absolute, precisely because of the centrifugal nature of all the elements. Absolute not to be understood in the vulgar sense, however: constantly at odds partly with the Estates, partly with rebellious feudal lords and towns; the Estates nowhere abolished; thus better described as an Estate monarchy (still feudal, decaying feudal and embryonic bourgeois).

He continues:

> Victory of revolution No. 1, which was much more European than the English one, and became European much more quickly than the French one.[381]

Thus, for Engels, the bourgeois revolution was a long process, which saw the "embryonic" bourgeoisie at the time of the German Reformation grow in strength and numbers until it was a force that could challenge the old feudal order for dominance. So what does it mean for Marxists to say that the Reformation and the Peasants' War were movements bourgeois in character?

Here what matters is not the class position of those fighting the struggle, but the struggle itself. Writing in *The Peasant War in Germany*, Engels makes this clear when he notes that the peasants could not win a revolution, and the *only* people to benefit were the enemies of both the peasantry and the emerging capitalists, the princes.[382] The defeat of the Peasants' War meant that serfdom was not destroyed, and feudal society was further entrenched.

But for Engels that was not surprising. Germany's limited economic development as well as the decentralised nature of its political structures meant that any move towards a more centralised nation was doomed to failure at this point in history. This was for several reasons – the most important was that not only was Germany split into many different provinces, but each of these was also "broken up into a multifold structure of estates and fractions of estates". Each of these provinces contained different groups (Engels lists princes, priests, nobles, peasants, patricians, burghers and plebeians), or estates, with competing interests vying with each other. Added into this mix were the international interests of the Emperor and the Church. Engels concludes:

> each estate opposed the line indicated by circumstances for the national development, that each estate acted on its own, coming into conflict not only with all the conservative, but also with the other opposition estates, and that it was bound to fail in the end. That was the fate of

the nobility in Sickingen's uprising, or the peasants in the Peasant War, and of the burghers in all of their insipid Reformation. Thus, even the peasants and plebeians in most parts of Germany failed to unite for joint action and stood in each other's way.[383]

The Peasants' War, and its wider Reformation context, was a class struggle that saw different classes fighting for their interests. Within this, the peasant rising, in part because of this classes' numerical significance, took on the form of a revolution against the existing order – even if that revolution could not be successful. The smashing of the rebels in 1525, and the continuation, and renewal, of serfdom afterward only strengthened the position of the feudal rulers, delaying Germany's further economic development, and eventually leading to stagnation.

When Luther came out against the peasants' rising, many people, including thousands of peasants, were shocked. Luther's class position led him to oppose the rising, even while he continued to attack those the peasants were rebelling against. While his writings and actions had given encouragement to the peasantry, his identification with the rich and powerful, and his belief in the fundamental importance of an authority, led him to side with those who repressed the rebellion, even when they did not agree with his religious beliefs. Engels skewered Luther for this:

> Luther had put a powerful tool into the hands of the plebeian movement by translating the Bible. Through the Bible he contrasted the feudalised Christianity of his day with the moderate Christianity of the first centuries, and the decaying feudal society with a picture of a society that knew nothing of the ramified and artificial feudal hierarchy. The peasants had made extensive use of this instrument against the princes, the nobility and the clergy. Now Luther turned it against the peasants, extracting from the Bible such a veritable hymn to the God-ordained authorities as no bootlicker of absolute monarchy had ever been able to match. Princedom by the grace of God, resigned obedience, even serfdom, were sanctioned with the aid of the Bible.[384]

However, the Reformation, like religious ideas in general, offered different things to different people. On the one hand, for the emerging capitalist class it was, in the words of British Marxist Neil Davidson, the "first ideology of bourgeois revolution",[385] but for the lower orders it was a legitimisation of their anger and frustration at their social position, exploitation and poverty. As we have seen, leading radical thinkers, such as Thomas Müntzer, were able to develop these arguments further into revolutionary ideas.

We must therefore caution against a crude understanding of the Reformation which sees it as a construction of the discontented capitalist class as a tool to justify and mobilise for the overthrow of the feudal order. Davidson points out that it was wrong to see "the capitalist economy producing Protestantism as a form of ideological legitimation", but it is also wrong to see "Protestantism as an independent factor that inadvertently provided the psychological motivation for believers to undertake capital accumulation".[386]

European society in the early sixteenth century was a time of great uncertainty, crisis and economic instability. Protestantism was a reaction to this in the sense that it seemed to offer an explanation of the root of the crisis – the failings of the Pope and the Church – and an alternative. Criticisms of the Church were not new. Luther drew on some of the thinkers who preceded him. The difference was that in 1517 and after ideas critical of the Church took root in significant sections of European society. In Germany, it opened the door to mass peasant rebellion, but as Davidson points out, it offered, "assurance of salvation in a world where assurance was gone, and it did so by asking believers to look into their hearts for proof that they were among the saved".[387]

The general flourishing of debate within the Reformation movement itself, and between Luther and the defenders of the existing Church and among the Reformation movement, was a reflection of the way that the Reformation had different interpretations for different people. One group that was particularly inspired in this way was Engels' "embryonic bourgeoisie",[388] for whom further development of their economic interests was held back by the Church and its behaviour, Marx notes that the Reformation was revolutionary in how people thought about themselves and their faith:

> Luther, we grant, overcame the bondage of piety by replacing it by the bondage of conviction. He shattered faith in authority because he restored the authority of faith. He turned priests into laymen because he turned laymen into priests. He freed man from outer religiosity because he made religiosity the inner man. He freed the body from chains because he enchained the heart.[389]

Faith, then, under Protestantism, became an individual's property, an ideological break suitable for a bourgeois outlook on the world.

Luther's anger and polemic against the Church in 1517, particularly around the question of indulgences, was not abstract. The needs of the Church to raise funds through the sale of indulgences, the levying of tithes and the exploitation of peasants on church lands, meant there was an economic basis to the Reformation. This was one reason why a mass movement developed from below. But for the emerging bourgeois class in particular, the Church was a barrier to their interests in other ways. The historian Michael Mann identifies three of these:

> First, there was a tension between the centralised authority of the Catholic Church and the decentralised decision-making required in a market system by those who owned the means of production and exchange. Second, there was a tension between a fixed order of statuses legitimated by the church and the requirements of commodity production, in which nothing apart from property ownership is given a fixed and authoritative status… Third, a tension existed between the social duty of the rich Christian to be 'luxurious' (i.e. to maintain a large household, provide extensive employment, and give to the poor) and the capitalist's need to claim private ownership rights over the surplus so as to provide a high level of reinvestment.[390]

The Peasants' War was bourgeois in character insofar as it represented the beginnings of a struggle for a new social order across Europe. The low level of German economic development and its political and social fragmentation meant that the development of the bourgeoisie and its rebellion against feudal society was slower than elsewhere in Europe. Indeed, when the Reformation spread from Germany elsewhere, the capitalist class in countries such as England and the Netherlands surpassed them in their struggles against feudalism because they had developed much further.[391]

Luther's Reformation created the space for discontent to develop and crystallise in the writings and speeches of radicals. In part, this was because he was a rebel himself, against the Church and the Pope. But Luther, at least in the earlier stage of the Reformation, also had to appeal to the masses by expressing at least some of their discontent. For instance, Luther, in his 1520 pamphlet *To the Christian Nobility of the German Nation concerning the Reform of the Christian Estate*, criticised those who made money without working.

> We must put a bit in the mouth of the Fuggers and similar companies. How is it possible in the lifetime of one man to accumulate such great possessions, worthy of a king, legally and according to God's will? I don't know. But what I really cannot understand is how a man with one hundred gulden can make a profit of twenty in one year. Nor, for that matter, can I understand how a man with one gulden can make another – and all this not from tilling the soil or raising cattle.[392]

Such arguments would have appealed to the great mass of the labouring population, even as they would have alienated those who wanted to accumulate wealth from others' labour. But Luther's ideas, rooted as they were in his close reading of the Bible, also furnished ammunition and religious justification for those arguing for "Godly Law".

This is why Luther could be attacked by his enemies as having encouraged rebellion, and simultaneously rush to denounce and attack those who rose up under the Reformation banner. It is why the historian James M Stayer is correct to describe the Peasants' War as "the expression of the Reformation in the countryside".[393] It is also why the nobility from both the Protestant and Catholic wings of the Reformation debates could put aside their religious differences and unite to crush the peasantry.

Luther himself never shirked from encouraging the violent

repression of the peasantry and aggressively defended his position afterward. In *An Open Letter on the Harsh Book against the Peasants*, written just weeks after the peasants had been crushed, Luther defended his earlier demand that they be violently suppressed. He wrote "rebellion is a crime which deserves neither a court trial nor mercy, whether it be among heathen, Jews, Turks, Christians, or any other people; the rebel has already been tried, judged, condemned, and sentenced to death and everyone is authorised to execute him".[394]

Luther feared the revival of resistance and rebellion. In 1527 he warned that "Müntzer is dead but his spirit has not been rooted out".[395] These warnings were not unwarranted. At the end of 1527 the town council of Erfurt uncovered a planned rebellion, led by a former follower of Müntzer. In their report about the plan, they note that the rebels considered Müntzer and Pfeiffer "true teachers [who] were unjustly slain".[396]

The end of the peasant rebellion saw no reforms or changes that made any material difference to the lives of the vast majority of the population. Indeed, the repression and punishment of the rebellion made the situation worse. So, Luther's fear of further discontent was well warranted. But following the slaughter at Frankenhausen and elsewhere, this discontent would not be expressed through mass rebellion, despite the hopes and plans of a small number of isolated rebels.

As Andrew Drummond concludes, "after the defeats of 1525, the desire for these changes did not disappear, but the immediate means to attain them did; social militancy was therefore mostly sublimated into religious dissent, which found considerable support among the lower classes".[397] We look further at how this took place later, when we consider the end of the radical Reformation and the Anabaptist movement.

Those who crushed the peasantry and their allies wanted revenge for the defeats they had received at the movement's hands. But they also wanted to ensure that further radical change was not forthcoming. Such change was expressed in the radical preaching and writing of figures like Müntzer, but it was far from the reality in places where the radical Reformation and peasants' revolt was, temporarily, triumphant. As Engels notes of Müntzer's base in Mühlhausen, during the rebellion it

> [r]emained a republican imperial city with a somewhat democratised constitution, a senate elected by universal suffrage and controlled by a forum, and with a hastily improvised system of care for the poor. The social upheaval that so horrified its Protestant burgher contemporaries actually never went beyond a feeble, unconscious and premature attempt to establish the bourgeois society of a later period.[398]

But even these changes were too much and were rolled back immediately after the defeat of the peasantry. Nonetheless, for thousands of peasants, the radical ideas espoused by Müntzer and others inspired them to take up arms against powerful enemies. Let us now explore this radicalism further.

Chapter 13
All Things in Common

The Peasants' War has left historians with hundreds of documents detailing the demands of the rebels. This rich material gives a real insight into the concerns of the mass of the population of Germany. But some rebels went much further articulating a vision of a socially equal society wherein the products of peasant labour were equally distributed, with everything held in common, not seized by a minority of the ruling class. In this chapter, we will look more closely at these revolutionary demands and discuss whether such a society could have been created out of the German Peasants' War.

In September 1524, Thomas Müntzer and Heinrich Pfeiffer published the Mühlhausen Articles, a declaration of how a new government should be elected that would base itself on God's Word. The first article called for a "completely new council" and the second read:

> That righteousness and justice be exercised in accordance with the Bible or command of the holy Word of God. Why? To ensure that the poor are treated in the same way as the rich, as in Zechariah 7, Leviticus 19 and 26, John 7, Matthew 5, Luke 18.[399]

Like many other texts produced by the rebels in 1524 to 1525, this was an example of the way that many of them wanted to transform how society was organised. The basis for the new order should be God's Law, as written down in the Bible. In February 1525, the Baltringen band declared, "Whatever this same word of God grants us or takes from us we will gladly accept and suffer whatever good or pain comes from it".[400] Peter Blickle, emphasising the revolutionary nature of this step, writes:

> Godly law was potentially dynamic in three senses. First, demands of any kind could be submitted, so long as they could be supported from the Bible. Secondly, corporate barriers, which had formerly divided

peasants from townsmen, could be dissolved. And thirdly, the social and political order of the future now became an open question.[401]

With the adoption of "Godly Law" as the ambition of the peasants, we see a fusing of Reformation ideas with the programme of the rebels. Who could deny a demand that was backed up by the Bible? Who could justify behaviour that went directly against the teaching of God's word?

Two surviving oaths of the Christian Association of the Baltringen, Allgäu and Lake Constance bands are focused on a new social and political order to protect the changes the peasants were fighting for. Blickle describes them, cautioning that "the peasants and their leaders were still too bound up in feudal relations even to imagine a radical alternative to the existing order":

> In the first version we find an oath aimed at establishing the gospel and godly law and at protecting existing governmental and seigneurial rights within this framework; in the second version, the peasants aimed at the replacement of governmental powers with the statement that they wanted no other lord than the emperor.[402]

As with Müntzer and Pfeiffer's articles, this Christian Association's Federal Ordinance[403] contained references to Godly Law as the highest legal authority:

> This Christian Union and alliance has been founded to the praise and honour of Almighty God, invoking the holy Gospel and Word of God, also to assist justice and godly laws, without prejudice or harm to any spiritual or secular person, in so far as is contained in and may be demonstrated by the Gospel and godly law, and especially to increase brotherly love.

The Ordinance continues with a series of demands against debts, for a fairer sharing of resources similar to a number of other sets of Articles from the rebellion. Interestingly, point five of the Ordinance says that:

All persons in the service of princes and lords should relinquish and renounce their oaths [to their lords]. Once they have done so, they shall be admitted to this union. Whoever will not do so, however, shall gather up his wife and children and not darken this region again.

Peasants and servants were here encouraged to join the new social order through an explicit break with the past. But what of Godly Law itself? What was it? The importance of the Bible to sixteenth century German society meant it had enormous authority. However, Godly Law was problematic in that it was a nebulous concept. It was not spelt out and required interpretation.

One rebel statement of the Association, states:

> We desire men of skill and understanding in holy Scripture to preach and teach us the holy Gospel and Word of God, purely and clearly, with all its fruits and without the addition of human teaching.[404]

The authors of the Federal Ordinance of the Christian Association called for several theologians, including Martin Luther, his close collaborator Philip Melanchthon and Ulrich Zwingli, to take on the role of interpreting God's Law. They refused, Melanchthon replying "since the Gospel requires obedience to the government and forbids rebellion even if the princes behave wickedly, and since it also requires that one suffer injustice, the peasants are acting against the Gospel".[405]

Effectively this meant that no one really knew what Godly Law was, and the matter was open to interpretation. Without interpretation, Godly Law became the most radical approach to unanswered questions for the rebels, particularly under the influence of the most revolutionary of preachers and thinkers inside the movement. The Christian Association's armies now stormed castles and monasteries in their region. Blickle concludes:

> Once the peasants acknowledged the godly law, they no longer aimed only at the abolition of concrete grievances but pushed more for a new political order, even if it was still only a vague idea. This new order would remove all differences of status and build on such local and

regional corporations as village and urban communities, local courts, and territorial assemblies. Instead of eliminating these older corporations, the new order would use their experience with elections to work toward a broader political union based on the same electoral principle.[406]

As we have seen, this led to a variety of different attempts, or proposals, to reorganise villages, towns and communities along democratic lines. Though, as Engels criticises, these never "went beyond a feeble, unconscious and premature attempt to establish the bourgeois society of a later period".[407] But this is not to deny that there was a genuine radicalism to these attempts. Indeed, they provided the framework for communities to select their own clerics, refuse to pay taxes, destroy records of feudal servitude and much more. While this was rarely real democracy from below, it was a step beyond the restrictions of feudal organisation.

Here lies the contradiction of the rebellion. Countless rebel articles and demands could call for a new way of organising key aspects of society, but implementing the change permanently was impossible. Take the fourth of the Twelve Articles, which concerned the rights of everyone to hunt, fish and trap animals to help feed their families:

> It has hitherto been the custom that no poor man has been empowered or permitted to catch game, wildfowl, or fish in flowing water, which we consider quite improper and unbrotherly, indeed selfish and contrary to the Word of God. In some places the lords keep game in defiance of [our wishes] and to our great detriment, for we must suffer the dumb animals wantonly and unnecessarily to devour our crops... For when the Lord God created man he gave him dominion over all creatures, over the birds in the air and the fish in the water. Therefore it is our request that whoever has waters for which he has adequate documents to prove that they have been unwittingly bought by him, should not have them taken from him by force, but rather that Christian consideration be shown for the sake of brotherly love; but whoever cannot provide adequate proof, should surrender them to the community in a reasonable manner.[408]

Similarly, the sixty-two Articles of the Peasants of Stühlingen, where the rebellion broke out in the summer of 1524, included a long complaint (article 41) demanding "game should be free". It complained about the injustice suffered by peasants whose crops were damaged by game kept for lords to hunt and noted that anyone who tried to hunt these animals and protect their livelihood risked their eyes being "put out" in punishment. The Stühlingen peasants pleaded to be allowed to "hunt, shoot, catch and use for our own needs, all game, high or low", and that they should not have to "give anything to the forester for allowing us to carry crossbows and muskets to hunt".[409]

As early as May 1524, the people of Forchheim rioted over the right to fish the ponds of the local cathedral. Peasant demands that they should be allowed to hunt, fish and trap as required were a common feature of rebellions of this era. They reflect the tension that existed within a society based on a land-owning minority, whose serfs worked land on sufferance from their lords, with limited legal recourse to protect their rights.[410]

The fourth article of the Twelve Articles and the other similar demands, expressed a deep-seated frustration, but no appeal to the lords' "brotherly love" or selfishness would resolve this issue. German society was based on the idea that a minority of people owned the land, with the rest of the population labouring on it for the benefit of the upper classes. Central to this was the idea that private ownership of land conferred on the owner the right to use that land. In fact, increasing his wealth often saw the lord destroying common land or taking away peasant rights precisely because they were a barrier to how feudalism functioned for the wealthy. Thus for the peasants to win the right to hunt, shoot or catch game and fish, to satisfy their needs required a direct challenge to the central principles of existing society. No matter how kind, or unselfish, a lord might be, or how worried he was that his castle would be burnt down, giving in to these demands other than in the short term was impossible.

So, the demand for "Godly Law" could help unleash revolutionary forces, but it could not articulate a new, classless, social order. Those like Michael Gaismair or, in a different context, Gerrard Winstanley, who did imagine such a new society, could not see it realised. This is because constructing such a new society required both the destruction of the old order and the development of an economic basis sufficient to support a classless world.

Marx wrote that the history of class society is the history of class struggle. Because class societies are based on antagonistic, exploitative social relations, they generate class struggle. But this struggle takes place irrespective of whether or not it is possible for the oppressed and exploitative societies to win through. In the German Peasants' War, the mass struggles of the oppressed groups were a challenge to the existing social order, and they created an environment within which individual thinkers could imagine a peasant utopia based on equitable distribution of goods and local democracy. But they could not break through to create that new social order.

The reasons for this lay in the nature of peasant society and the limited economic development of sixteenth century German society. As we have seen, the economic and social base of Germany at the time was the peasantry. It was peasant agricultural production that supported both the local lords and the small towns of Germany. Enough agricultural surplus was produced to support the extravagant lifestyle of the lords, princes and monarchs as well as those in villages and towns who were producing other goods essential to the agricultural economy. These peasants had a shared experience of oppression and exploitation. There were, therefore, inevitably moments when collective responses, such as risings and protests, would bring the peasant community together into rebellion against their common oppressors – the church, landowners and the monarch for instance. Such movements could raise common demands about land ownership, access to natural resources and land, or opposition to limitations on the rights to hunt or trap game. But what was absent was the potential for a collective alternative. This is because production within peasant communities is an isolating experience. It is worth reading Marx's comments on the French peasantry to illuminate this:

> The small-holding peasants form a vast mass, the members of which live in similar conditions but without entering into manifold relations with one another. Their mode of production isolates them from one

another instead of bringing them into mutual intercourse... Their field of production, the smallholding, admits of no division of labour in its cultivation, no application of science and, therefore, no diversity of development, no variety of talent, no wealth of social relationships. Each individual peasant family is almost self-sufficient; it itself directly produces the major part of its consumption and thus acquires its means of life more through exchange with nature than in intercourse with society. A smallholding, a peasant and his family; alongside them another smallholding, another peasant and another family. A few score of these make up a village, and a few score of villages make up a department. In this way, the great mass of the French nation is formed by simple addition of homologous magnitudes, much as potatoes in a sack form a sack of potatoes.[411]

The isolation of the peasants within self-contained smallholdings based on family production inevitably meant that they were incapable of, in Marx's words, "enforcing their class interests in their own name". While they could lead revolutionary movements, the peasantry in Germany were unable to push those movements through into the construction of a new society. Thus the best that could be achieved were reforms to the existing order – limitations on their own exploitation, some redistribution of wealth and legal changes.

The idea of "common ownership" has been central to numerous utopian visions throughout the centuries. But it was not until modern capitalism developed, concentrating production into huge workplaces and factories, that a vision of "common ownership" could have real meaning. Implementing it will require the overthrow of capitalist society through the smashing of the capitalist state, with the workers taking control of the "means of production" and organising, collectively, in their class interest. This was not an avenue available to the German peasantry.

So while peasant demands of 1524 and 1525 were littered with references to "Godly Law", some activists went further to envisage a new social, communal, order. The main demands were for just such a redistribution of wealth and for limits to the exploitation of the peasantry. In Wassertrudingen in Franconia, for instance, rebels told the mayor, "You great fool, you must share your wealth with us and everyone must be as rich as everyone else". In Wurzburg, other rebels declared, "if we are all to become brothers, then let's start right away making the rich share with the poor and redistribute above all what the rich have taken from the poor by trade and retail".[412] Within the rising there were numerous examples of peasants spontaneously redistributing wealth by taking the contents of the castles, monasteries and wealthy homes that they had stormed. But this movement could not proceed to defeat the feudal order.

Also visible in the peasants' struggle was the yearning for a society where property and land were held in common. This latter view is particularly associated with the ideas of Müntzer. As we have seen, this is extremely unlikely to have been something that Müntzer believed or said.

This is not to say that Müntzer was not a revolutionary. It is clear from his articles as well as his role in leading peasant armies, that he understood that change had to come through the breaking of the existing society through mass revolutionary force. Indeed, there was a deep pedigree to the idea of a world where "All things are held in common" in German theology which went back to the Bible. The very early Christian movement began as a communal movement, and this is reflected in a couple of places in the Bible. Famously, in Acts 2:44-45, followers of Jesus are described as living communally: "All who believed were together and had all things in common; they would sell their possessions and goods and distribute the proceeds to all, as any had need." Even more powerfully for the poor and radicals steeped in Christian theology, Acts 4:32-35 read:

> Now the whole group of those who believed were of one heart and soul, and no one claimed private ownership of any possessions, but everything they owned was held in common... There was not a needy person among them, for as many as owned lands or houses sold them and brought the proceeds of what was sold. They laid it at the apostles' feet, and it was distributed to each as any had need.[413]

During the Reformation and the Peasants' War, this was revolutionary for two reasons. Firstly, it furnished a ready set of arguments against those who called themselves Christian yet lived in luxury in the midst mass poverty. Secondly, it was a vision of a society run on a communal basis, where private property was abolished and everyone shared wealth. The desire to implement Godly Law drove the revolutionary movement forward. While this was not realisable, the fact that the exploited fought back against their exploitation five hundred years ago, has been, and continues to be, an inspiration to all those who fight today for a society free from oppression and exploitation.

Almost a decade after the defeat of the peasantry, radical Christians in one city in German tried to implement a society based on a strict, radical, reading of the Bible. In the next chapter we will look at the story of Anabaptist Münster.

Chapter 14
Anabaptism: the End of the Radical Reformation

Today, Münster, in Westphalia, Germany, is a large university town of about three hundred thousand people. It is relatively unremarkable, similar to many other such towns in western Germany. The centre is dominated by the Gothic St Paul's Cathedral, but nearby is another church, the Catholic church of St Lambert's. Looking up at St Lambert's today, you see an extraordinary sight: three cages hanging from the spire. These cages are replicas of those erected in 1536 which held, for several decades, the remains of three men: Jan van Leiden, Bernhard Knipperdolling and Bernhard Krechting. They were executed for their leading roles in the last major act of the radical Reformation in Germany: the Münster Rebellion. These men were Anabaptists and the rising that they were part of began as an attempt to construct a radical Christian society based on a "community of goods" and other ideals. Its degeneration, and the deprivation caused by the enemies' siege of Münster, led to trauma and death on a huge scale. Inside the besieged city, and in response to the deprivation of war, a system of common ownership and polygamy was implemented from the top down. Tragically the isolation of Münster quickly saw its degeneration.

Today the Anabaptists are mostly known as small religious groups such as the Mennonites, Amish or Hutterites. But their origins lie in the religious turmoil of the early Reformation era, and their ideas were shaped through a radical reading of the Bible that emphasised the alleged ideas of the early Christian followers, described by the sections of Book of Acts discussed in chapter thirteen. While the early Anabaptist movements were marked by a variety of different interpretations of the Bible, some shared characteristics include a commitment to a "community of goods", groups where "all things were in common", a rejection of infant baptism and belief in the baptism, or rebaptism, of adults.

In the excitement and turmoil of the early Reformation the Anabaptists were not particularly noteworthy – they were one of many different groupings and sects that were thrown up. The commitment of many of their followers to converting others, which often saw Anabaptist preachers travelling from village to village converting, and rebaptising, people they met, helped the group to spread and gain a following. The remaining isolation of these groups led to doctrinal differences among followers. But, as one historian explains, "the same social and economic impulses that inspired local peasant unrest fuelled the religious dissent of the early Anabaptists".[414] James M Stayer, another historian of the early Anabaptist movement, argues that they were the "most important groups of radicals in the sixteenth century 'revolution in consciousness' which we call the Reformation".[415]

Early Anabaptism has come to be associated with the Peasants' War for several reasons. The first is the direct connection between some radicals of the Peasants' War and leading Anabaptists – later we will meet Hans Hut, for instance, an associate of Thomas Müntzer, whose radicalism shaped Hut's ideas and practice. The second reason is that the ideas of shared goods and communal living were associated, particularly by the movement's enemies, with the revolutionaries of the peasant rising. In fact, one socialist historian of the movement, Ernest Belfort Bax, goes so far as to describe the Münster Rising as the "culminating effort of Christian communism".[416]

In the aftermath of the counter-revolutionary destruction of the Peasant Rising in 1525, there was limited space for radical movements to develop and prosper. As a result, social discontent became even more focused on religious belief and organisations. The Anabaptists were the most significant group to benefit from this, appealing to discontented and poverty-stricken peasants and town dwellers alike through their rejection of the status quo and their demand for a Church stripped of the trappings of wealth and power. The close parallels between the areas where Anabaptism grew and those of the peasant rising, as well as the fact that many former rebels became Anabaptists, makes it likely that "Anabaptism was to some degree a religious after-effect of the Peasants' War".[417]

This meant that even in its earliest days Anabaptism was shaped by theological divisions. For instance, there were differences in opinion over key questions such as pacifism, the communal sharing of goods and whether or not authority had power over Christian believers. One significant debate among Anabaptists was the theological question of "the Sword". This was a contested concept that evolved out of different biblical readings relating to the use of power. Were there two powers of "coercive jurisdiction", the civil and ecclesiastical? Or just one, wielded solely by the temporal (non-religious) regime? The Anabaptists and many other Reformers held to the latter, which meant that for them "the one, temporal, Sword stood for all the authority and force necessary to cement a social order comprised of individuals assumed to be in the vast majority radically wicked, egoistic and, hence, unresponsive to the common good". The concept of the Sword troubled the Anabaptists because it was closely tied up with ethics, and as Stayer argues, led to multiple ideas about whether or not it was right to use force to protect oneself, or one's beliefs, or use violence to promote those same ideas.[418]

Leading Anabaptists had initially been followers of Luther and other reformers around him. In Zurich, where the group first coalesced, the Anabaptists originally grouped around Ulrich Zwingli, though they eventually broke with him. This initial break took place over the question of church tithes, which Zwingli acknowledged had been abused by the Pope and the Church hierarchy, but nonetheless were, he thought, important for the continued functioning of society.[419] Zwingli thought that opposing tithes would be a direct challenge to authority and would lead to violence. He criticised the hierarchies of the Church who had abused their position and failed ordinary Christians, but he was also deeply concerned about the growing radical movement. As one biographer of Zwingli notes, he

> also referred to the new threat to social and religious harmony at home – the extremist evangelicals, self-confident, highly critical of others, lacking in charity, opposing the established civil government, quarrelsome, envious, back-biting hypocrites. To the baptism of children they were utterly opposed, and by their constant discussions at every street corner and their open-air preaching, the Gospel was in danger of being brought into disrepute. It was an indication of the existence of a religious left wing in Zurich that was long to trouble church and state.[420]

As a result of debates like these, from 1525 onwards, the Anabaptists found themselves at odds with both wings of the Christian movement, and very much in a minority position, though one growing in strength.

This is not the place for a detailed history of Anabaptism. But several things are worth noting. Firstly, the rejection of infant baptism and the need for "rebaptism" were central to the Anabaptist idea that an individual had to come to the Church through their own belief. The rebaptism of followers of the Anabaptists first took place in January 1525, and was directly in contradiction to existing Church belief. The Catholic Church had long held the idea that rebaptism was impossible and a blasphemous offence punishable by death. The effect was that the Anabaptist movement was immediately under threat of persecution, for both its religious beliefs and its practice. The second effect was that the Anabaptists saw themselves as separate from other Christians, denying the validity of their beliefs, their religious figures and even their churches – they kept themselves separate from the rest of society. This extended even to their rejection of the existing state, and led to what Bax called a "genuine attempt to carry out logically, principles of the Gospel-teaching and the idea of a return to a supposed primitive Christianity".[421]

This independence cultivated self-reliance and an element of subterfuge in how they organised and spread their ideas. This was not surprising. In the years following the period of the Peasants' War, thousands of Anabaptists were persecuted, imprisoned, tortured and executed – often in the grossest of ways. The oppression of the Anabaptists illustrates an important point about religious belief in this period. There was no concept of tolerance of other religious groups, and violent persecution was central to the approach taken by the authorities to their opponents.

As a result of this persecution, the Anabaptists were frequently forced to become refugees. This helped spread their ideas, and likely strengthened their resolve and their belief that they were the elect, the true group of Christians. Understanding the early Anabaptist movement, however, requires a brief exploration of the idea closely associated with them by friends and enemies alike, the "community of goods".

The idea of the "community of goods" was closely associated with the radicalism of the Peasants' War. As we have seen, many rebels saw the rebellion as the beginnings of realising a new form of religious society. In rejecting the existing Church – with all its wealth and power – these rebels looked for different ways of organising their religion and many were inspired by Biblical depictions of early Christians, principally those described in Acts 2 and 4. But there is enough ambiguity in these passages to allow for slightly different conclusions by different groups of Anabaptists. Stayer, in his account of the Anabaptist "community of goods" and the Peasants' War, identifies roughly four different groups of Anabaptists, separated geographically as well as theologically. Stayer argues that the "artisan leaders" of Anabaptism, "simply articulated the economic and religious ideals of pre-capitalist, pre-industrial rural and semi-rural commoners generally".[422] Some of them interpreted the "community of goods" as meaning the sharing of goods and wealth within single-family households. Others, such as the Swiss Anabaptists, "took Christian community of goods to be an expression of divine law" and that meant "sharing with the needy and…forbade human exploitation". For them, the church was "a congregation of commoners who worked with their hands, in which no rulers or rentiers with their special privileges disturbed the unity of the brotherhood".

Other Anabaptists, according to Stayer, in south and central Germany, were influenced by the most radical ideas of the peasant rebellion. To them, the community of goods was realised through "subsistence economics". Finally, Anabaptists in Moravia (now in the east of the Czech Republic), which became a haven for persecuted Anabaptists, took the most radical interpretation, influenced by the ideas of Michael Gaismair, and wanted a "self contained, relatively egalitarian society of commoners".[423]

For some Anabaptists "community of goods" was a revolutionary rejection of existing society, and an attempt to construct a new social order. For others it was about living in a better, more egalitarian and less oppressive way. But what matters here is less the detail of how different groups of Anabaptists interpreted the Bible and implemented different ways of living, but rather the strong sense of communal living inherent to Anabaptist religious life.

Anabaptism threw up many fascinating characters whose radical Christian ideas became a source of inspiration to tens of thousands of people. One of these was Hans Hut, a travelling book dealer who had distributed and sold the works of Thomas Müntzer. Hut was drawn to Anabaptism and became a significant figure in the movement in southern Germany and Austria. He had been at Mühlhausen with Müntzer and marched to Frankenhausen where he had heard Müntzer make his final speech. Escaping the slaughter, he was captured and eventually released. Despite the defeat, he preached afterwards that "We subjects should slay all our rulers. This is the right moment because we have power in our hands".[424]

But the most significant Anabaptist in this period was Melchior Hoffman, who became closely associated with a radical millennialism in the city of Strasbourg in the early 1530s. While the Anabaptist movement grew in Moravia, it was in the north-west of Germany where it began to take on a new character. Strasbourg afforded the early Anabaptists in the later 1520s a fertile area to grow. Authorities in this Imperial City seem to have been more lenient, allowing the first preachers who arrived to carry on with relatively little restriction. Anabaptism here initially grew along "the old theological lines",[425] until the arrival of Hoffman. Hoffman was an artisan, a skinner, who had taught himself the Bible and travelled widely in northern Germany along the Baltic coast, even, it seems, preaching in Stockholm. He arrived in Strasbourg in 1529 and joined the Anabaptists, quickly becoming regarded as a prophet. Hoffman then travelled into the Netherlands where he helped spread Anabaptism, but eventually returned to Strasbourg. Hoffman seems to have broken with the prevailing doctrines of non-violence to which the majority of Anabaptists adhered. He began to preach that the elect should take up the "two-edged sword" and use it against unbelievers. Hoffman's influence was localised to Strasbourg, the Netherlands and significantly, Münster, where his Melchiorite Anabaptism would become significant to the rebellion.

Hoffman himself came to a tragic end. He saw Strasbourg as a New Jerusalem and believed that it would be the site for the coming of the Lord, who would introduce the "reign of the saints". Hoffman predicted that the Lord would arrive in 1533, and his return to the city led to the development of a huge movement, with thousands coming to hear him preach. The authorities, fearful of wider unrest, arrested and imprisoned Hoffman. He continued to preach the end of the world from his prison tower. But as the year ended, it became clear that the saints were not coming to Strasbourg, and Hoffman's followers looked instead to Münster, which had seen an enormous growth in the radical Reformation movement. Perhaps, they believed, the people of Strasbourg had failed God and Münster was to be his chosen place. Hoffman, however, could not follow. He was imprisoned in the city for the rest of his life, dying in his cell ten years later.[426]

In the 1530s Münster was a significant town of about fifteen thousand people. Its inhabitants were caught up in an intense battle of ideas between Catholics, Protestant followers of the orthodox Reformation and radicals. The town was part of the Prince-Bishopric of Münster, one of three run by Bishop Franz von Waldeck. In 1533, however, the town won significant reforms and privileges that gave substantial power to the elected town council and the right to be Lutheran. This created a "three-cornered struggle over religion" in the city, between the Catholics, the orthodox Lutherans "around the Council" and the followers of Bernhard Rothmann, a radical Reforming minister in Münster. He was not yet an Anabaptist but was moving rapidly in that direction under the influence of radical refugees arriving in the city.[427]

The early Anabaptist arrivals organised in secret. New arrivals would meet Rothmann and be baptised, until there were so many that they could act in public, as Heinrich Gresbeck, an eyewitness to the Münster rebellion, explains:

> The priest first of all performed the baptism secretly, and he would also preach secretly in his house, baptising many people (men, women, and maidens). In this way, the number of rebaptisers in the city grew to be so large that they began to openly baptise anyone who wished to have himself baptised… The rebaptisers had a secret token among themselves for men and women. They wished to be very saintly and were unwilling to address the other burghers and women. Be it mother or father, they were unwilling to address anyone. When men met each

other on the street, they gave each other their hand and kissed each other on the mouth, saying, "Dear brother, God's peace be with you." The other answered, "Amen." The womenfolk who'd been baptised also had a secret token among themselves. They would go around without any head scarf. They went around in a wimpel, and this wimpel had a covering over the head. The wimpel was their secret token, and you could recognise female rebaptisers by it. These rebaptisers and female rebaptisers would treat each other like brothers and sisters, so great was the love that they had among themselves. This is how the priest held his rule over the city.[428]

There was a fraught atmosphere in the city. The Council called in a Lutheran theologian to strengthen their position and planned to expel Rothmann and other radicals. In November 1533 the Catholics tried to launch a violent attack on the radicals, but it was defeated by armed followers of Rothmann who assembled at St Lambert's Church.[429] As Stayer explains, Rothmann was deprived of his position and couldn't preach, but to prevent him, the city's Council had to rely on the Catholics. While not yet aligned with Anabaptism, the use of arms at this stage by the followers of Rothmann demonstrated how far the movement was from the non-violence associated with contemporary Anabaptism.

The radicalism of Rothmann's movement would only develop further.[430] In January 1534, Rothmann and other leading radicals were baptised and took up Anabaptism, and quickly Anabaptism became the dominant religion in the city. While the city had won the right to be Lutheran the previous year, the bishop was hostile and the Council was only able to hold this position because it had the support of a nearby prince. With the rise of the Anabaptists, who were then illegal everywhere in the Empire, the town Council was under threat from two sides – the Anabaptists themselves, and the bishop. At the start of 1534, rumours that the bishop was marching on Münster to suppress the Anabaptists led to a series of armed confrontations in the city centre, as different forces demonstrated their strength in preparation for the bishop's expected arrival. On 9 and 10 February 1534, a further rumour that the bishop was coming led to the Anabaptists gathering in strength, and a confrontation with the city Council, who organised a united force of Lutherans and Catholics to oppose them. The Anabaptists were heavily outnumbered. The Council had brought in outside forces including a thousand peasants opposed to the Anabaptists. This overwhelming threat forced Rothmann's followers to take up arms, despite their previous belief in non-violence. However, perhaps because of their belief in non-violence, they made a tactical offer to lay down their arms in the name of peace. As Stayer explains, the Council's burgomaster seems to have grabbed the opportunity, convincing the rest of the Council to accept peace in order "to attempt to carry on the affairs of the city on the basis of mutual religious toleration".[431]

It was a brief respite. The bishop began military preparations to capture the city, in fear of a siege and the Anabaptists themselves, the Catholics and Lutherans began to leave. At the same time Anabaptist refugees began to pour into Münster. On 23 February, the annual council elections were due to take place. Every seat was won by an Anabaptist.

Anabaptists now came to Münster in huge numbers, preparing for the "rule of the saints". Taking control of the city had required the Anabaptists there to take up arms. While there had been little violence, it was a powerful display of force, though as Stayer points out they had "come to power legally".[432]

But immediately they were in power, the Anabaptist leadership began to pressure those who didn't agree to either convert or leave. The only surviving account of events in Münster comes from Heinrich Gresbeck, who was eventually to flee the town and go over to its besiegers. His account was written to justify his own actions, and, as the quotes below will show, he was hostile to Anabaptism, despite playing a leading role in the rebellion. But Gresbeck gives a sense of what happened. Here is his account of the agitation:

> When it began to get dark in the evenings, the rebaptisers would run through the streets and shout, "Confess and repent! God is going to punish you!" and "Improve yourselves!" They shouted, "Father, Father, grant, stamp out, stamp out the godless! God will punish them!"... Some people in the city would say that the rebaptisers had hired the criers to cry this way through the streets in the evenings and nights so

that they would terrify the people and lead them astray. They would also preach at night in houses. They would gather together at night, and wouldn't preach during the day. For they didn't yet have possession of the city, but they did have sufficient possession of it. They had the keys to all the city gates, and every night they closed off all the streets and lanes with iron chains. They kept on with this closing until they chased away their opposition, which they eventually did. As soon as they'd chased away the burghers and clergy, both young and old, they no longer closed off any streets at night. Then they were a single people and were lords of the city of Münster. Whoever didn't wish to remain had to depart from the city or they would have killed them.[433]

A number of key Anabaptist figures now shaped events in Münster. One of these was Jan Matthys, an Anabaptist who had been converted by Hoffman, who came to Münster among the refugees entering the city, as the Lutherans and Catholics left to escape the bishop's siege. Another Anabaptist was Jan van Leiden (born Jan Bockelson), who would prove to be an important figure in the subsequent history. These leaders sent messengers everywhere inviting other Anabaptists to join them in Münster, which would, they predicted, soon become the New Jerusalem.

While Anabaptism in the city was very much the religion of the poorest communities, it also had its wealthier supporters, followers who felt that the Lutheran Reformation had not gone far enough. Among these was the powerful figure Bernhard Knipperdolling (or Knipperdollinck), the head of the town's guilds. Knipperdolling had been powerful enough a few years before to lead a challenge to the bishop and was clearly not afraid of challenging authority over religious issues. The closeness of leading figures in the rebellion is demonstrated by the marriage between Jan van Leiden and Knipperdolling's daughter during the rebellion.

Münster rapidly came under the control of Jan van Leiden and Matthys, who instituted a theocratic state. Matthys would have executed all non-Anabaptists, Catholic and Protestant alike. But under the urging of less extreme figures, they were expelled instead. The expulsion was akin to a pogrom; hundreds of people, old and young, healthy and unwell were ejected from Münster into a snowstorm. They left behind their wealth and possessions, and those that remained were rebaptised in a three-day ceremony.[434] As Norman Cohn points out, by 3 March "there were no 'misbelievers' left in Münster; the town was inhabited solely by the Children of God".[435]

These events urged the authorities into action. The bishop began a siege of Münster, whose inhabitants built earthworks, fortified the town and organised ordinary citizens as defenders. The Anabaptists complained that there had been no "declaration of war" and that the bishop, as the authority over the city, should have given the city's Council a hearing before starting a war.[436] Stayer notes how the events at the beginning of the siege fitted the ideas of the Anabaptist followers of Hoffman:

> If the initial resistance of Münster was not inconsistent with Hoffman's belief in the right of a Christian magistracy to use the Sword for legitimate, worldly purposes, the siege produced a mood of apocalyptic urgency that transformed the Melchiorite doctrine of the Sword. For instance, the escape of the Anabaptists from military disaster on 10 February was soon understood as a literally miraculous event.

Rothmann claimed that there had been miraculous fires and multiple suns in the sky that had protected the Anabaptists from slaughter. Reports of these were sent out to Anabaptists in areas around Münster, helping to justify events in the city by implying they were supported by God, thus encouraging more Anabaptists to come to the city.

But the Anabaptist leadership organised a highly repressive rule, though it was one whose support rested on the thousands of Anabaptists who remained. Their participation in mass religious events and communal action helped legitimise and strengthen the town's situation. Gresbeck reports that one dissenting city member, Hubert Smit, was arrested for making critical statements and tried "in the ring" by a common assembly, which found him guilty and sentenced him to death. Jan van Leiden then stabbed him. He died from his wounds a week later.[437]

The city government was also scrapped, and power rested in the hands of Jan Matthys, who had opponents imprisoned and punished.

Executions of opponents were common through the siege, and increased as it drew on and in the aftermath of attempts to topple the leadership. Knipperdolling was to admit that "he had performed eleven or twelve decapitations while the King [Jan van Leiden] credited himself with seven or eight".[438]

The use of force was a direct result of both the stringencies of the siege and the religious ideology of the figures at the heart of the Anabaptist regime. Stayer concludes that the Anabaptists in Münster "believed that God had miraculously revealed that they had been given the Sword for an apocalyptic crusade through which the world should be punished and their Kingdom made universal".[439]

All of Münster's inhabitants had a role during the siege, male and female, young and old. To keep the city functioning with limited resources, the Anabaptist leaders instituted a communal order, redistributing possessions and food that had been left behind, and created central stores where the poor and needy could apply for items they needed – from bedding to clothing. Communal dining areas were created where people ate together while listening to readings from the Bible. It is worth quoting Gresbeck's account of these events:

> So the prophets and preachers, along with the whole council, took counsel and wished to have all property in common. They first issued a proclamation that all those who had copper money should bring it up to the council hall. A different kind of money would be given to them in return. That is what happened. Next, they came to an agreement and decreed that all property should be common, that everyone should bring up his money, silver and gold, just as each had done the last time. After the prophets and preachers reached this agreement with the council, they had it announced in the preaching that all property should be common and that one person should have as much as the next. Whether they'd been rich or poor, they should all be equally rich, the one having as much as the next.
>
> So they said in the preaching, "Dear brothers and sisters, now that we're a single folk, brothers and sisters, it's absolutely God's will that we should bring together our money, silver and gold. The one person is to have as much as the next. So everyone should bring his money

up to the registry next to the council hall. The council will sit there and receive the money." The preacher Stutenberent continued, "It's not appropriate for a Christian to have any money. Be it silver or gold, it's unclean for a Christian. Everything that the Christian brothers and sisters have belongs to one person as much as to the next. You shall lack nothing, be it food or clothing, house and hearth. What you need you shall get, God will not let you lack anything. One thing should be just as common as the next, it belongs to us all. It's mine as much as yours, and yours as much as mine." This is how they convinced the people, so that they (some of them) brought their money, silver and gold, and all that they had. But in the city of Münster, the idea that the one person was to have as much as the next turned out unfairly.[440]

This policy was closely associated with Jan van Leiden, and violence was used against those who did not comply.[441]

While implemented from the top down, there is no doubt that these policies were popular among the poorest. Cohn quotes a scholar from Antwerp writing to the Dutch theologian and humanist Erasmus in Rotterdam: "We in these parts are living in wretched anxiety because of the way the revolt of the Anabaptists has flared up. For it really did spring up like fire. There is, I think, scarcely a village or town where the torch is not glowing in secret. They preach community of goods, with the result that all those who have nothing come flocking".[442]

Unsurprisingly the authorities mobilised to isolate and defeat the Anabaptists. Anabaptism "was made a capital offence not only throughout the diocese of Münster but in the neighbouring principalities, the Duchy of Cleves and the Archbishopric of Cologne". Cohn continues, "during the months of the siege countless men and women in the towns were beheaded, drowned, burnt or broken on the wheel".[443]

The Münster Anabaptists' commitment to the "community of goods" should not blind us to the repressive measures of the theocratic state. Books, other than the Bible, were banned and, together with charters and documents from the previous regime, burnt in a fire that Gresbeck says lasted eight days. Churches and monasteries were desecrated and destroyed, and while five or six schools were opened, they only taught religious subjects.[444]

But it was on the siege that Münster's inhabitants were mostly focused. They began the manufacture of gunpowder, firing on the besieging troops and led night-time raids against them, capturing prisoners and spiking cannon and stealing some guns. On 25 May 1534 the bishop's forces tried to storm Münster but were unsuccessful. Revealingly Gresbeck tells us that the defenders began to adopt "traditional military practices".[445] Initially the defenders did not have captains, or drums and pipes as these were considered unchristian. But under pressure of events, the Anabaptist leaders had a "revelation from God that the children of Israel had had units and all sorts of instruments. This they found in the Bible."

The siege was long, hard, and characteristic of how mediaeval warfare was changing with the arrival of cannon and guns. These allowed fortifications to be attacked, and long-range firing to be relatively accurate (Gresbeck tells of a cannon shot directed at a piper on the town walls). But mostly the siege was characterised by attempts to undermine the defences and counterattacks: the Anabaptists built catapults to fire at attackers, for instance. It was a war of attrition with casualties on both sides but one where the attackers had the advantage – they had food and supplies. Those inside the town began to suffer dramatically from hunger and shortages. There were a number of centralised plans to deal with this, including the seizure of any remaining food stores. But eventually the defenders were forced to eat cats, dogs and rats. There was a centralisation of power in the hands of Jan Matthys, who increasingly saw himself as a prophet. This was to be his undoing. In April 1534 he had a vision that he would defeat the enclosing forces with a small band of just twelve – the number no doubt relating to the number of Jesus's apostles. The small group rode out from Münster, but Matthys and these disciples were easily overwhelmed and killed by the besiegers.

Power now lay in the hands of Jan van Leiden, who declared himself King. This was to lead to a deepening of the theological influence on the running of the state. Jan van Leiden was prone to visions, which he would use in startling ways. In one instance he stood naked in the town square in a trance for three days. On coming out of the trance he declared that God had revealed to him that the old order of the city was to be replaced by a completely religious one whereby he would rule with twelve elders, who included some existing councillors and guild representatives.[446]

One aspect of the siege of Münster that has provoked lurid speculation and discussion is the question of polygamy. Originally Anabaptists had only allowed marriage between two Anabaptists; marriage between an Anabaptist and a nonbeliever, as well as adultery, were punishable by death.[447] Van Leiden, however, instituted "polygamy". Firstly, let us have a look at what Gresbeck says happened, while remembering that he is writing a hostile account of Anabaptism:

> Now, Jan van Leiden took matrimony in hand with the preachers and the twelve elders, so that one man was supposed to have more than one wife. The prophets, the preachers, and the twelve elders took matrimony in hand, secretly for as long as they were of one mind. The prophets and preachers found in the Bible the phrase "grow and increase yourselves." There were also some Old Fathers, such as Abraham, David, and Helkmaen [Elkanah] and others of them, and they had more than one wife. They wished to go on according to this practice and accepted matrimony. So the prophets and preachers proclaimed matrimony in their preaching, how it was God's will that they should accept a kind of matrimony in which God would have a good pleasure, so that man should increase the world – for God wanted to establish a new world – and that it was God's will that each brother should have more than one wife and increase the world.

He continues:

> Jan van Leiden with his bishop, preachers, and the twelve elders proclaimed the matrimony, saying that it was God's will that they should increase the world, that everyone should have three or four wives, as many of them as he wanted, but they were to live with the wives in a godly way, as you'll eventually hear. This pleased the one and not the other. There were men and women opposed to this, so that they wouldn't uphold the matrimony, and for this reason many a person would eventually have to die.[447b]

Jan van Leiden's justification for instituting polygamy rested on a reading of events in the Old Testament, wherein key figures such as Noah had more than one wife, and the biblical incitement to "go forth and multiply". He himself had fifteen or sixteen wives.

After the siege, the institution of polygamy was used to attack the Anabaptists, demonstrating in the eyes of their enemies their lack of morals. This, we should note, is the grossest hypocrisy, coming from people who cheered on the suppression, torture and mass slaughter of the Anabaptists. But we should not view Münster's polygamy as being about sexual liberation in any form. Some have explained the decision as being a result of the disproportionate number of women to men in the town, resulting from men suffering a higher death rate[448] and because many men fled town to avoid execution, leaving their wives behind to look after their property.

While some women were actively involved in the "evangelical movement" before the Münster rising and were active within the besieged city as Anabaptists (including one woman who tried to kill Bishop Frank in emulation of Judith in the Old Testament, who supposedly killed a general besieging her city), most women took no part. Some, including nuns, were opposed to both the Reformation and Anabaptism and others only accepted rebaptism "under duress" while staying loyal to their faith.[449] The forceful rebaptism of all Münster's population meant that anyone who could not leave the city essentially became considered Anabaptist even if they did not accept those beliefs. Finally, it was the poorest who could not leave, which included many "single working women – spinsters, widows, and young servant girls".[450] All these factors help explain the large number of women in the city.

In trying to explain the introduction of polygamy some historians have suggested it was done to protect these women by tying them into marriage. It should be noted that this justification does not appear in Gresbeck's account of events. Rather we need to understand polygamy in Münster as reflecting the ideas and interests of the city's Anabaptist leaders. Gresbeck says that quickly the decision of polygamy led to men taking as many wives as they wanted, specifically younger women and, he says, "little girls". He continues "So they slept first with one wife and then with the other. They did all this with a holy pretense, so that they would increase the world".[451]

This was not in fact polygamy, as that would suggest that women could take multiple husbands. It is better described as polygyny (men could take multiple wives, but not women). This is underlined by the declaration of the Münster Anabaptist authorities:

> All womenfolk, virgins, maidens, and widows, all those who are marriageable, whether they be noble or non-noble, spiritual or secular, they should all take husbands, and the wives who have husbands outside the city who've fled from us should also take other husbands, since their husbands are godless and have fled from the Word of God and aren't our brothers. Dear brothers and sisters, for so long did you live in heathendom in your marriage, and it was not a real marriage.[452]

Thus women were forced into marriage. While it seems that some women married willingly, many did not. Reading Gresbeck's account of these events is distressing.[452b] It is clear there was great discontent. In fact, according to Cohn, the introduction of polygamy led to a small uprising against the Anabaptist rule that saw Jan van Leiden and Knipperdolling briefly imprisoned before their rescue. Fifty rebels against the Anabaptists were executed. There was also great discontent among the women within households and Gresbeck suggests that at least one unnamed woman may have committed suicide or been killed. Others were executed for refusing or opposing forced marriage. The discontent was strong enough that the Anabaptist leadership retreated on polygamy. Gresbeck says they declared, "marriage should be voluntary", but that it was too late.[453]

The historian Ronnie Po-chia Hsia argues that the turn to "polygamy" had less to do with Biblical ideas and was more a method of control within Münster when the majority of the population could not be trusted. It tied women to men and prevented them getting salvation, except through the "double intermediacy of men and Christ". Hsia concludes that events in Münster were an "attempt to subjugate women by restricting their social and religious roles, by transforming them, ultimately, into obedient (and protected) wives and daughters of a polygamous, patriarchal, and sacred tribe".[454]

As the siege drew on, and life became increasingly desperate, power was centralised in the hands of van Leiden, who declared himself "king over New Israel and the whole world, and would be next to God. In the whole world, there would be no king or lord but Jan van Leiden, and in the whole world there would be no government but Jan van Leiden".[455]

Notably, Gresbeck suggests that not everyone agreed with this. The common man, he says, "kept quiet", but it was "The leaders in the city of the rebaptisers – the preachers along with Knipperdolling and Bernhard Krechting and Henry Krechting and Tilbeck and even more of them – agreed about this".[456]

Cohn describes the increasingly wild decisions made by the appointed king: "streets and gates in the town were given new names; Sundays and feastdays were abolished and the days of the week were renamed on an alphabetical system; even the names of new-born children were chosen by the king according to a special system. Although money had no function in Münster a new, purely ornamental coinage was created… A special emblem was devised to symbolise Bockelson's [Jan van Leiden's] claim to absolute spiritual and temporal dominion… The king himself wore this emblem, modelled in gold, hanging by a gold chain".[457]

Jan van Leiden now concentrated wealth in his own hands, living in requisitioned mansions with his multiple wives, a huge retinue and special guards. He took on all the trappings of the medieval monarchy and sat in state and judgement on a special throne in the marketplace.[458] More and more goods were confiscated to fund this lavish lifestyle, while the mass of the people of Münster suffered more and more.

Terror now became reality – those who did not obey the king or his appointed officers faced execution. The whims of the ruler dominated life – one example being a mass muster called on the blowing of a trumpet. The people had to assemble immediately, ready to leave the city and fight the besiegers. They were promised superhuman strength and inevitable victory. Thankfully, this did not take place. Cohn describes how the terror was first used against women: "One was beheaded for denying her husband his marital rights, another for bigamy…and a third for insulting a preacher and mocking his doctrine". Cohn also suggests that the terror was principally used by Jan van Leiden against the native population of Münster who did not support him as strongly as the Anabaptist immigrants. These formed his guard and had special privileges.[459]

By the end of 1534 the besiegers were preparing to destroy the Münster Anabaptists completely. The bishop got agreement from nearby states to supply money, arms and troops to attack the city. The siege was now solid, but a few Anabaptists were able to escape to continue to spread propaganda. This was so successful that in January 1535 a thousand armed Anabaptists from the Netherlands planned to march on Münster to relieve it, but were defeated before they got close. On another occasion, eight hundred Anabaptists captured a monastery in West Frisia before being killed.[460] Inside the town things were getting desperate. Gresbeck describes how the leaders had plenty, but the masses had almost nothing:

> They began to eat horses first – the head with the feet, and the liver and the lungs. They ate cats, dogs, mice, rats, great big mussels, frogs, and grass. Greens were their bread. So long as they had salt, this was their wheat. They also ate ox hides, and they laid old shoes in the malting trough and ate them… Their children were dying, the old people were dying, one dying first, the other next. But the criminal (the king) with his councilors and the leaders, they had enough to eat and let the other folk starve to death. Whoever at that time could steal something from one person or another, they did so – food and dogs and cats. Where they could steal, there they were and ate it. That was their prey. If the king was informed at this time that someone wanted to flee from him, he cut his head off or had him hung from a linden up at the cathedral square.[461]

In May, van Leiden responded to the desperation by allowing many people to leave the town. Tragically the younger men were promptly killed by the besiegers, who refused to allow the others to leave. The women, elderly people and children were left to suffer, trapped between the town walls and the besieging armies. For five weeks hundreds of them starved to death, having only grass to eat and unable to escape. Eventually the bishop after discussion with his allies, relented – those considered Anabaptists were executed and the remainder banished.[462]

The town survived until June 1535, eighteen months after the Anabaptists had taken control. Gresbeck was one of two people to escape from the town. Having likely played a key role in events (which he does not describe in his own account) and being a military leader, he turned traitor. Captured by the besiegers he provided a plan to enter the town undetected. This was successful. The bishop's forces entered the town on the night of 24 June 1535, fighting their way through and killing hundreds. Despite promises of safe conduct, many Anabaptists were killed after their capture, and all the rebels had their property confiscated. Leading figures such as the "king", Jan van Leiden, were tortured and eventually executed. This included women such as Jan van Leiden's wife and "queen" Divara van Haarlem. In January 1536, van Leiden, Knipperdolling and Bernhard Krechting were publicly tortured to death in the centre of Münster, each body placed in a cage and hung from the tower of St Lambert's Church.

Some accounts of Münster, notably those of leftists such as Ernest Belfort Bax, whose history of the events was published in 1903, have tried to draw close parallels with later working-class rebellions. The fact that the Anabaptist leaders tried to implement a "community of goods" and the authorities responded with siege and massacre has an obvious parallel with the working-class Paris Commune of 1871. But it is wrong to give Anabaptist Münster too much of a revolutionary colouring.

While many ordinary people in Münster suffered appallingly as a result of the ideas of their leaders, particularly after Jan van Leiden declared himself king, it is also true that many Anabaptists, coming from the mass of the poor in north-west Germany and the Netherlands, had high expectations that a millennial moment was coming and hoped to benefit from the redistribution of wealth from the rich to the poor. Indeed, throughout the months of Anabaptist rule in Münster, there was a strong identification among poor Anabaptists that the city was the site of the millennium. Preachers and emissaries were sent out from Münster to spread the word about events and encourage people to join. As a result, large numbers of people headed towards Münster. In March 1534 dozens of ships with thousands of Anabaptists from the Netherlands responded to a call to assemble at a meeting point near the port of Kampen. The Dutch authorities prevented them travelling, executed some of the leaders and imprisoned most of them before sending the rest home. In a decision reminiscent of more contemporary treatment of refugees, the authorities had initially threatened to execute the Anabaptists by sinking their boats. Interestingly the decision not to do this was based on the conclusion that they were "poor, naive people" and to "avoid the depopulation of the land".[463] In May 1535 an attempt at a rising in Amsterdam, involving the seizing of the town hall by sixty Anabaptists, saw most of the rebels killed after none of the Protestant population supported the insurrection. Stayer suggests that Jan van Geel, who led this, knew it was hopeless but saw it as a last chance to support beleaguered Münster.[464]

In other cities emissaries from Münster raised some support, but this was followed by repression. The town of Warendorf declared for Münster but capitulated after the bishop arrived with an army. Münster's messengers were executed.[465] In January 1535 planned Anabaptist risings in Wesel, Maastricht, Utrecht and Leiden were prevented, despite elaborate plans.[466] While there was clearly enthusiasm and sympathy for Münster from the oppressed Anabaptists across the region, and particularly among the poor, this was not a mass revolutionary movement based on emancipatory politics. Rather it was one expecting the millennial second coming, which was prepared to use the Sword to defend the true believers until that moment arrived.

So we must be careful not to draw too close a parallel with later revolutionary movements. This is not to say that there were no aspects of radical social thought to Anabaptism at this time, or even among the leadership in Münster. But Münster was not an early prototype of later urban revolutionary movements. The most obvious modern parallel is the Paris Commune. But what distinguished the Paris Commune was mass participation in the revolution. It was an armed workers' movement that redistributed wealth and property and created new working class institutions. Democracy was central to the Paris Commune, which ensured that elected officials were paid the average wage and were instantly recallable. No such democracy or accountability existed in Münster, nor was there a mass movement from below creating new social structures. Instead, the distribution of wealth was implemented from above, albeit with the willing support of many of Münster's ordinary citizens, but it was not enfranchising. The isolation of the Münster Anabaptists and the violent siege no doubt forced the leadership to make difficult decisions such as imposing a violent logic in their rule. But ultimately, Münster's self-declared "king" lived in luxury, while his followers starved.

*

The storming of Anabaptist Münster, and the mass murder and execution of those who remained inside was the end of the radical Reformation. Anabaptism never regained its strength or mass support, though its religious descendants remain today, holding on to their beliefs in communal identity and pacifism. After 1535, there were no more mass scale attempts to use the Reformation to construct a "community of goods" within existing society.

By destroying the Peasant Revolution in 1525 through massacre and repression, the German authorities had left only one outlet for discontent – religion. Their bloody destruction of Münster, and the suffering of thousands during the nearly eighteen months of siege, was an attempt to shut that avenue down too. In this, they were mostly successful. The Reformation in Europe lost its mass nature and became in many places a Reformation from above. Indeed, in England, Henry VIII's Reformation was met by discontent and resistance from ordinary people who rejected his religious reforms and fought to retain their old Church.[467]

Despite the destruction of the Anabaptist movement by the defeat at Münster, vestiges of radicalism remained in Germany and the Netherlands. Small sections of those who had been inspired by Melchior Hoffman continued to organise. In December 1535, for instance, a small group of sixty Anabaptists attempted an uprising in Hazerswoude, South Holland, but were quickly defeated.[468] Around Christmas 1538 there were expectations, or rumours, of a renewed rising among the remaining Anabaptists in the Netherlands. But within a few years some of the remaining radical, or revolutionary, Anabaptists seem to have descended into criminal gangs, robbing churches on the justification that they were attacking the Catholic Church. As late as the 1570s one band continued this activity, its leader even printing one of Rothmann's pamphlets and taking multiple wives. These were, however, the dying flare-ups of a movement whose main force had been destroyed in Münster. The destruction of the Anabaptists was thus the end of the radicalism that had emerged during the Peasants' War.

Many of the most radical organisers and thinkers of the Peasants' War had close links to the Anabaptist movement. One of these was Heinz Kraut, a veteran of the Peasants' War in Thuringia. Captured in December 1536, he was interrogated by none other than Philip Melanchthon. At his trial Kraut refused to acknowledge the superiority of those in authority. He demonstrated that for all the bloodshed, the ideas that inspired hundreds of thousands of men and women to fight for freedom and equality had not been extinguished. He was sentenced to death. Just before his execution he recited an old couplet that had been on the lips of peasant rebels for centuries: "When Adam delved and Eve span, who then was the gentleman?".[469] It is individuals like Kraut, prepared to put their lives at risk in the struggle for a better world, that we should remember today.

Conclusion

As the peasant rebellion spread throughout Germany, alongside the burning castles and captured cities, there were various attempts to change society. But, as Friedrich Engels noted, none of these went beyond the sort of democracy that would become common during the bourgeois era. Why could the peasants not realise a communal society?

In part the failure lay in the limited power of the movement. Some of this was circumstantial. Peasant movements are frequently limited by the localism inherent in peasant society. It was possible, at least temporarily, to satisfy a peasants' needs by expelling the local landowner and dividing up their lands among local families; this has been a feature of peasant risings across the globe throughout history. This localism, however, does not encourage a vision of a wider state organised on a communist basis. Secondly, there were practical limitations to the power of the peasant movement and their ability to defeat feudalism. Their military weakness, despite their anger and numbers, was repeatedly demonstrated throughout 1525 as band after band was violently smashed by the nobles, who were able to deploy their wealth and resources to hire mercenary armies, putting aside their differences to defeat their common enemy. The peasantry, however large their armies were, was not powerful enough to defeat the forces of the feudal ruling class, who were wealthier, better armed, more experienced and usually more ruthless.

Finally, the establishment of a communist society requires a material basis. It needs a level of economic development that can free up a surplus to allow everyone to live communally. The peasant economy of sixteenth century Germany was not developed enough to do this. Isolated, local peasant communes could not survive within feudalism, and the peasants' movement could not overthrow feudal society. Defeating feudalism needed the further development of capitalist interests within the old order.

Engels described the peasants' rebellion during the German Reformation as the most crucial component of the first stage of the bourgeois revolution. This was because it arose out of contradictions that would crystallise in later mediaeval society as the new economic order was beginning to emerge.

The inability of the revolutionary movement to break through was summed up by Engels in his famous description of the trap that Thomas Müntzer found himself in:

> The worst thing that can befall the leader of an extreme party is to be compelled to assume power at a time when the movement is not yet ripe for the domination of the class he represents and for the measures this domination implies. What he can do depends not on his will but on the degree of antagonism between the various classes, and on the level of development of the material means of existence of the conditions of production and commerce upon which the degree of intensity of the class contradictions always reposes. What he ought to do, what his party demands of him, again depends not on him, but also not on the degree of development of the class struggle and its conditions.
>
> He is bound to the doctrines and demands hitherto propounded which, again, do not follow from the class relations of the movement, or from the more or less accidental level of production and commerce, but from his more or less penetrating insight into the general result of the social and political movement. Thus, he necessarily finds himself in an unsolvable dilemma. What he can do contradicts all his previous actions and principles and the immediate interests of his party, and what he ought to do cannot be done. In a word, he is compelled to represent not his party or his class, but the class for whose domination the movement is then ripe. In the interests of the movement he is compelled to advance the interests of an alien class, and to feed his own class with talk and promises, and with the asseveration that the interests of that alien class are their own interests. He who is put into this awkward position is irrevocably lost.[470]

Engels did not study the 1525 events purely for historic interest but to understand the cowardice of the German bourgeoisie in the revolutions of his own time. In 1848, mass revolutionary movements exploded across Europe, seeking to sweep away the remnants of the old aristocratic, feudal order. In theory, this would give the new bourgeoisie the opportunity to profit from the accumulation of capital without any hindrances. In Germany, however, fear of further revolt from below prompted bourgeois elements to back off from a final confrontation with the old order and side with the aristocracy against the workers' movement.

In 1525, the German bourgeoisie was not yet powerful enough to enforce its interests, although there were some small, hesitant steps in this direction. Remember how in 1525 some rebellious towns and cities produced articles inspired by peasant demands with an economic agenda of their own. They called for changes to taxation that would benefit the emerging forces of merchant and manufacturing capital.

This was the basis for Engels' remark that "under the circumstances, the princes alone had benefited from the Peasants' War". It is easy to see who lost out – the Church suffered dramatically, as did the local nobles, through the burning of hundreds of monasteries, churches and castles. The towns gained little – those "burghers" who used the occasion of the rebellion to raise their own demands, were repressed and their "opposition was broken for a long time". As Engels points out, the old order was re-established "tying up commerce and industry hand and foot up to the time of the French Revolution".

Finally, of course, and most tragically, the peasants lost out. Tens of thousands were killed, many more injured. They were imprisoned, tortured, branded, fined or expelled. Their leaders were put to death in the most hideous of ways; their organisation was almost, though not entirely broken. The rebellion was crushed.

As Engels concluded, the princes, benefitted

> not only relatively, from a weakening of their opponents – the clergy, nobility and the towns – but also absolutely, since they carried off the spolia opima (the main spoils) of all the other estates. The church estates were secularised in their favour; part of the nobility, fully or partly ruined, was obliged gradually to accept vassalage; the indemnities they received from the towns and peasant communities swelled their treasuries and, furthermore, the abolition of so many town privileges now afforded much greater scope to their favourite financial operations.[471]

Yet, five hundred years after the revolution, the Peasants' War continues to speak to us. Those who rose up and rebelled, knowing they were putting their lives at risk in a fight against oppression and exploitation, did so because they thought that their resistance could win. Those who were inspired by the revolutionary words of Thomas Müntzer or Michael Gaismair lived in a world where a tiny minority of people owned almost everything, while the masses laboured in poverty. Ordinary people felt squeezed by the demands of the rich and powerful, fearful of disease and war, and sick of corruption and waste. They wanted a world where humanity could be free to use nature's resources in the most equitable way for the benefit of everyone, and within this, they wanted freedom to practise their religion without restriction, without a corrupt, incredibly wealthy Church pushing its own agenda and squeezing them still further.

The parallels with today are obvious. But five hundred years after the German Peasants' War the world is very different. Bourgeois society has triumphed globally. But now billions of people face war, destitution and environmental destruction because of a world driven by capital accumulation. However, capitalism, as Marx pointed out, has produced a class with the potential to be its gravediggers. In sixteenth century Europe it was the hard labour of peasants that created the wealth that built beautiful cathedrals, huge castles and glittering palaces. Today, it is the labour of billions of workers' which fills the pockets of the shareholders of multinational corporations and the bank accounts of billionaires.

When the peasants rebelled, the best that could happen was that they would divide up the land previously owned by a rich landowner or the Church. They hoped to win back some communal land, or rights to hunt, fish or gather wood in the local forests. Maybe they hoped that a particularly oppressive lord or noble would be killed. Sometimes they were successful, but these were always temporary victories. Today, workers' collective labour in factories, offices, call centres and other workplaces creates the potential for a different outcome to the struggle. A society where we own and control the means of production collectively, where the fruits of human labour are shared on the basis of need, and where society is democratically organised in the collective interest of all. This is not just necessary; it is possible in a way that the peasants of 1525 could not realise.

The fact that people have always fought to try to change the world is inspirational for those struggling against capitalism today. This is why the German Peasants' War remains an important touchstone. While the religious language from sixteenth century Germany is dated, there is no doubt that the sentiment of Michael Gaismair's revolutionary constitution echoes today:

> You should root out and expunge all godless men who persecute the Word of God, burden the common man, and hinder the common good.[472]

Capitalism has shown the productive potential of human society. But alongside this wealth, it breeds poverty, hunger and human suffering on an enormous scale. It certainly burdens the common people and "hinders the common good". As we face environmental collapse, economic crisis and endless war, there is an ever greater urgency to the struggle to replace capitalism with a more just society organised for the "common good". As Thomas Müntzer understood, the need for revolutionary change is forced upon people by the reality of society. As he said in 1524,

> it is the lords themselves who make the poor man their enemy. If they refuse to do away with the causes of insurrection how can trouble be avoided in the long run? If saying that makes me an inciter to insurrection, so be it![473]

The time for the harvest has come.

Afterword
The strange afterlife of the German Peasants' War

As a Marxist, one of the most fascinating aspects to studying the German Peasants' War is its political afterlife. In 1850 Friedrich Engels, the lifelong friend and collaborator of Karl Marx, published a short account of the event, which drew heavily on the work of the nineteenth century German historian Wilhelm Zimmermann. Engels' book was less a detailed study of the events and more an attempt to understand the defeat of the 1848 German Revolution in its historical context. Some years later, Engels wrote that the "parallel between the German Revolution of 1525 and that of 1848–49 was too obvious to be altogether ignored at that time". Despite the parallels however, Engels was clear that the two revolutions were fundamentally different. One was an early attempt to overthrow feudal society, doomed to failure. The latter was a revolution that threatened to spill over into the transformation of society. In this sense the revolution of 1848 was a project that remained uncompleted, because of the growing power of the working class. The "Revolution of 1848-50 cannot end like the Revolution of 1525" he concluded.[474]

Engels' position as Marx's lifelong friend and collaborator gave his analysis enormous importance to subsequent Marxists. In the late nineteenth century, two of these, Ernest Belfort Bax and Karl Kautsky, wrote their own accounts of the Peasants' War and its context, which drew heavily on Engels' analysis. In 1910, the German Marxist Franz Mehring also wrote on the events in *Absolutism and Revolution in Germany (1525–1848)*.

But interest in the Peasants' War was not limited to the left. One of the most significant German historians of these events was Günther Franz, whose 1926 publication *Der Deutsche Bauernkrieg 1525: Herausgegeben in Zeitgenössischen Zeugnissen* remains one of the most complete collections of archival material relating to the rebellion.

Franz joined the Nazi Party in May 1933. In 1935, he moved from the SA to the SS Race and Settlement Main Office, before getting an academic post in 1936. Franz regularly wrote and lectured for the Nazi regime. One of his contributions to a training book for the SS from 1937-38 explained that the "blame" for the German Peasants' War lay with the Jews. He made other antisemitic and completely incorrect claims about the Reformation, the Thirty Years War and the Catholic Church and was central to attempts to link historic events to contemporary antisemitism. Franz became a key figure in the Nazi regime, promoted to SS-Hauptsturmführer in November 1943 for his contribution to the development of racial ideology and history. Despite his work for the Nazi regime throughout the Nazi dictatorship, Franz was "denazified" after the Second World War and eventually returned to teaching, maintaining that he had not been taken in by the Nazis, though this flies in the face of evidence of his work for the regime.[475]

In the aftermath of the Second World War, the rebellion took on renewed importance, especially as the 450th anniversary approached in 1975. During the Cold War, the Peasants' War became part of an ideological battleground. The division of Germany between the victorious allies after the war eventually, in 1949, saw the Soviet zone of occupation become East Germany. The German Democratic Republic (GDR) was closely linked to the Soviet Union and was established as a "socialist" state.[476] Its historians considered Engels' work and analysis of the German Peasants' War enormously important – both as Marxist historiography and in terms of a foundational text for their own state. In studying the Peasants' War, they drew and built on the work of Engels and other socialist historians. This work was frequently contested by Western historians who usually rejected a Marxist approach, even when they did celebrate the movement from below. This meant that much scholarship of the Peasants' War in the twentieth century was framed through a reading of Marx, and Marxism, and a resultant antagonism between historians of the West and East framed by Cold War rivalries.[477]

For a Marxist like myself, this has raised several issues. On the one hand, it is rare to find such a plethora of material about historical events written by authors who use, or claim to use, a Marxist approach. This has naturally offered insights. On the other hand, the version of Marxism of official GDR ideology is far from the self-emancipatory Marxism that characterised the work of Marx and Engels themselves – and certainly is not one that I adhere too. As such, the insights of East German Marxist historians do not necessarily coincide with my own views, something I hope will be clear from this book. It is a tragedy of history that the events of 1525 have been celebrated by regimes that claimed to rule in the name of "working people" yet offered little to those people in terms of democratic rights and participation in managing the economic system itself.

While seeking to legitimise themselves as a "workers' government" by celebrating the events of 1524 and 1525, the East German government would, however, have repressed and hated anyone who dared to echo Thomas Müntzer's words critiquing the concentration of wealth into the hands of a tiny minority by taking it from the mass of the producers. The East German regime officially celebrated the events of the Peasants' War in order to help legitimise their claim to be a socialist government. In contrast to this "socialism from above", I hope my own account of the Peasants' War, and the struggle for justice, equality and democracy that was at the heart of those events, encourages and inspires a renewed interest in the project of mass, revolutionary emancipation.

Appendix
The Twelve Articles
of the Peasants[478]

The fundamental and correct chief articles of all the peasants and of those subject to ecclesiastical lords, relating to these matters in which they feel themselves aggrieved.

Peace to the Christian Reader and the Grace of God through Christ.

There are many evil writings put forth of late which take occasion, on account of the assembling of the peasants, to cast scorn upon the gospel, saying: Is this the fruit of the new teaching, that no one should obey but all should everywhere rise in revolt and rush together to reform or perhaps destroy altogether the authorities, both ecclesiastic and lay?

The articles below shall answer these godless and criminal fault-finders, and serve in the first place to remove the reproach from the word of God, and in the second place to give a Christian excuse for the disobedience or even the revolt of the entire Peasantry.

In the first place the Gospel is not the cause of revolt and disorder, since it is the message of Christ, the promised Messiah, the Word of Life, teaching only love, peace, patience and concord. Thus, all who believe in Christ should learn to be loving, peaceful, long-suffering and harmonious. This is the foundation of all the articles of the peasants (as will be seen) who accept the Gospel and live according to it.

How then can the evil reports declare the Gospel to be a cause of revolt and disobedience? That the authors of the evil reports and the enemies of the Gospel oppose themselves to these demands is due, not to the Gospel, but to the Devil, the worst enemy of the Gospel, who causes this opposition by raising doubts in the minds of his followers, and thus the word of God, which teaches love, peace and concord, is overcome.

In the second place, it is clear that the peasants demand that this

Gospel be taught them as a guide in life and they ought not to be called disobedient or disorderly. Whether God grant the peasants (earnestly wishing to live according to His word) their requests or not, who shall find fault with the will of the Most High? Who shall meddle in His judgments or oppose his majesty? Did He not hear the children of Israel when they called upon Him and saved them out of the hands of Pharaoh? Can He not save His own to-day? Yes, He will save them and that speedily. Therefore, Christian reader, read the following articles with care and then judge. Here follow the articles:

The First Article
First, it is our humble petition and desire, as also our will and resolution, that in the future we should have power and authority so that each community should choose and appoint a pastor, and that we should have the right to depose him should he conduct himself improperly. The pastor thus chosen should teach us the Gospel pure and simple, without any addition, doctrine or ordinance of man. For to teach us continually the true faith will lead us to pray God that through His grace this faith may increase within us and become part of us. For if His grace work not within us we remain flesh and blood, which availeth nothing; since the Scripture clearly teaches that only through true faith can we come to God. Only through His mercy can we become holy. Hence such a guide and pastor is necessary and in this fashion grounded upon the Scriptures.

The Second Article
According as the just tithe is established by the Old Testament and fulfilled in the New, we are ready and willing to pay the fair tithe of grain. The word of God plainly provided that in giving according to right to God and distributing to His people the services of a pastor are required. We will that, for the future, our church provost, whomsoever the community may appoint, shall gather and receive this tithe. From this he shall give to the pastor, elected by the whole community, a decent and sufficient maintenance for him and his, as shall seem right to the whole community (or, with the knowledge of

the community). What remains over shall be given to the poor of the place, as the circumstances and the general opinion demand. Should anything further remain, let it be kept, lest anyone should have to leave the country from poverty. Provision should also be made from this surplus to avoid laying any land tax on the poor. In case one or more villages themselves have sold their tithes on account of want, and each village has taken action as a whole, the buyer should not suffer loss, but we will that some proper agreement be reached with him for the repayment of the sum by the village with due interest. But those who have tithes which they have not purchased from a village, but which were appropriated by their ancestors, should not, and ought not, to be paid anything further by the village which shall apply its tithes to the support of the pastors elected as above indicated, or to solace the poor as is taught by the Scriptures. The small tithes, whether ecclesiastical or lay, we will not pay at all, for the Lord God created cattle for the free use of man. We will not, therefore, pay further an unseemly tithe which is of man's invention.

The Third Article

It has been the custom hitherto for men to hold us as their own property, which is pitiable enough, considering that Christ has delivered and redeemed us all, without exception, by the shedding of His precious blood, the lowly as well as the great. Accordingly, it is consistent with Scripture that we should be free and wish to be so. Not that we would wish to be absolutely free and under no authority. God does not teach us that we should lead a disorderly life in the lusts of the flesh, but that we should love the Lord our God and our neighbour. We would gladly observe all this as God has commanded us in the celebration of the communion. He has not commanded us not to obey the authorities, but rather that we should be humble, not only towards those in authority, but towards every one. We are thus ready to yield obedience according to God's law to our elected and regular authorities in all proper things becoming to a Christian. We, therefore, take it for granted that you will release us from serfdom as true Christians, unless it should be shown us from the Gospel that we are serfs.

The Fourth Article

In the fourth place it has been the custom heretofore, that no poor man should be allowed to catch venison or wild fowl or fish in flowing water, which seems to us quite unseemly and unbrotherly as well as selfish and not agreeable to the word of God. In some places the authorities preserve the game to our great annoyance and loss, recklessly permitting the unreasoning animals to destroy to no purpose our crops which God suffers to grow for the use of man, and yet we must remain quiet. This is neither godly or neighbourly. For when God created man he gave him dominion over all the animals, over the birds of the air and over the fish in the water. Accordingly it is our desire if a man holds possession of waters that he should prove from satisfactory documents that his right has been unwittingly acquired by purchase. We do not wish to take it from him by force, but his rights should be exercised in a Christian and brotherly fashion. But whosoever cannot produce such evidence should surrender his claim with good grace.

The Fifth Article

In the fifth place we are aggrieved in the matter of wood-cutting, for the noble folk have appropriated all the woods to themselves alone. If a poor man requires wood he must pay double for it (or, perhaps, two pieces of money). It is our opinion in regard to wood which has fallen into the hands of a lord whether spiritual or temporal, that unless it was duly purchased it should revert again to the community. It should, moreover, be free to every member of the community to help himself to such fire-wood as he needs in his home. Also, if a man requires wood for carpenter's purposes he should have it free, but with the knowledge of a person appointed by the community for that purpose. Should, however, no such forest be at the disposal of the community let that which has been duly bought be administered in a brotherly and Christian manner. If the forest, although unfairly appropriated in the first instance, was later duly sold let the matter be adjusted in a friendly spirit and according to the Scriptures.

The Sixth Article
Our sixth complaint is in regard to the excessive services demanded of us which are increased from day to day. We ask that this matter be properly looked into so that we shall not continue to be oppressed in this way, but that some gracious consideration be given us, since our forefathers were required only to serve according to the word of God.

The Seventh Article
Seventh, we will not hereafter allow ourselves to be further oppressed by our lords, but will let them demand only what is just and proper according to the word of the agreement between the lord and the peasant. The lord should no longer try to force more services or other dues from the peasant without payment, but permit the peasant to enjoy his holding in peace and quiet. The peasant should, however, help the lord when it is necessary, and at proper times when it will not be disadvantageous to the peasant and for a suitable payment.

The Eighth Article
In the eighth place, we are greatly burdened by holdings which cannot support the rent exacted from them. The peasants suffer loss in this way and are ruined, and we ask that the lords may appoint persons of honour to inspect these holdings, and fix a rent in accordance with justice, so that the peasants shall not work for nothing, since the labourer is worthy of his hire.

The Ninth Article
In the ninth place, we are burdened with a great evil in the constant making of new laws. We are not judged according to the offense, but sometimes with great ill will, and sometimes much too leniently. In our opinion we should be judged according to the old written law so that the case shall be decided according to its merits, and not with partiality.

The Tenth Article
In the tenth place, we are aggrieved by the appropriation by individuals of meadows and fields which at one time belonged to a community. These we will take again into our own hands. It may, however, happen that the land was rightfully purchased. When, however, the land has unfortunately been purchased in this way, some brotherly arrangement should be made according to circumstances.

The Eleventh Article
In the eleventh place we will entirely abolish the due called *Todfall* (that is, heriot)[*] and will no longer endure it, nor allow widows and orphans to be thus shamefully robbed against God's will, and in violation of justice and right, as has been done in many places, and by those who should shield and protect them. These have disgraced and despoiled us, and although they had little authority they assumed it. God will suffer this no more, but it shall be wholly done away with, and for the future no man shall be bound to give little or much.

Conclusion
In the twelfth place it is our conclusion and final resolution, that if any one or more of the articles here set forth should not be in agreement with the word of God, as we think they are, such article we will willingly recede from when it is proved really to be against the word of God by a clear explanation of the Scripture. Or if articles should now be conceded to us that are hereafter discovered to be unjust, from that hour they shall be dead and null and without force. Likewise, if more complaints should be discovered which are based upon truth and the Scriptures and relate to offenses against God and our neighbour, we have determined to reserve the right to present these also, and to exercise ourselves in all Christian teaching. For this we shall pray God, since He can grant these, and He alone. The peace of Christ abide with us all.

---

[*] A death duty or kind of inheritance tax

Bibliography

All Biblical quotes are from *The New Revised Standard Version of the Bible*, 2017 (Cambridge University Press)

Anderson, Erich B, 2017, "Wildcards: Landsknechts in the German Peasant Armies", *Medieval Warfare*, Vol. VI, issue 6, pp15-19.

Aston, T.H & C.H.E. Philpin, 1995, *The Brenner Debate* (Cambridge)

Austin, Kenneth, 2020, *The Jews and the Reformation* (Yale)

Bainton, Roland Herbert, 1950, *Here I Stand: A Life of Martin Luther* (Abingdon-Cokesbury)

Bak, Janos (ed), 2014, *The German Peasant War of 1525* (Routledge)

Bax, E Belfort, 1899, *The Peasants War in Germany, 1525-1526* (Swan Sonnenschein)

Bax, E Belfort, 1903, *Rise and Fall of the Anabaptists* (Swan Sonnenschein)

Baylor, Michael G, 1991, *The Radical Reformation* (Cambridge University Press)

Baylor, Michael G, 2012, *The German Reformation and the Peasants' War: A Brief History with Documents* (Bedford/St Martins)

Behringer, Wolfgang, 1999, "Bauern-Franz und Rassen-Günther. Die politische Geschichte des Agrarhistorikers Günther Franz (1902–1992)". In Winfried Schulze and Otto Gerhard Oexle (eds), 1999, *Deutsche Historiker im Nationalsozialismus* (Fischer)

Blickle, Peter, 1981, *The Revolution of 1525* (Johns Hopkins)

Blickle, Peter, 1979, "The 'Peasant War' as the Revolution of the Common Man – Theses", in Scribner & Benecke, 1979.

Blickle, Peter, 1992, *Communal Reformation: The Quest for Salvation in Sixteenth-Century Germany* (Humanities Press)

Boer, Roland, 2013, *Criticism of Earth: On Marx, Engels and Theology* (Haymarket).

Boer, Roland, 2014, "'All things are in common': theology and politics in Luther Blissett's Q", *International Socialism* journal, 141, Winter 2014. https://isj.org.uk/all-things-are-in-common-theology-and-politics-in-luther-blissetts-q/

Boer, Roland, 2017, "Luther and Marxism", in Alberto Melloni (ed), 2017, *Martin Luther: A Christian between Reforms and Modernity* (Cambridge University Press).

Brandi, Karl, 1996, *The Emperor Charles V* (Jonathan Cape).

Callinicos, Alex, 1989, "Bourgeois Revolutions and Historical Materialism", *International Socialism* journal, 43, Summer 1989. www.marxists.org/history/etol/writers/callinicos/1989/xx/bourrev.html

Cliff, Tony, 1988, *State Capitalism in Russia* (Bookmarks).

Cohn, Henry J, "The peasants of Swabia", in Bak, 2014.

Cohn, Norman, 1970, *The Pursuit of the Millennium* (Paladin)

Davidson, Neil, 2012, *How Revolutionary Were the Bourgeois Revolutions?* (Haymarket)

Drummond, Andrew, 2024, *The Dreadful History and Judgement of God on Thomas Müntzer: The Life and Times of an Early German Revolutionary* (Verso).

Empson, Martin, 2017, "A common treasury for all: Gerrard Winstanley's vision of utopia", *International Socialism* journal, 154, Spring 2017. https://isj.org.uk/a-common-treasury-for-all

Empson, Martin, 2018, *Kill all the Gentlemen: Class Struggle and Change in the English Countryside* (Bookmarks)

Endres, Rudolf, 1979, "The Peasant War in Franconia", in Scribner & Benecke, 1979.

Engelberg, Ernst, "Engels' Peasant War in Germany", in Bak, 2014.

Engels, Friedrich, 2006 [1850], *The Peasant War in Germany* (International).

Firnhaber-Baker, Justine, & Dirk, Schoenaers, 2017, *The Routledge History Handbook of Medieval Revolt* (Routledge)

Firnhaber-Baker, Justine, 2021, *The Jacquerie of 1358* (Oxford)

Friedrichs, Christopher R, 1997, "German Social Structure 1300-1600", in Scribner (ed), 1996.

Gimpel, Jean, 1976, *The Medieval Machine* (Penguin)

Gluckstein, Donny & Janey Stone, 2024, *The Radical Jewish Tradition* (Bookmarks)

Harman, Chris, 1998, *Marxism and History* (Bookmarks)

Harman, Chris, 1999, *A People's History of the World* (Bookmarks)

Herrer, Hipolito Rafael Oliva, 2017, "Interpreting large-scale revolts: some evidence from the War of the Communities of Castile", in Firnhaber-Baker & Schoenaers, 2017.

Hilton, Rodney, 1986, *Bond Men Made Free: Medieval Peasant Movements and the English Rising of 1381* (Methuen)

Howell, Martha, C, 1986, *Women, Production and Patriarchy in Late Medieval Cities* (Chicago University Press)

Hoyer, Siegfried, 1979a, "Arms and Military Organisation in the German Peasant War", in Scribner & Benecke, 1979.

Hoyer, Siegfried, 1979b, "The Rights and Duties of Resistance in the Pamphlet to the Assembly of the Common Peasantry (1525)", in Scribner & Benecke, 1979.

Hsia, R. Po-Chia (ed), 1988, *The German People and the Reformation* (Cornell)

Kaufmann, Thomas, 2023, *The Saved and the Damned: A History of the Reformation* (Oxford).

Kautsky, Karl, 1959 (1897), *Communism in Central Europe at the Time of the Reformation* (Russell & Russell)

Klaassen, Walter, 1978, *Michael Gaismair: Revolutionary and Reformer* (Brill)

Laube, Adolf, 2014, "Precursors of the Peasant War: 'Bundschuh' & 'Armer Konrad'- Popular Movements at the Eve of the Reformation", in Bak, 2014.

Leon, Abram, 2012, *The Jewish Question* (Pathfinder)

Luther, Martin, 1524a, "A Letter to the Princes of Saxony Concerning the Rebellious Spirit", www.andydrummond.net/muentzer/PDFs/luther_letter_princes.pdf (accessed Oct 2024).

Luther, Martin, 1524b, "An Open Letter to the Honourable and Wise Mayor, Council and Whole Community of the Town of Mühlhausen", www.andydrummond.net/muentzer/PDFs/luther_letter_muhlhausen.pdf (accessed Oct 2024).

Luther, Martin, 2007, *Selected Writings of Martin Luther* (four volumes) (Fortress)

MacCulloch, Diarmaid, 2004, *Reformation: Europe's House Divided 1490-1700* (Penguin)

MacKay, Christopher S, 2016, *False Prophets and Preachers: Henry Gresbeck's account of the Anabaptist Kingdom of Münster* (Truman State University Press)

Marx, Karl, 1843, "A Contribution to the Critique of Hegel's Philosophy of Right", www.marxists.org/archive/marx/works/1843/critique-hpr/intro.htm

Marx, Karl, 1852, "The Eighteenth Brumaire of Louis Bonaparte", in Marx, 1991.

Marx, Karl, 1991, *Selected Works* (Progress)

Marx, Karl & Friedrich Engels, 1990, *Collected Works* volume 26 (International Publishers)

Marx, Karl & Friedrich Engels, 2004, *Collected Works* volume 50 (International Publishers)

Matheson, Peter (editor), 1988, *The Collected Works of Thomas Müntzer* (T&T Clark)

Miller, Douglas, 2009, *Armies of the German Peasants' War 1524-1526* (Osprey)

Ming, Wu, 2010, *Thomas Müntzer: Sermon to the Princes* (Verso)

Oman, CWC, 1890, "The German Peasant War of 1525", *The English Historical Review*, Vol. 5, No. 17, p65-94

Packull, Werner, O, 1986, "In Search of the 'Common Man' in Early German Anabaptist Ideology", *The Sixteenth Century Journal*, Vol. 17, No. 1, p51-67.

Packull, Werner, O, 2008, *Mysticism and the Early South German-Austrian Anabaptist Movement 1525-1531* (Wipf & Stock)

Pascal, R, 1933, *The Social Basis of the German Reformation* (Watts)

Pettegree, Andrew, 2016, *Brand Luther* (Penguin)

Potter, G.R, 1984, *Zwingli*, (Cambridge University Press)

Rapp, Francis, 1979, "The Social and Economic Prehistory of the Peasant War in Lower Alsace", in Scribner & Benecke, 1979.

Roper, Lyndal, 1987, "'The Common Man', 'The Common Good', 'Common Women': Gender and Meaning in the German Reformation Commune", *Social History*, Jan 1987, Vol. 12, No. 1, pp1-21.

Roper, Lyndal, 2016, *Martin Luther: Renegade and Prophet* (Vintage)

Rösener, Werner, 1996, "The Agrarian Economy, 1300-1600", in Scribner (ed), 1996

Scott, Tom, 1986, *Freiburg and the Breisgau: Town-Country Relations in the Age of Reformation and Peasants' War* (Clarendon).

Scott, Tom, 1989, *Thomas Müntzer: Theology and Revolution in the German Reformation* (Palgrave)

Scott, Tom, 1996, "Economic Landscapes", in Scribner (ed), 1996.

Scott, Tom and Bob Scribner, 1991, *The German Peasants' War: A History in Documents* (Humanities)

Scribner, Bob (ed), 1996, *Germany: A New Social and Economic History: 1450-1630* (Arnold)

Scribner, Bob & Gerhard Benecke, 1979, *The German Peasant War 1525: New Viewpoints* (Allen & Unwin)

Stalnaker, John C, 1979, "Towards a Social Interpretation of the German Peasant War", in Scribner & Benecke, 1979.

Stayer, James M, 1976, *Anabaptists and the Sword* (Coronado Press)

Stayer, James M, 1994, *The German Peasants' War and Anabaptist Community of Goods* (McGill-Queen's University Press)

Steinmetz, Max, 1979, "Theses of the Early Bourgeois Revolution in Germany, 1476-1535", in Scribner & Benecke, 1979.

Stanford, Peter, 2017, *Martin Luther: Catholic Dissident* (Hodder & Stoughton)

Thompson, EP, 1971, "The Moral Economy of the English Crowd in the Eighteenth Century", *Past & Present*, No. 50, p76-136.

Trotsky, Leon, 1992, *The History of the Russian Revolution* (Pathfinder)

Ward, A.W, Prothero, G.W & Leathes, Stanley, 1903, *The Cambridge Modern History Volume II: The Reformation* (Cambridge)

Williams, George Huntston, 1992, *The Radical Reformation* (Truman State University Press)

Wohlfeil, Rainer, 2014, "*The Peasant War in Germany* by Friedrich Engels – 125 years after", in Bak, 2014.

Wiesner, Merry E, 1996, "Gender and the Worlds of Work", in Scribner (ed), 1996

Wunder, Heide, 1979, "The Mentality of Rebellious Peasants: the Samland Peasant Rebellion of 1525", in Scribner & Benecke, 1979

Endnotes

Introduction
The German Peasants' War?

1 Quoted in Matheson, 1988, p335.

2 In what follows I use terms such as Germany and Europe. These are somewhat anachronistic for the period. However, they will make the text easier to follow. When describing particular places, I have tried to give a sense of where they are on a modern map, but readers should be careful to note that the borders of modern European nation states frequently do not match those of the sixteenth century, even when there were separate nations.

3 Endres, 1979, p77.

4 Endres, 1979, p68.

5 Scott & Scribner, 1991, p9. A tithe was a tax that was supposed to support the Church. It was usually supposed to be a tenth of the harvest or other income.

6 The rising in Samland is rarely discussed but one exception is Wunder, 1979.

7 Hilton, 1986, p35-36.

8 Blickle, 1979, p19. Also Blickle, 1981, p105-124. Here we must note a problem with the "Common Man" thesis which is that its gendered language implies the absence of women from these events, even though, as we shall see women were involved.

9 Trotsky, 1992, pxvii.

10 Matheson, 1988, p370-371.

Chapter 1
Germany on the Eve of Revolution

11 Scott, 1996, p3-5.

12 Rösener, 1996, p70.

13 This summary of the multiplicity of changes to German agriculture in the sixteenth century, based on Rösener, 1996, p70-78.

14 Rösener, 1996, p74.

15 Rösener, 1996, p76.

16 Scott, 1996, p10.

17 Friedrichs, 1996, p249.

18 Gimpel, 1976, p78-79.

19 Harman, 1999, p179.

20 Pettegree, 2016.

21 Scott, 1996, p9. In feudal society, the "demesne" was manorial land specifically for use by the lord. This is contrasted to other land that was let out to others.

22 Scott, 1996, p11.

23 Indulgences were remissions against God's punishments for sins someone committed during their lifetime, often understood to mean a reduction of time in "purgatory", the state of punishment and purification a soul was understood to be in after death but before entering heaven.

24 Harman, 1998, p96.

25 Pascal, 1933, p18. Here Pascal uses the word proletariat to mean urban wage labourers. But this term, in the Marxist sense, is not really applicable to the pre-capitalist era before a class of workers had developed that were collectively exploited by capitalist bosses.

26 Harman, 1998, p96.

27 Rösener, 1996, p74-76.

28 Harman, 1999, p182.

29 Wiesner, 1996, p218. Merry E. Wiesner's article is a brilliant introduction to the question of work and gender in Germany in this period.

30 Wiesner, 1996, p228-229.

31 Wiesner, 1996, p215.

32 Wiesner, 1996, p214-215.

33 Wiesner, 1996, p215-216.

34 Quoted in Wiesner, 1996, p214.

35 Kautsky, 1959, p2.

36 The Hussites were a radical Czech Christian movement which arose in the fifteenth century following the Bohemian Reformation, a precursor to the Protestant Reformation. The Hussites followed the teachings of Jan Hus, a Catholic priest who argued for significant reforms to the Church. After his execution for heresy in 1415, his followers rose in military rebellion and defeated the Papal "crusading" armies sent against them. The wars ended with a compromise that allowed Bohemia to use a reformed version of Christianity.

37 Kautsky, 1959, p102-103.

38 Scott, 1986, p166.

39 Cohn, 1970, p234 and Scott, 1986, p166 who gives more detail and other examples from the fourteenth and fifteenth century.

40 On antisemitism in the Bundschuh, see Scott, 1986, p167 and p169, especially footnote 17.

41 Scott, 1986, p174.

42 Quoted in Baylor, 2012, p35. I discuss the concept of Godly Law later in this book.

43 Baylor, 2012, p36-38 and Scott, 1986, p174.

44 Scott, 1986, p176-182.

45 Laube, 2014, p50. As Laube notes, there are interesting parallels with other peasant rebellions here. In 1354, for instance, a French peasant rising saw the rebels take up the patronising name "Jacques Bonhomme" – James Goodman – and make it their own, leading to the rebellion becoming known as the Jacquerie. On this great rebellion, see Firnhaber-Baker, 2021.

46 Scott, 1986, p186.

47 Scott, 1986, p187.

48 Scott, 1986, p188.

49 Laube, 2014, p51-52.

50 Pascal, 1933, p18.

51 Marx, 1843.

52 Engels, 2006, p13.

Chapter 2
Martin Luther and the German Reformation

53 Roper, 2016, p27. Roper's book is indispensable on Luther's early life and the importance of this to understanding him.

54 Roper, 2016, p26-27.

55 MacCulloch, 2004, p88.

56 MacCulloch, 2004, pp 97-105.

57 Quoted in Stanford, 2017, p110.

58 Pascal, 1933, p45.

59 Pascal, 1933, p49.

60 Stanford, 2017, p110-112.

61 All quotes from the *Theses* are from Luther, 2007, volume 1, p51-59. Marcus Licinius Crassus was a general and statesman in ancient Rome, considered the richest Roman ever, who made a fortune from slavery and real estate, including buying fire-damaged property on the cheap, even while it was burning. Luther would have used Crassus' name as a shorthand for corruption and violence, as well as extreme wealth.

62 Roper, 2016, p97. Thomas More was Henry VIII's Lord High Chancellor from 1529 to 1532 and a strong opponent of the Reformation.

63 Stanford, 2017, p312.

64 This is not the place for a full history of the German Reformation, or indeed, the Reformation beyond the Empire. Two excellent introductions are MacCulloch, 2004 and Kaufman, 2023.

65 Gluckstein, 2023, p23.

66 Roper, 2016, p389.

67 Roper, 2016, p392. Roper's account of Luther's antisemitism [389-396] details his horrific racism and his appalling language, including his belief that he was made ill by travelling through villages [80] with Jewish communities, and further extremely offensive comments. She notes that while some of his contemporaries rejected Luther's ideas others "propagated it" [395], with at least one example of officials in Saxony using Luther's arguments at this time to encourage the seizure of Jewish property.

68 Roper, 2016, p395-396. Luther's antisemitism was virulent enough for the Nazis to use it to justify their own attacks on Jewish people. Kristallnacht, the Nazi pogrom against Jewish businesses in Germany on the night of 9-10 November 1938, was described by participants as a "birthday present for Luther", who was born on 10 November 1483. At the Nuremberg trials, Julius Streicher, the Nazi owner of the virulently antisemitic newspaper *Der Stürmer*, used Luther's pamphlet in his defence, "arguing that he had added nothing to the reformer's original message" and that Luther would also be on trial if he were alive. See Austin, 2020, pxii-xiii.

69 Boer, 2013, p145. Roland Boer argues that Marx had a "soft spot for Luther", seeing him as a forerunner for contemporary revolutionaries. See, for instance, Boer, 2013, p31-32.

70 Luther, 2007, volume 3, p354.

71 Luther, 2007, volume 3, p352, p353 & p354.

72 Stanford, 2017, p311.

73 Quoted in Bainton, 1950, p80.

74 Harman, 1999, p178.

Chapter 3
The Beginning of the Revolt

75 Brandi, 1996, p95.

76 Scott & Scribner, 1991, p221. The rebellious articles [See Scott & Scriber, 1991, p221-223] raised by mine workers in May 1525 in Joachimsthal, now in the Czech Republic, do not concern themselves with wage rates, but rather with tolls, tithes and similar complaints to those raised by urban rebels elsewhere. It is better to understand miners in sixteenth century Germany as self-employed tradesmen, rather than workers in the modern sense. My thanks to Andrew Drummond for his comments on this point.

77 Rapp, 1979, p58 & p59. Francis Rapp gives an example of fluctuating prices: "In the first half of the fifteenth century, the price of a quarter of cereal fluctuated between 40 and 90 pfennig. In the second half…it went as low as 26 pfennig and as high as 160 pfennig", p58.

78 Ward & others, 1903, p176.

79 Figures from Endres, 1979, p63-65.

80 Scott & Scribner, 1991, p121-122.

81 For ease, I refer to the events of the "German Peasants' War" as a revolt, rebellion or uprising. I will discuss whether they deserve the description "revolution" later. I also use the term "peasants" as a catch-all description to include all those who took part in the uprising – though as I have already acknowledged these individuals went

beyond those who are commonly understood as peasants today.

82 Scott & Scribner, 1991, p65-72.

83 All quotes from the Stühlingen Articles are from Scott & Scribner, 1991, p65-72.

84 This account is quoted from Cohn, 2013, p24-25. The village of Baltringen would become the centre of the revolt and gave its name to one of the armed peasant groups, the Baltringer Haufen.

85 Cohn, 2013, p13.

86 Scott & Scribner, 1991, p20.

87 Quoted in Bax, 1899, p44.

88 Quoted in Scott & Scribner, 1991, p115.

89 Quoted in Scott & Scribner, 1991, p116.

90 Quoted in Scott & Scribner, 1991, p116.

91 Scott & Scribner, 1991, p118.

92 Scott & Scribner, 1991, p119.

93 Scott & Scribner, 1991, p21.

94 Ward & others, 1903, p179.

95 Scott & Scribner, 1991, p25.

96 Scott & Scribner, 1991, p25-26. The leadership of a mass peasant revolt by a landowner might seem contradictory. In this case it is likely that Hurlewagen took leadership in order to contain the revolt. I have discussed this phenomenon and the wider contradictory role of elite leaders of peasant revolts in the English context in Empson, 2018.

Chapter 4
The Twelve Articles

97 Cohn, 2013, p11. The Twelve Articles repay reading. But their importance and fame has meant that the extensive other collections of grievances, demands and articles, produced by the rebels from 1524 onwards have often been neglected. We have already encountered the Sixty-two articles produced by the rebellious peasants of Stühlingen. Hundreds of other examples have survived.

98 Cohn, 2013, p11.

99 This section follows the text of the Twelve Articles in Scott & Scribner 1991, p253-7.

100 Quoted in Cohn, 2014, p21.

101 Scott & Scribner, 1991, p103.

102 A point made by Harman, 1999, p187. See Engels, 2006, p50.

Chapter 5
Fear and Loathing at a Peasant Revolution

103 Luther, 2007, volume 3, p351-352.

104 Scott & Scribner, 1991, p158.

105 Scott & Scribner, 1991, p159.

106 Quotes from von Eck are from Scott & Scribner, 1991, p151-152.

107 Blickle, 1979, p21.

108 All quotes from *To the Assembly of the Peasantry* are from Baylor, 1991, p102-129. For more on the pamphlet see Hoyer, 1979b.

109 Hoyer, 1979b, p136.

110 Note that here I have omitted the references to biblical verses.

111 The Swiss Confederation was sometimes held up as a model of community organisation for German peasants. It was based on a political system wherein local republican communities (cantons) came together for common interests (e.g. defence) but retained their independence and self-organisation. This had arisen from a series of rebellions from below against feudal lordship. Note however that the Swiss Confederation was contradictory. Free communities existed alongside those run by lords,

and all overseen by the Emperor. It remained a feudal system.

112 Hoyer, 1979b, p110.

113 Detail on Salzburg from Blickle, 1981, p101-103. Salzburg retained a feudal order from which "most German cities were free". Ward & others, 1903, p183.

Chapter 6
The Spread of the Rebellion

114 Ward & others, 1903, p181.

115 Quoted in Bax, 1899, p105.

116 The Landsknechts were mercenary troops on which the counter-revolutionary forces were heavily reliant. I discuss their organisation and importance for the rebellion later.

117 Miller, 2009, p21.

118 Ward & others, 1903, p182.

119 Scott & Scribner, 1991, p156.

120 Scott & Scribner, 1991, p156-157.

121 Ward & others, 1903, p182.

122 Ward & others, 1903, p181. Ulrich was eventually restored as Duke of Württemberg in 1534, an event of considerable importance to the history of the Reformation as he suppressed the monasteries, and encouraged support for Lutheran ideas. This fascinating story illuminates the complexities of feudal alliances during this period but is far beyond the scope of this book.

123 Scott & Scribner, 1991, p28, the map on p30 of this book gives a sense of the route taken by the Württemberg rebels.

124 Scott & Scribner, 1991, p141-142.

125 Detail of Battle of Böblingen from Miller, 2009, p33 & p34.

126 Scott & Scribner, 1991, p243-244.

127 Quoted in Scott & Scribner, 1991, p206.

128 Scott & Scribner, 1991, p32-33.

129 Bax, 1899, p146-157. Bax's use of the term "city-proletariat" here is anachronistic. Like many socialists of his era, he was keen to portray the Peasant War as a precursor to modern workers' revolutions. But while there had been wage labourers and day workers for centuries, no "proletariat" as Marx understood it, a class of workers under capitalism, existed in sixteenth century Germany. Bax also is mistaken as there were forty-six demands demanded by the rebels of Frankfurt. See Scott & Scribner, 1991, p170-174.

130 Summary of the Bildhausen band's inglorious history based on Scott & Scribner, 1991, p34-35.

131 Scott & Scribner, 1991, p35.

132 An excellent summary of the economic background to the revolt in the Alsace can be found in Rapp, 1979.

133 Rapp, 1979, p59.

134 Rapp, 1978, p60.

135 Scott & Scribner, 1991, p44 & p189.

136 Details on earlier Alsace revolts from Laube, 2014, p50-51.

137 Scott & Scribner, 1991, p45.

138 The Jewish Marxist historian Abram Leon notes that in the mediaeval era, "in certain cities, principally in Germany and in Italy, the Jews became primarily loan-makers to the popular masses, the peasants, and the artisans. In this role as petty usurers exploiting the people, they were often the victims of bloody uprisings." See Leon, 2012, p88.

139 Scott & Scribner, 1991, p45. See their map on p46-47 for a sense of the huge scale of the revolt in Alsace.

140 Scott & Scribner, 1991, p193. The Franciscans where a religious order

founded by Francis of Assisi in the thirteenth century marked by a life of poverty supposed to be close to that of the original Apostles.

141 The white veil was either a symbol of mourning, or as Scott and Scribner suggest, a death veil. This was a threat of violence.

142 Scott & Scribner, 1991, p194-195.

143 This summary is based on Scott & Scribner's account on p48-49.

144 Drummond, 2024, p215.

145 Scott & Scribner, 1991, p265.

146 Scott & Scribner, 1991, p308.

147 Scott & Scribner, 1991, p49.

148 Margrave was the title given to some princes in the Holy Roman Empire who were military commanders.

149 Scott & Scribner, 1991, p49.

150 Blickle, 1981, p113. My thanks to Andrew Drummond for helping clarify this point.

Chapter 7
The Peasants' War in the Towns

151 For the Frankfurt Articles see Scott & Scribner, 1991, p170-174.

152 These actions are reminiscent of the struggles described in EP Thompson's classic article "The Moral Economy of the English Crowd in the Eighteenth Century", which argued that there were a set of social norms around food production, sales and distribution that were considered acceptable to the rural and urban poor. Any challenge to these, such as price rises, or any "outrage to these moral assumptions, quite as much as actual deprivation, was the usual occasion for direct action." Thompson was mostly writing about eighteenth-century England, but the parallels with sixteenth century German peasant struggles and demands are interesting. See Thompson, 1971.

153 Austin, 2020, p56-57.

154 Quoted in Bainton, 1950, p379.

155 There have been a number of attempts to have this offensive sculpture removed, but this has been blocked by German courts, most recently in 2022. In the 1990s a number of display boards contextualising the sculpture and explaining the Holocaust were placed nearby, though in my opinion the sculpture should be removed to the local Luther museum.

156 It should be noted that others, such as the radical Thomas Müntzer, were not antisemitic. Indeed, Müntzer held the position that both Jews and Muslims could be part of the Elect. See Drummond, 2024, p168.

157 Scott & Scribner, 1991, p177-178.

158 For the Erfurt Articles and Luther's commentary see Scott & Scribner, 1991, p174-176.

159 Quoted in Pettegree, 2016, p243. It is worth noting that Luther was sent these articles in September 1525, long after the movement had been crushed. This did not dampen his dislike.

Chapter 8
Thomas Müntzer and the Revolt in Thuringia

160 Engels, 2006, p71-72.

161 The best introduction to Müntzer's life and politics is Andrew Drummond's recent biography, see Drummond, 2024. This is closely followed by Tom Scott's book, Scott, 1989.

162 Here I follow Drummond, 2024, chapter 2, for biographical details.

163 Drummond, 2024, p37.

164 Scott, 1989, p9.
165 Quoted in Drummond, 2024, p39.
166 Scott, 1989, p11.
167 Drummond, 2024, p44-46.
168 Scott, 1989, p17-18.
169 Drummond, 2024, p49.
170 Scott, 1989, p22.
171 Drummond, 2024, p63-64.
172 Drummond, 2024, p50.
173 Drummond, 2024, p65.
174 Drummond, 2024, p66. The elect, in its Christian meaning, are those individuals chosen (elected) by God to perform particular tasks or for salvation. In Müntzer's view, the elect were those Christians who would "perpetuate the 'living Gospel' in themselves as people predestined to execute the will of God on earth". Drummond, 2024, p53.
175 Andrew Drummond's book details the way that Müntzer's battle with Egranus was developing tensions with those around Luther in Wittenberg, who were still supporting Müntzer in these debates. Drummond, 2024, p67, and Scott, 1989, p23, for instance, quote Johannes Agricola, a close supporter of Luther, critiquing Müntzer for acting only with "threats and bloodshed", suggesting that he needed to be more careful in how he conducted his arguments. Müntzer did not listen.
176 Scott, 1989, p21.
177 Drummond, 2024, p61. Drummond argues that Storch and Müntzer had an important effect on each other, particularly exposing the latter to important radical ideas such as Hussitism and Taboritism. But after Müntzer left Zwickau, it seems there was no further contact. Contrast this, however, with Scott, 1989, p26-27, who downplays the relationship, casting Storch as "pupil" to Müntzer. I tend to see Drummond's position as more likely, with Müntzer developing his ideas in engagement with existing radicalism.
178 Drummond, 2024, p68.
179 Drummond, 2024, p69.
180 Thanks to Rosemarie Nünning for this information.
181 Drummond, 2024, p78.
182 Ming, 2010, p2.
183 Ming, 2010, p5-6.
184 Ming, 2010, p7.
185 Drummond, 2024, p83.
186 Ming, 2010, p7.
187 Ming, 2010, p10-11.
188 Drummond, 2024, p87.
189 Drummond, 2024, p91.
190 See the discussion of this letter in Drummond, 2024, p95-97.
191 Matheson, 1988, p43-44 & p46.
192 Drummond, 2024, p97.
193 Scott, 1989, p42-43.
194 Matheson, 1988, p162.
195 Drummond, 2024, p107.
196 Drummond, 2024, p112.
197 Quoted in Matheson, 1988, p66-67.
198 Interestingly the Protestation by Müntzer includes reference to the Koran, suggesting a familiarity with it, or at least knowledge of some of its contents.
199 Scott, 1989, p65.
200 Scott, 1989, p67.
201 Daniel 2:2-16.
202 Daniel 2:31-35.
203 Daniel 2:36-45.
204 Daniel 2:46.
205 Ming, 2010, p28.
206 Ming, 2010, p31.

207 Ming, 2010, p34-35.

208 Drummond, 2024, p147-151.

209 Quoted in Drummond, 2024, p149.

210 Quoted in Drummond, 2024, p151.

211 Drummond, 2024, p151.

212 Drummond, 2024, p153.

213 Quotes from this letter are from Matheson, 1988, p88-90.

214 Here Müntzer's refers to the Turks, as Muslims, representing non-Christian unbelievers.

215 All quotes from the letter from Luther, 1524a.

216 Romans 13: "Let every person be subject to the governing authorities; for there is no authority except from God, and those authorities that exist have been instituted by God." Again, contrast the position in the May 1525 *Appeal to the Common Peasantry*.

217 Engels, 2006, p16-p17.

218 Matheson, 1988, p116.

219 Drummond, 2024, p181.

220 See Luther, 1524b.

221 Drummond, 2024, p187.

222 Quoted in Drummond, 2024, p183. Here Müntzer signs his work "Thomas Müntzer with the Hammer". This is a reference to Jeremiah 23:29, "Is not my word like fire, says the Lord, and like a hammer that breaks a rock in pieces?" It is not difficult to find symbolic meaning in Jeremiah 23 for Müntzer himself. Take for instance, Jeremiah 23:30, "See therefore, I am against the prophets… who steal my words from one another."

223 Drummond, 2024, p183.

224 The complete pamphlet is in Matheson, 1988, p260-323.

225 Drummond, 2024, p185.

226 Matheson, 1988, p309.

227 Matthew, 9:37-38.

228 Matheson, 1988, p312.

229 Matthew, 13:24-30.

230 Matthew, 13:36-43.

231 Matheson, 1988, p327-p350.

232 Matheson, 1988, p350. See Scott, 1989, p108.

233 Drummond, 2024, p192.

234 Drummond, 2024, p191.

235 Scott & Scribner, 1991, p37 & p103-105.

236 Drummond, 2024, p218 onward explores what little we know of Müntzer's activities in this period. Drummond dismisses the idea that Müntzer was responsible for writing the Twelve Articles.

237 Drummond, 2024, p225.

238 Drummond, 2024, p228. Note the women invaded the convent while Müntzer was out of town. We know very little about Ottilie, but this implies she was committed to similar radical politics and was organising and active independently from her husband.

239 Scott, 1989, p143-145.

240 Scott, 1989, p145.

241 Drummond, 2024, p232.

242 Quoted in Drummond, 2024, p232.

243 Scott, 1989, p146-147.

244 Quoted in Scott, 1989, p147.

245 Scott, 1989, p148.

246 Quotes from "The Letter to the League at Allstedt", from Baylor, 2012, p98-100.

247 Matheson, 1988, p142-143.

248 Matheson, 1988, p143-145.

249 This account of Müntzer's actions before arrival in Frankenhausen is based on Drummond, 2024, p235-250.

250 Drummond, 2024, p242.

251 Scott, 1989, p156-157 & Drummond, 2024, p243-245.

252 Drummond, 2024, p245-246.

253 Drummond, 2024, p246.

254 Matheson, 1988, p146-147.

255 Matheson, 1988, p147-148.

256 Matheson, 1988, p148.

257 Matheson, 1988, p151 & Drummond, 2024, p248-249. Hesse was an unpleasant character. He married a Catholic daughter, Christine, of Duke Georg, in 1523 fathered ten children, but then bored of a wife saying that she was "unfriendly, ugly, and smelled bad", with the agreement of Luther and Melanchthon he married bigamously again. Then had a further nine children with his second wife and three more with Christine. Detail from Drummond, 2024, p249-250.

258 Scott & Scribner, 1991, p160.

259 Drummond, 2024, p253.

260 Drummond, 2024, p254.

261 Scott & Scribner, 1991, p200-201.

262 Drummond, 2024, p257.

263 Matheson, 1988, p156.

264 Bax, 1889, p261.

265 Drummond, 2024, p262.

Chapter 9
Military Organisation

266 On the risings of 1381 and 1450s see Empson, 2018. On Castile, see Herrer, 2017.

267 See Anderson, 2017.

268 See Miller, 2009, p12, p13 & p22.

269 See Miller, 2009, p10 and p23.

270 Hoyer, 1979a, p99.

271 Anderson, 2017, p18.

272 See Hoyer, 1979b.

273 Scott & Scribner, 1991, p274-275.

274 Bright band is a translation of "Heller Haufen", the name given to the regiments of peasants and Landsknechts. For the full *Ordinances,* see Baylor, 2012, p93-97.

Chapter 10
The End of the Rising

275 Scott & Scribner, 1991, p292. Heldrungen was the location of Ernst von Mansfeld's powerful castle, about fifteen kilometres from Frankenhausen, where many lords who had fled the rebellion were hiding and which was the assembly point for counter-revolutionary forces in the region.

276 Drummond, 2024, p264-265. The text of the letter and ultimatum is available in Matheson, 1988, p159-160.

277 Scott, 1989, p166.

278 Scott & Scribner, 1991, p290.

279 Scott & Scribner, 1991, p291.

280 Matheson, 1988, p160-161.

281 Drummond, 2024, p275.

282 Written on the 21 May 1525. Scott & Scribner, 1991, p291.

283 Scott & Scribner, 1991, p293.

284 All quotes from the Confession in Matheson, 1988, p433-438.

285 Ward & others, 1903, p189. Götz's own account of his participation is a self-serving explanation of how he came to be in a leading position of the rebellion, designed to escape punishment. It is worth reading for what it tells us about the struggle in Franconia and peasant organisations. See Scott & Scribner, 1991, p203-205.

286 Scott & Scribner, 1991, p294. See also Miller, 2003, p36-37.

287 Scott & Scribner, 1991, p295.

288 Scott & Scribner, 1991, p295.

289 Bax, 1899, p295.

290 Scott & Scribner, 1991, p295-296.

291 Scott & Scribner, 1991, p295-296 and Bax, 1899, p296.

292 Scott & Scribner, 1991, p297.

293 On the defeat at Würzburg and the punishments, see Scott & Scribner, 1991, p297-298.

294 Miller, 2003, p37-38.

295 Bax, 1899, p304.

296 Scott & Scribner, 1991, p301.

297 Details of the Battle at Leubas from Miller, 2003, p38. Various accounts including Bax, 1899, p308-312 and Oman, 1890 give much higher figures for the number of rebels at Leubas. Bax says twenty-three thousand and Oman fourteen or fifteen thousand. These figures seem improbably high for this stage in the rebellion, but if they are true, Bax would be justified in concluding that had the rebels "never had a more favourable opportunity" and had they defeated Truchsess Georg they could have reversed the tide and the "rebellion might still…have been saved". Readers wanting to learn more are warned that the battle is usually described as taking place at the river Leubas (spelt Luibas in older texts) but the Leubas is a much smaller waterway, best described as a creek.

298 Scott & Scribner, 1991, p115-119 and Scott, 1986, p202-204.

299 Scott, 1986, p206.

300 Scott & Scribner, 1991, p187.

301 Scott, 1986, p208-209.

302 Scott & Scribner, 1991, p189.

303 Scott, 1986, p209.

304 My account of events in Freiburg is based on Scott, 1986, p217-219.

305 Scott & Scribner, 1991, p233.

306 See the full list in Scott & Scribner, 1991, p306-307.

307 Ward & others, 1903, p191.

308 Scott & Scribner, 1991, p301.

309 Scott & Scribner, 1991, p303-304.

310 Material on the Diet of Speyer and suggested reforms are based on Blickle, 1981, p165-169.

311 Blickle, 1981, p169.

Chapter 11
Michael Gaismair's Unchristian, Horrible Order against the Royal Domain of Tyrol

312 A critical title given to Gaismair's vision of a new Tyrolean society by an opponent, the full description reads, "Michael Gaismair's unchristian horrible order and unjustified, terrifying and inhuman intention against the royal domain of Tirol". See Klaassen, 1978, p58, footnote 268.

313 Bax, 1899, p326.

314 Material on Dietrichstein and Schladming from Bax, 1899, p326-330. On the revolt in Austria see also Scott & Scribner, 1991, p49-53.

315 Williams, 1992, p169. This description is perhaps slightly inaccurate as it reflects the radical position developed by Gaismair after the main rebellion was defeated in 1526. However, it is the vision Gaismair hoped to bring to Tyrol in the years immediately following the Peasants' War, before his assassination in 1532.

316 Engels, 2006, p77. Note Engels gives an incorrect year for Gaismair's death.

317 Klaassen, 1978, p58.

318 Note that Klaassen, 1978, p143 incorrectly describes this as a Wehrmacht Regiment (i.e. the regular German Army) but it was an SS unit.

319 The only detailed biography of Gaismair in English is Klaassen, 1978, which this section draws heavily on.

320 Klaassen, 1978, p14.

321 For material on Gaismair's employment see Klaassen, 1978, p14-16.

322 Quoted in Klaassen, 1978, p161-7.

323 Klaassen, 1978, p23.

324 Klaassen, 1978, p5.

325 Klaassen, 1978, p7.

326 Klaassen, 1978, p12.

327 Klaassen, 1978, p23.

328 Klaassen, 1978, p26.

329 Scott & Scribner, 1991, p50 and Klaassen, 1978, p27-29.

330 Klaassen, 1978, p35.

331 All quotes from the Merano Articles are from Scott & Scribner, 1991, p86-95.

332 Quoted in Scott & Scribner, 1991, p90. The three named companies were extremely wealthy banks and mercantile families.

333 Klaassen, 1978, p33.

334 Klaassen, 1978, p29. Many peasant rebels in the Middle Ages believed that the monarch was well intentioned but surrounded by corrupt and greedy officials and advisors who needed to be removed. This thinking had proven to be a fatal flaw for the peasantry during the English Uprising of 1381, as well as in Tyrol in 1525-26.

335 Klaassen, 1978, p36.

336 Klaassen, 1978, p36.

337 Klaassen, 1978, p37-38.

338 Quoted in Klaassen, 1978, p42.

339 Summary here based on Klaassen, 1978, p43-45.

340 Klaassen, 1978, p46.

341 Klaassen, 1978, p55.

342 Klaassen, 1978, p57-58.

343 This can be contrasted with the utopian vision of "Communism of Distribution" produced by the English revolutionary Gerrard Winstanley, in his 1649 *The New Law of Righteousness*. See my discussion of this in Empson, 2017.

344 Quoted in Klaassen, 1978, p133.

345 Klaassen, 1978, p134.

346 It is worth comparing this to the similar storehouses proposed by Winstanley in 1649. See Empson, 2017.

347 Klaassen, 1978, p135-136.

348 Klaassen, 1978, p136.

349 Klaassen, 1978, p121.

350 Klaassen highlights the likely important "general" influence of Zwingli in producing the Constitution. See, for instance, Klaassen, 1978, p92-94.

351 Summarised from Klaassen, 1978, p62-65.

352 Klaassen, 1978, p69.

PART TWO
CAUSES AND CONSEQUENCES

Chapter 12
The Reformation, the German Peasants' War and the Bourgeois Revolution

353 Steinmetz, 1979, p9.

354 Marx & Engels, 2004, p166. See www.marxists.org/archive/marx/works/1893/letters/93_07_14.htm

355 Steinmetz, 1979, p15-18.

356 Engels, 2006, p83.

357 Engels, 2006, p83.

358 Engels, 2006, p83.

359 Blickle, 1979 and 1981.

360 Blickle, 1979, p19.

361 Blickle, 1992, p4.

362 Roper, 1987, p21.

363 Roper, 1987, p20.

364 Roper, 1987, p12.

365 Howell, 1986, p123-127.

366 Roper, 1987, p14.

367 Blickle, 1992, p170.

368 Blickle, 1992, p153.

369 Blickle, 1992, p199.

370 Blickle, 1992, p153.

371 Blickle, 1992, p15.

372 Quoted in Blickle, 1992, p122.

373 Blickle, 1992, p123.

374 Blickle, 1992, p100.

375 Blickle, 1992, p103.

376 Scott & Scribner, 1991, p94 & p254-255.

377 See, for instance, Neil Davidson's lengthy discussion in Davidson, 2012. It is worth acknowledging the extensive debates among Marxists about the "transition from feudalism to capitalism". Most importantly this includes the so-called "Brenner debate" following Robert Brenner's influential 1976 article on "Agrarian class structure and economic development in pre-industrial Europe". See Aston & Philpin, 1995. My framework is influenced by the approach of Chris Harman, outlined particularly in his *Marxism and History*, see Harman, 1998.

378 Callinicos, 1989.

379 Wohlfeil, 2014, p102.

380 Quoted in Engelberg, 2014, p103-104.

381 Marx & Engels, 1990, p554-555. These notes are extremely brief, and their existence is usually forgotten. It demonstrates that Engels wanted to return to the importance of the Reformation, the Peasant War and the Bourgeois Revolution later in life. Sadly, all that was completed were a couple of pages of fragmentary notes.

382 Engels, 2006, p83. "Who profited from the Revolution of 1525? The *princes*." [Engels' emphasis]

383 Engels, 2006, p82. The Sickingen Rising (1522), also known as the Knights' War, was a rising led by Franz von Sickingen, a lower noble, which was an attempt to reform and restructure the Empire, in the interest of the knightly class. The Rising ended in failure and Sickingen died from wounds received in the siege of his castle in 1523.

384 Engels, 2006, p20.

385 Davidson, 2012, p565.

386 Davidson, 2012, p566.

387 Davidson, 2012, p569.

388 See discussion in Davidson, 2012, p569-570.

389 Quoted in Boer, 2017, p961.

390 Quoted in Davidson, 2012, p569.

391 It's worth noting Davidson's point that in countries such as France, Italy and Spain, the existing ruling class did not adopt Protestantism because they were economically powerful enough to "dominate the Catholic world from inside". He thus concludes that the "centre of the Reformation" was in the least developed countries of Europe. Davidson, 2012, p570.

392 Luther, 2007, volume 1, p350.

393 Stayer, 1994, p5.

394 Luther, 2007, volume 3, p381-382.

395 Quoted in Roper, 2016, p315.

396 Scott & Scribner, 1991, p328.

397 Drummond, 2024, p286.

398 Engels, 2006, p72.

Chapter 13
All Things in Common

399 Scott & Scribner, 1991, p103. For an example of the meaning of these Biblical references, Zechariah 7:8-10 tells how God instructed his followers to "show kindness and mercy to one another; do not oppress the widow, the orphan, the alien, or the poor; and do not devise evil in your hearts against one another".

400 Blickle, 1981, p91.

401 Blickle, 1981, p92.

402 Blickle, 1981, p99.

403 The full text of the Ordinance is in Scott & Scribner, 1991, p130-132.

404 Scott & Scribner, 1991, p132.

405 Quoted in Blickle, 1981, p99.

406 Blickle, 1981, p100-101.

407 Engels, 2006, p72.

408 Quoted in Scott & Scribner, 1991, p255.

409 Scott & Scribner, 1991, p70-71.

410 Such concerns remained a feature of the antagonism between rich landowners and peasants, agricultural smallholders and labourers into the modern era. The massive criminalisation of poaching and hunting for the non-landowning class in eighteenth and nineteenth-century England was an example of the way that nature was commodified with the rise of capitalism as part of the transition to a wage-labourer economy in the countryside. See Empson, 2018.

411 Marx, 1991, p163-164.

412 Endres, 1979, p77.

413 Acts 2 & 4 were also of great importance to the early Anabaptist movement, which we will discuss later. See Stayer, 1994, chapter 4.

Chapter 14
Anabaptism: the End of the Radical Reformation

414 Packull, 2008, p19.

415 Stayer, 1976, p1.

416 Bax, 1903, pv.

417 Stayer, 1994, p72 & p89. Stayer makes the links between the Peasants' War and the Anabaptist movement clear.

418 Stayer, 1976. p1-2.

419 Potter, 1984, p161-166.

420 Potter, 1984, p166.

421 Bax, 1903, p63.

422 Stayer, 1994, p10.

423 All quotes on different versions of Anabaptism from Stayer, 1994, p10-12.

424 On Hans Hut, see Stayer, 1994, p78-79 from where this quote is taken.

425 Bax, 1903, p99.

426 Based on Bax, 1903, Chapter 4.

427 Note that in Gresbeck's accounts, Rothmann is often called Stutenberent, a derogatory nickname that means "White Bread Bernie", reflecting Rothmann's practice of using ordinary bread instead of communion wafers. See Mackay, 2016, p50, note 3. James M. Stayer details the various radical ideas that were influencing figures like Rothmann, making the point that they were not followers of Melchiorite, but "taught but did not practice baptism on confession of faith". See Stayer, 1976, p228-229.

428 Mackay, 2016, p62.

429 Stayer, 1976, p229.

430 Section on the capture of Münster by the Anabaptists based on Stayer, 1976, p228-234.

431 Stayer, 1976, p233.

432 Stayer, 1976, p234.

433 Mackay, 2016, p52.

434 Cohn, 1970, p262-263.

435 Cohn, 1970, p263.

436 Stayer, 1976, p235.

437 Mackay, 2016, p77-78. Mackay notes that essentially the same story appears in the only other roughly contemporary account of the siege by Hermann von Kerssenbrock, albeit it one written decades later.

438 Stayer, 1976, p256.

439 Stayer, 1976, p239.

440 Mackay, 2016, p81-82.

441 Mackay, 2016, p83.

442 Quoted in Cohn, 1970, p266-267.

443 Cohn, 1970, p267.

444 Mackay, 206, p97-99.

445 Mackay, 2016, p105-106.

446 Cohn, 1970, p268.

447 Cohn, 1970, p269.

447b Mackay, 2016, p110-111.

448 Hsia, 1988, p59.

449 Hsia, 1988, p58.

450 Hsia, 1988, p58-59.

451 Mackay, 2016, p113.

452 Mackay, 2016, p113. Note that Mackay here says that the translation from German of marriageable means "sexually mature".

452b Gresbeck says that many young women and girls were repeatedly raped, several of whom died as a result. See MacKay, 2016, p124.

453 Cohn 2016, p269 & Mackay, 2016, p118.

454 Hsia, 1988, p59 & p60.

455 Mackay, 2016, p134.

456 Mackay, 2016, p134.

457 Cohn, 1970, p272.

458 Cohn, 1970, p273.

459 Cohn, 1970, p275-276.

460 Cohn, 1970, p276-277.

461 Mackay, 2016, p254-255.

462 Cohn, 1970, p278.

463 Stayer, 1976, p262-263.

464 Stayer, 1976, p274-275.

465 Stayer, 1976, p266.

466 Stayer, 1976, p269.

467 See my account in Empson, 2018. Discontent against Henry VIII saw a coming together of religious, economic and social demands, involving tens of thousands of people in open rebellion, particularly in the north-east of England in 1536-7.

468 Stayer, 1976, p287.

469 For more on Heinz Kraut, see Stayer, 1994, p81-83 from where this account and quote are taken. The couplet was associated with the English radical priest John Ball, a leader of the 1381 rising and was known in Germany almost two centuries later. Werner O. Packull notes that the meeting hall of the weavers' guild in Augsburg had displayed "When Adam Delved and Eve Span" "since the fifteenth century", Packull, 1986, p56.

Conclusion

470 Engels, 2006, p71.

471 Engels, 2007, p81.

472 Scott & Scribner, 1991, p265.

473 Matheson, 1988, p335.

Afterword

474 Engels, 2007, pviii and p83.

475 Information on Günther Franz's career from Behringer, 1999. I am indebted to Rosemarie Nünning for information on these points.

476 This is not the place for a discussion on the nature of the East European regimes created in the aftermath of the Second World War. Suffice to say that, for me, the analysis of them as State Capitalist, as described by Tony Cliff, remains the most convincing. See Cliff, 1988.

477 The fractious nature of these debates is evident in several of the chapters in Janos Bak's important 1976 collection of essays on the Peasants' War. See Bak, 2014. Good overviews of the debates are in Stalnaker, 1979 and Blickle, 1981.

Appendix

478 Available at https://www.marxists.org/archive/marx/works/1850/peasant-war-germany/index.htm

Index

Acta Augustana 36

Acts (Biblical book) 185, 187, 191

Africa 1

Against the Robbing and Murdering Hordes of Peasants (Luther pamphlet) 35

Agriculture 2, 7-10, 11, 12, 14, 16, 17, 24, 239 (footnote 410); Agricultural workers 77

Allgäu 46, 133; Allgäu Band 46, 179

Allstedt 90, 94, 96, 97, 99, 102-104, 124; Allstedt League 99, 100

Alsace 7, 37, 69-71, 74, 78, 119

Amish 187

Amsterdam 207

Anabaptism 96, 176, 187-209

An Open Letter on the Harsh Book against the Peasant (Luther pamphlet) 176

Antisemitism 20, 33-34, 71, 79, 216, 220 (footnote 67 & 68)

Articles of Allegiance of the Stühlingen Peasantry 138-139

Austria 3, 13, 37, 41, 44, 52, 64, 73, 142-157

Baltringen 43, 44, 46, 47, 62, 178, 179, 230 (footnote 84)

Baptism 96, 187, 189, 190, 193, 240 (footnote 427)

Bax, Ernest Belfort 188, 190, 206, 215, 236 (footnote 297)

Bildhausen Band 68-69

Black Forest, The 46, 64, 134, 135

Blickle, Peter 4, 56, 74, 141, 161-164, 166, 178, 180

Böblingen, Battle of 15, 66, 129, 167

Boer, Roland 229 (footnote 69)

Bourgeois Revolution 159-160, 168, 170-177; Bourgeois Revolution No.1 (Engels) 170-171

Brandenburg 29

Bundschuh Rebellions 19-22, 67, 70, 135, 228 (footnote 40)

Callinicos, Alex 168

Capitalism 4,5, 16, 18, 23 , 85, 168-169, 184, 213-214, 239 (footnote 410)

Cohn, Henry J, 47

Cohn, Norman 197, 204-205

Columbus, Christopher 1, 7, 11, 17

Communal Reformation 162-163, 166

Communion 90-91, 220

Commons, The 115, 148

Common Ownership 184, 187

Concerning the Rebellious Spirit (letter by Martin Luther) 102

Constance, Lake 41, 45, 46, 120

Charles V (Holy Roman Emperor) 37-38, 156

Christian Union, The (Evangelical Brotherhood) 46, 135, 136, 137, 179

Crusades, The 20, 28

Daniel (Biblical King) 97-98

Demesne land 12, 13, 38, 227 (footnote 21)

Devil, The (see Lucifer)

Egranus, Johann Wildenauer 86-88

Eisleben 27

Engels, Friedrich 5, 24, 51, 83, 103, 127, 143, 159-161, 168, 170-173, 181, 210-212, 215-217

Erasmus, Desiderius 28, 70-71, 199

Erfurt 80, 92, 176; Erfurt Articles 80-81

Evangelical Brotherhood, see Christian Union

Explicit Exposure of False Faith, Presented to the Faithless World, An (Muntzer article) 104

Famine 1,38

Ferdinand, Archduke of Austria 44, 63, 139, 145, 146, 147, 149-151, 156, 157

Feudalism; Feudalism to Capitalism (transition) 23, 168-169, 238 (footnote 377)

Fifth Lateran Council, The 26, 28

Fishing (or Fish) 21, 76, 112, 181, 182, 213, 221

France 1, 2, 3, 24, 37, 65, 69, 110, 151, 168, 239 (footnote 391)

Franconia 39, 66-69, 74; Franconian band 64, 114, 120, 122

Frankenhausen 111, 113-116, 123, 159; Frankenhausen, battle of 15, 84, 117, 123, 125, 129; Frankenhausen, massacre 126, 167, 176

Frankfurt 75, 76, 78, 79, 84; Frankfurt Articles 75, 76, 77, 80

Franz, Günther 215-216

Freiburg im Breisgau 13, 21, 64, 134-137

French Revolution 168, 170, 212

Fritz, Joss 20, 22, 70

Fuggers, The 14, 15, 16, 29; Fugger Bank 29, 145, 146, 148, 151, 155, 175

Gaismair, Michael 16, 56, 71, 143-145, 146, 149-157, 182, 191, 213, 236 (footnote 315)

Geel, Jan van 207

German Democratic Republic (GDR) 216-217

Geyer, Florian 64, 67, 131

Gresbeck, Heinrich 193, 195, 196-206

Harman, Chris 11, 16, 17, 238 (footnote 377)

Helfenstein, Count Ludwig von 53, 62

Heilbronn 53, 54, 62

Henry VIII 31, 208, 240 (footnote 467)

Heriot Tax 50, 223

Hilton, Rodney 3-4

Highly Provoked Vindication and a Refutation of the Unspiritual Soft-Living Flesh in Wittenberg, A (Muntzer pamphlet) 106

Holy Roman Empire, The 1, 2, 15, 23, 37, 69, 73, 140

Hsia, Ronnie Po-chia 203

Hunting 21, 49, 115, 138

Hut, Hans 124, 188, 192

Hutterites 187

Italy 37, 65, 110, 118, 120, 143, 231 (footnote 138)

Indulgences 17, 26-32, 36, 84, 174, 227 (footnote 23)

Infant Baptism (see Baptism)

Jack Cade's Rebellion 117

Jews 33-34, 71, 78-79, 95, 176, 216, 231 (footnote 138), 232 (footnote 156)

Jüterbog 29, 84

Karlstadt, Andreas 90-91

Kautsky, Karl 19, 215

Lake Constance 41, 45, 46, 120

Lake Constance Band 179

Landsknecht 62, 118-120, 133, 134, 145, 231 (footnote 116)

Large Committee of the Diet of Speyer 140-141

Leiden 207

Leiden, Jan van 187, 196-206

Lucifer 24, 35, 53, 59, 100, 101, 218

Luther, Martin 2, 11, 17, 24, 25, 26-36, 37, 53, 55, 57, 78, 80-81, 83, 84, 86-94, 102, 123, 160, 164, 165, 167, 173, 180; Luther and antisemitism 33-34, 78-79; Luther's responses to Müntzer 102, 104; Luther's class position 172; Luther in Wittenberg 11-12, 31, 37, 79, 233 (footnote 175)

Maastricht 207

Mansfeld 27, 97, 113; Mansfeld, Count von 94, 111, 115, 235 (footnote 275)

Margrave (title) 232 (footnote 148)

Marx, Karl 34, 168, 173, 183, 213, 215, 216, 217, 229 (footnote 69), 231 (footnote 129)

Marxism 12, 24, 159, 213, 216, 217, 238 (footnote 377)

Melanchthon, Philip 37, 73, 92, 93, 114, 180, 209

Memmingen 1, 47, 120, 133

Mennonites 187

Merchants 11, 13, 14, 77, 78, 85, 86, 155, 161, 169, 170; Merchant capital 16, 212; Merchant class 77, 162

Metzler, Georg 64, 66-67, 129

Matthys, Jan 196, 197, 200

MacCulloch, Diarmaid 28

Miners/Mining 4, 7, 11, 27, 28, 38, 85, 97, 110, 115, 119, 144, 153, 155, 156, 229 (footnote 76)

Mühlhausen 69, 83, 103-114, 125, 126, 128, 177, 192; Mühlhausen Articles 50, 106, 178; Mühlhausen, Eternal Council 83, 106, 107, 108

Müller, Hans 44, 45, 46, 64, 71, 134, 135, 136, 137

Müntzer, Thomas 50, 71, 72, 80, 83-116, 123-128, 157,160, 176, 178, 185, 188, 211, 213, 217; Müntzer's Confession 127-128; Müntzer in Wittenberg 84; Müntzer's Prague Manifesto 5, 88-90; Müntzer's Sermon to the Princes 96-98

Ninety-five Theses 26, 27, 30-32, 35, 84, 160

Nürnberg/Nuremberg 27, 107; Nuremberg Trials 229 (footnote 68)

Paris Commune 108, 206, 207

Peasant, see serfs/serfdom

Pfeiffer, Heinrich 50, 106-109, 111, 114, 128, 176, 178

Pike 118

Poland 3, 37

Polygamy 187, 201-203

Pollard, AF 46, 61, 62

Poor Conrad 22, 64, 65

Pope, the 2, 14, 21, 28, 29, 30-36, 88, 90, 157,173,175,189; Pope Julius II 28; Pope Leo III 37; Pope Leo X 29

Portugal 1

Prague 85, 88, 90, 91; Prague Manifesto 5, 88-90

Printing Press 11, 28, 164

Prussia, Duchy of 3

Redistribution of wealth 184, 206

Rents 9, 33, 49, 55, 70, 222

Revolt of the Comuneros 117

Revolution of the Common Man 4, 56, 161, 163

Rhineland 7, 20

Roper, Lyndal 27, 34, 162, 163

Rothenburg ob der Tauber 3, 66, 133

Rothmann, Bernhard (Stutenberent) 193-194, 197, 199, 240 (footnote 427)

Russia 3, 4; Russian Revolution 4, 108

Saint Anna 28

Saint Peter's Basilica 29, 30, 31, 35, 36

Salzburg 60, 142

Samland 3

Sangerhausen 99, 100, 112, 113

Serfdom 8-11, 16, 17, 43, 48, 49, 60, 167, 169, 171, 172, 220; Serfdom, second 10; Serfs 8, 9, 10, 13, 20, 38, 49, 50, 136,138,167,182,220

Sermon to the Princes, The (Pamphlet) 96-98

Slovakia 37

Slovenia 37

Soviet Union 216

Spain 1, 2, 239 (footnote 391)

Stayer, James M 175, 188, 189, 191, 194, 195, 198

Storch, Nikolaus 87-88, 91, 233 (footnote 177)

Stühlingen 41-44, 134, 137-139; Stühlingen Articles 41, 42, 43, 44, 182

Stutenberent (White Bread Bernie), see Rothmann, Bernhard)

Stuttgart 53, 62, 65

Swabian League 52, 61, 62, 64, 65, 66, 129, 133, 143

Switzerland 1, 3, 37, 41, 65, 71, 151

Sword, The (Christian concept) 189, 192, 197, 198, 207

Tetzel, Johann 29, 30, 84

To the Assembly of Common Peasantry (pamphlet) 56-60

Trotsky, Leon 4

Truchsess Georg 61, 62, 63, 65-66, 129-130, 133, 134

Index

Tyrol 16, 37, 63, 142-157

Twelve Articles, The 1, 2, 41, 47-52, 53, 56, 68, 70, 73, 75, 78, 133, 140, 141, 165, 166, 181, 182, 218, 223

Upper Swabia 41-46, 47, 56, 61, 133-134, 137

Utraquism 91

Utrecht 207

van Haarlem, Divara 206

von Gersen, Ottilie 96, 107, 234 (footnote 238)

Warendorf 207

Wars of the Roses 117

Wiesner, Merry E. 17-18, 228 (footnote 29)

Weinsberg Massacre 51, 52-54, 62, 68

Wesel 207

Women 17-19, 73, 85, 97, 107, 120, 121, 126, 142, 162-163, 209; Women's economic role 17-19, 85, 162-163; Women in Munster 193-194, 199, 201-204

Wool 7, 38, 41

Workers 4, 27, 38, 39, 77, 85, 87, 143, 155, 156, 169, 207, 213

Wittenberg 12, 26, 29, 31, 37, 79, 84, 85, 87, 88, 90, 91, 94; Wittenberg, antisemitic sculpture 79, 232 (footnote 155)

Württemberg 62-66; Württemberg band 66; Württemberg, Ulrich Duke of 22, 53, 61, 64-65, 231 (footnote 122)

Würzburg 54, 67, 68-69, 129, 130, 132, 133, 150, 185

Zimmermann, Wilhelm 215

Zwickau 85-88, 91-92